Is Stalinism Really Dead?

ALEXANDER S. TSIPKO

Translated from the Russian by
E. A. Tichina and
S. V. Nikheev

 HarperSanFrancisco
A Division of HarperCollins*Publishers*

FIRST EDITION

Library of Congress Cataloging-in-Publication Data

Tsipko, Aleksandro Sergeevich.
    Is Stalinism Really Dead? / Alexander S. Tsipko : translated
from the Russian by I. Tichina. — 1st ed.
        p.   cm.
    Includes bibliographical references.
    ISBN 0-06-250871-7
    1. Soviet Union—Politics and government—1985-   2. Perestroïka
I. Title.
DK288.T75   1990
947.085′4—dc20   89-24718
                                                                      CIP

90 91 92 93 94 RINAM 10 9 8 7 6 5 4 3 2 1

Contents

To the Reader

I had to write this book twice. At first I conceived it as a story about changes in our views on socialism, the world, and our postrevolutionary history. It seemed that this sort of quiet narrative was exactly what the publishers were expecting of me—to describe the philosophy of *perestroika* and the changes occurring in the bedrock of our world outlook.* I honestly covered that road in three hundred typewritten pages. Then I reread the whole thing.

Everything seemed to be there and correct. I had written about our new approach to general human values; how perestroika had reinstated biblical morality and freedom of conscience; how the 27th Communist Party Congress had rehabilitated the market and commodity-money relations and, along with them, cooperation, small-time private production, and economic initiative†; and how we were grappling with the arrears of ideological conservatism that had kept us tethered by the feet, hands, and even minds.

But, both as author and reader, I found the text boring and long-winded. As soon as you begin to vivisect perestroika for its constituent principles—such as the idea of diversity of forms of life and forms of property, the idea of self-value of human life, of trust in the individual, and of free dialogue—and begin to take them one by one, the living tissue of the intellectual process seems to disintegrate, the overall image of the current changes fades away, and the thought loses its resilience.

After all those labors, which proved in vain, I started to look for another key to describing the changes taking place in our society. Really, there must be some blanket idea, a blanket topic that would include the whole emotional and intellectual message of our present moral revolution.

I feel the reader has already guessed what topic I thought of. I eventually arrived at the conclusion that the changes occurring in our society come down to the renunciation of Stalinism and its moral, political, and economic heritage. I realized that the renunciation of Stalinism, which was a side-

---

* This concept is used to refer to the political, economic, and ideological transformations that began after the April 1985 Plenary Meeting of the Central Committee of the Communist party. *Perestroika* has brought about *glasnost*, the abolition of ideological censorship, rehabilitation of Stalinist reprisal victims, restoration of the freedom of assembly and demonstrations, and restitution of the rights of the church. The results of perestroika in the economy of the country are more modest.

† The 27th Congress of the CPSU took place in late February–early March 1987. In his landmark report to the congress, Mikhail Gorbachev criticized Stalin's dogmatic notions of socialism for the first time and called attention to crisis phenomena in the development of the country.

line topic in the first version of the book, could provide penetrating insight into the causes, motives, and the ultimate goals of the burgeoning moral revolution. This was my decision as I started working on the new text, which I now submit to the judgment of the English-language reader.

The change of the vantage point on the philosophy of perestroika immediately helped me overcome a number of obstacles that until then had held back my writing. Previously an onlooker and a recorder of changes taking place, I could now become actively involved in them and set out my own views on the political and ideological sources of Stalinism. More important, I could voice my ideas about the current, at times fierce, arguments over the reasons for the horrors of Stalinism, the disastrous leftist leaps of the 1930s, especially the horrors of the forcible collectivization, and the causes of what I call in the book the Russian Apocalypse. Thus, I was able to write the new version of the book in a publicist manner,* which particularly fits my character, and thus better describe the moral atmosphere in the perestroika Russia of late 1988 and early 1989.

In fact, linking the philosophy of perestroika to criticism of Stalinism is justified from any standpoint, first of all that of substance. Why did the perestroika that Khrushchev launched in 1956 fail to produce a new vision of socialism and its destinies? For the simple reason that his criticism of Stalin's crimes did not evolve into criticism of the philosophical and economic foundations of the political regime that Stalin had built. The criticism of Stalin's personality in the latter half of the 1950s and early 1960s was self-defeating since it created insurmountable obstacles to studying the causes of what had happened. An illustration is that criticism of Stalin's personality cult and the repressions of the 1930s was continued at the 22d Communist Party of the Soviet Union (CPSU) Congress, but at the same time the new, third† program of the CPSU canonized the idea of Russia's accelerated progress toward communism that Stalin himself had formulated in 1939.

On the one hand, Khrushchev denounced Stalin as a personality, as the organizer and instigator of the repressions of the 1930s. But on the other hand, he defended and implemented Stalin's ideas about socialism and ways leading to it, the same ideas that had previously resulted in Stalin's forcible collectivization. Theoretically, Khrushchev was not so much a Leninist as a Stalinist, a dogmatic Marxist, convinced that capitalism was headed for an early and unavoidable economic collapse, that agricul-

---

* Publicistic writing represents a typically Russian variety of political journalism. Marked by a strong civic spirit, it has been widely used to criticize the government.
† The 22d Congress of the CPSU took place in February 1961. It adoped a left-wing utopian program of the building of communism in the USSR, an objective that was to be implemented by 1981. The then First Secretary of the Central Committee of the CPSU promised that "the present generation of the Soviet people shall live under communism."

tural, as well as industrial, work must be completely socialized, and that the market and commodity-money relations must be ousted. In their views on socialism, Leonid Brezhnev and Mikhail Suslov* were no different from the predecessor they had overthrown. In effect, up to the Plenary Meeting of the CPSU Central Committee in April 1985,† our official social science repeated the ideas of Stalin's work, *Economic Problems of Socialism in the USSR* (1952).

The new perestroika launched by Mikhail Gorbachev was directed, from the very beginning, against the ideological foundations of Stalinism, especially the idea of uniformity, forcible collectivization, and the subordination of life to a theoretical scheme. Essentially, it rejected the idea of noncommodity, total socialism as a twentieth-century illusion, and affirmed the priority of practice as the supreme criterion of truth. For this reason, the transformations that began in our country in April 1985 were, fundamentally, of the nature of a moral revolution signaling a cardinal reappraisal of values.

It must be admitted, however, that in the early phases of our present perestroika everybody failed to realize how powerful and formidable was Stalin's ideological heritage and how difficult it would be to live down. We were on the brink of repeating Khrushchev's mistake, if only the mirror image of it. Whereas the 20th Congress confined itself to the moral condemnation of Stalin's repressions, without taking the trouble to analyze the economic and political nature of Stalinism, we started out by rejecting Stalinism as an economic doctrine but desisted from serious criticism of Stalinism as political practice and a method of dealing with social problems and from a serious and critical analysis of the entire post-Lenin period of our history. In effect, it was not until February 1988 – a little less than three years after that watershed in March 1985 – that Mikhail Gorbachev's report to a Plenary Meeting of the CPSU Central Committee referred to what was called "Stalin's deformations of socialism" and to the fact that Stalin's political reality had, in effect, been of a criminal nature. But in 1985 and 1986 many were convinced that it was no use digging in the past or troubling the dead, that the truth about the past would be of no help, and that, instead, it was necessary to concentrate on the future and on urgent economic problems. Few realized that the deprivation of the human right to know one's national history, which was typical of Stalinism, the deprivation of the right to historical truth, was closely

---

* M. A. Suslov (1902–1982), the chief ideologue of the Brezhnev era, was a militant dogmatic.

† In March 1985, a Plenary Meeting of the Central Committee of the CPSU elected Mikhail Gorbachev its general secretary. He unveiled his political program a month later at the April Plenary Meeting of the Central Committee of the CPSU.

linked with Stalin's forcible alienation of the working people from the means of production and from political decision making; few realized that a rational and effective economy could never be built on half-truth or plain deception.

The controversy that developed over the Soviet film *Repentance*, by the Georgian director Tenghiz Abuladze, illustrates this. The film attempts to uncover the human-hating nature of Stalinism as a social phenomenon, as the incarnation of a person's moral corruption and all-permissive tyranny. Shot back in 1984, it was screened on a mass scale only in early 1987, under pressure from the artistic community.

All told, the moral revolution at this point in our history has again run against serious obstacles. Many hoped for too long that the ideological and moral crisis that struck the nation back in the late 1960s would be resolved with "few sacrifices" only by exposing the corruption and mismanagement of the Brezhnev period, or the so-called period of stagnation. Indeed, in the spring of 1985 the greatest desire was to get rid of the disgrace of the 1970s; to castigate the flattery, servility, and adulation; to name the rascals and punish the embezzlers and those who had insulted the dignity of an honest person and impugned the right to an honest and conscientious life. There was so much elan, so much delight in November 1985 when *Pravda* published readers' letters about the corrupting influence of the former political style and about the danger of flattery and servility. The appeals to cleanse our society's moral atmosphere of "all things alien and superficial" and "burn away such harmful phenomena as flattery, servility, bootlicking, cringing, etc." sounded so boldly in those days (November 20, 1985).

But very soon our society grew tired of exposing the abominations of the 1970s and criticizing individual crimes and violations. New exposures of legal abuse added nothing to what was already known, and condemnation as such no longer produced moral satisfaction. The causes of those things had to be explained.

It is my profound conviction that the breakthrough, which gave fresh impetus to perestroika and ensured an easier victory for common sense, came about when our society, the intelligentsia, secured the right to search for the causes of the crisis in the field of history, when it was realized that Brezhnev's stagnation had been a relapse into Stalinism and a follow-up to it. The mental breakthrough occurred when it became clear there was no way of reinstilling into the farmer a sense of social dignity, a sense of political validity (not to mention economic independence), until Stalin's forcible collectivization had been condemned, until it had been stated that the land had been taken away from the farmers without their consent. The mental breakthrough occurred when it became obvi-

ous that Russia stood no chance of reverting to a healthy moral and cultural life until condemnation had been meted out to the Stalinist, vulgar
class approach that had uprooted the peoples of our country, especially
the Russians, from their traditions, from the outstanding achievements of
Russian literature, philosophy, and religious thought.

Step by step, by unearthing new, deeper strata of Stalinism, we developed a new and more humanitarian vision of our history and built up the
philosophy of perestroika. All periods of Russian history merged in one,
and it became clear that by ignoring what had happened prior to 1917, we
could say nothing comprehensible about what was going on today, let
alone realize what we should strive for tomorrow.

For the first time in dozens of years, history has reentered our minds,
giving us back the lost sense of time and continuity, giving us the necessary moral support for sober-minded judgment about the present and
the future. It has turned out that perestroika cannot do without repentance and that, essentially, we depend on it for weeding out what still
remains of Stalinism in our hearts and our life, for returning to the people
the capacity for independent judgment that the great inquisitor took
away from them, for cleansing our hearts of the vestiges of slavery.

The outcome of the present moral revolution has largely been decided
by our protest, spontaneous as it has been in many ways, against the past
attempts to push history into oblivion. It is a protest against the most
ingrained feature of our moral slavery, against the unwillingness to know
the past, reflect on it, and learn from it. Now we know that the simplistic
logic "Let bygones be bygones" is from the devil, from those who want to
control our thoughts and deprive people of the right to learn from their
history. People learn primarily from their national history, for it is the
only thing they can identify with as a personality; it is their own history
and the life experience of their parents and ancestors.

We began to cure our disease by getting millions of people to think of
what has happened to us over the past seventy years, what Russia has
lived through, what it has achieved, and what it has lost. One can arrive
at the truth only through spoken word, through independent judgment
of oneself, the time, and the world.

In the four years since April 1985 we have become convinced that as
soon as things are called aloud by their names, the world changes and
starts moving. People change because they overcome their fears and, by
taking the plunge, each feels himself a free and thinking personality. The
truth gives one the key to social, public life (lies have never made anyone
a social being). In negotiating the earlier painful gap between word and
deed, between theory and life, a person restores the lost mental equilibrium. The possibility of calling evil evil, of calling absurdity absurdity,

contains a mighty stimulus for moral progress. The visibly recuperating moral health of people and society is priceless. That is why we are so impatient to know the truth and speak out on things that no desperado would have dared to say before 1985.

Today we are saying many things loud and clear in order to overcome our former fears of independent political judgment, temper our will-power, and cut off the road back to our past silence and moral inactivity. Learning the truth and getting rid of lies and illusions has never taken too long. People make haste because they want to shake off the shameful past as soon as possible; they make haste because they want to be different in their own lifetime. The starting point of our perestroika and our moral revolution was exactly the shame felt by many over their political behavior in the past, their thoughtless and humiliating servility, and our tolerating something that should have been decried and denounced. One should keep in mind that "shame is already revolution of a kind." To get rid of their sins, said Marx, people should talk of them and call them what they are in actual fact.[1]

Certainly, the new vantage point on perestroika I chose tends to be one-sided as well. The problems facing us are not confined to combating Stalinism or simply rejecting the way we lived prior to 1985. Ever more often, we have had to step over the limits of the already habitual paradigm "Stalinism–anti-Stalinism."

Yet, I believe, there is no other way to describe perestroika as an integral moral process. The desire of the morally healthy part of our society to shake off what remains of Stalin's heritage as soon as possible has remained perestroika's motive force—and the guarantee that the changes occurring in society are irreversible. Strange as it might seem, the less we have to travel toward the complete victory of common sense, the fewer people are willing to learn the full truth about our past and see our social history the way it has been. The time has now come when moral condemnation of Stalinism as a crime no longer takes us further toward understanding the society in which we live, toward comprehending what has happened to us and who is responsible for our troubles. Conversely, it has become a serious obstacle to learning the truth. This paradox was the mainspring that pushed out of me the text that I decided at last to put to the readers' judgment. So my book is not so much about the road of unmasking Stalinism that we have covered thus far as about the road that still lies ahead.

NOTE

1. K. Marx and F. Engels, *Collected Works*, (London: Lawrence & Wishart, 1975), 3:133.

CHAPTER 1

Was Stalin a Marxist?

Quite recently many of us, myself included, have believed that after we had told all the truth about Stalin and his epoch, after we had called a crime a crime and evil evil, there would no longer be any serious hurdles left to the progress of social thought and we would finally see the renaissance of a long-lost faculty for philosophical analysis and independent review of history, the world we live in, and our destiny. It seemed to us that if we were courageous enough to overturn the false idols, we would also have enough courage to expose false claims.

In the beginning, common sense managed to have the upper hand extremely easily. A few days of the 27th CPSU Congress and then of the January 1987 Plenum of the CPSU Central Committee destroyed the stronghold of ideological conservatism built for over fifty years.* We were nearly ready to say then: Our perestroika is the first revolution in history that does not entail the creation of new myths. On the contrary, it teaches people realism and gives them a chance to see the world as it is.

But today I see ever more clearly that such optimistic assessments were premature. We have really broken through former ideological conservatism. But alongside the truth, half-truths and even blatant lies have penetrated the resultant breach.

Bold, nearly revolutionary criticism of the past and the disowning of political and historical myths associated with Stalin's personality by themselves have not always and in all circumstances consolidated our ability to think and to realize who we are, what happened to us, and what we are to do next. In Russia the very possibility of forming an opinion about the state leader as if he were a mere mortal, the very chance of

---

* This is a reference to the dogmatic interpretation of socialism as a society based on public ownership, which excludes market relations, competition, and money. This interpretation can be traced back to Karl Marx.

calling a crime a crime and an absurdity an absurdity, has, of course, always been an enormous breakthrough. And today, after half a century of silence it would be a sacrilege to underestimate the spiritual and moral achievements of perestroika.

But in many instances the debunking of some easy-to-reveal political myths has led to the consolidation and popularization of other myths that are more plausible and, therefore, more dangerous. And frequently, emotional and honest criticism of the past has only diminished interest in its analysis and has hypnotized thought.

Is it not absurd that some of our writers have been trying to impose on us the idea that we, the Russians, are destined to build a "unique" and "specific" economy and to surprise the world by our ability to withstand hardship and to follow "the ideologists of self-denial" rather than to enjoy normal living standards and have good hospitals and computers?*

Is is not absurd that our so-called adult philosophy declares on the pages of some serious magazines that Stalin—that very Stalin who destroyed all the best in Russian peasants, who destroyed the Russian life-style with its traditions and sanctities—was nobody else but a covert Slavophile and expressed the interests of Russian patriarchal peasantry?†

I am of the opinion that many of those who write about Stalin and the thirties have completely lost touch with reality and common sense. Otherwise it would be impossible to hit upon the currently fashionable

---

* These views of Russian post-October history have been developed by the writer Alexey Prokhanov in his speeches and publicist articles. For example, speaking at the Plenum of the USSR Union of Writers on May 6, 1987, he tried to prove that our country's development could not be evaluated in terms of the universal values of modern civilization, that we had our peculiar criteria of advance. "There is rather a widespread view," Prokhanov said, "that perestroika was triggered off by our strategic lag behind Western civilizations. Soviet hospitals treat patients worse than Western hospitals, Soviet computers compute slower than Western computers, Soviet fields yield smaller crops than Western ones. And this underdevelopment harmful to our defence, social progress and all our national life urged us to pursue the policy of reforms. The challenge of perestroika is to catch up with the West, to reduce the lag following in its wake. Such a view . . . encourages us to tail Western civilization and makes us copy its models whether these are instruments, rock groups, methods of interviewing or managing and economic models."

Such imitation, in Prokhanov's opinion, deprives us of our sovereign way and gives rise to an inferiority complex. It suggests to this unique society, which has chosen socialism, trivial ways and means that foredoom us to depression. In contrast to traditional aims and methods of advance elaborated by civilization and "imitated strategic development objectives," he puts forward "original," "sovereign" ways "based on the ideals of socialist society." He believes that this program "will require from the people efforts equal to those that were once needed for our nuclear and space programs. It will ask for equal concentration and urgency." Hence, in Prokhanov's view, we may once again need in the future "thinkers advocating the idea of state stoicism, state self-denial"(*Literaturnaya Gazeta* [The literary gazette], May 6, 1987).

† A reference to Russian peasantry, their communal life-style, and predominantly natural form of production.

idea of our revolution's Thermidor, Stalin's counterrevolutionary coup at the end of the twenties—the idea that history and philosophy born in October 1917 died in 1929 and that the great change of those years meant a return to prerevolutionary Russia.*

I personally feel that, for example, a very fashionable myth today among the publicists about the peasant origin of Stalin's leftist leaps, including collectivization, was fostered precisely to make redundant the issue of the doctrinal causes of our failures in socialist construction and the responsibility of the party intellectuals and the working class for Stalinism.

The paradox of the current situation is that today, under perestroika, it has become even more difficult than in the recent past to purify Marxism of some typical mistakes of socialist thought of the nineteenth century.

When Soviet philosophers wrote several years ago that Marx had advanced the ideas of the complete elimination of small private farming, of transforming a peasant into an agricultural worker, and of large industrial farming, we had, in keeping with the views of that time, every ground to compare all these prognostic ideas with the actual results of their implementation and to think about the practical applicability of these ideas for the future.

True, there were some objections to such comparisons of socialist theory and practices, but they were not very serious and could generally be easily refuted. For instance, some philosophers used to say that it was not yet time to critically review "Critique of the Gotha Program" in which Marx had advanced the idea of pure, noncommodity, nonmarket socialism wholly based on the property of the entire people. These philosophers asserted it was too early to draw any conclusions, in the first place, because Marx's theoretical forecast was made for a longer period than our post-October experience of socialist construction.

Such an objection was not, however, accepted as a serious argument against the evaluation of historical fortunes and the already identified

---

* The gifted Soviet sociologist L. Ionin was also affected by the fashion to identify the change in 1929 with the Thermidor of the French Revolution. In his article "Conservative Syndrome," published in 1987 in the journal *Sotsiologicheskye Issledovaniya* (Sociological Studies), no. 5, he deliberately contrasted the ideology and policies pursued from 1917 to 1929 to the ideology and political practices characteristic of the period that followed the April 1929 Plenum of the party Central Committee. This author asserts that at first, beginning with October 1917, we resolutely and uncompromisingly broke with Russian conservatism and Russian etatism. Then "back at the end of the twenties the principle of organic development started regaining momentum though assuming a different—secularized, theoretical—aspect and, above all, acting in conjunction with the technocratic principle of rationality" (p. 26).

practical significance of Marxism. True, the experience we have gained in building socialism and communism is neither complete nor universal. And true, only the future global experience of socialist development will give us the right to dot all the i's and cross all the t's. Nevertheless, seventy years of life and work under new noncapitalist conditions plus nearly fifty years' experience of socialist construction in various regions of the world make a tangible historical experience whose cognitive importance can hardly be overemphasized. It is equally true that our experience in building and developing socialism has a significant advantage over possible future experience since it already exists, whereas future experience is just a probability and hope for the confirmation of the theory. Today's experience is, of course, academically much more representative. It can tell us how correct or erroneous some of the ideas are, whereas hope can never be an argument in an academic debate.

So comparison of Marxist theory with practice was considered a necessary and normal thing a few years ago. Today, if we take on trust the assertions of current critical publicism, we are deprived of the right to judge Marxism in the context of our socialist history. Similarly, if we agree to the statement of the author of the article "Which Street Leads to the Church?" that the socialism built by Stalin has nothing to do either with Marx's socialism or with the socialism of Trotsky, that this Stalin's socialism is the product of the inflamed consciousness of a patriarchal peasant, then we virtually have no right to compare scientific socialism with the real one.[1]

This ban is, probably, valid not only for our country but for the whole of the socialist bloc, since socialism there also developed in keeping with Stalin's pattern for a new society. The process of renovating economic and political structures carried from the Soviet Union to the national soil of other socialist countries has just started. Moreover, some parties in the international Communist movement still believe that in principle the command model of socialism and the total socialization of the means of production achieved in Stalin's time reflect most adequately the substance of scientific socialism.

Today we are greatly tempted, of course, simply to efface the memory of Stalin with his political practices and ideas of socialism from the history of Marxism and the international Communist movement. We are greatly tempted to compare Stalin's victory over his opponents in the Politburo of the CPSU(B)* Central Committee to the Thermidor or to

---

* The Politburo of the Central Committee of the CPSU is elected by a Plenary Meeting of the Central Committee. During the Stalin period it wielded absolute power both in the party and the country as a whole.

present it as a counterrevolutionary coup, as a complete break with the ideology and the ideals of Russia's revolutionary proletariat.

Once you yield to this temptation, all the problems are immediately solved: Stalin is condemned, faith in the ideal is preserved, and the "purity" of the theory is restored, etc.

The author of the above-mentioned article, "Which Street Leads to the Church?," I. Klyamkin, must have been guided by this reasoning when he contrasted variform Bolshevism of the twenties as a whole to Stalinism and insisted that the socialism built by Stalin differed from both the left wing's and the right wing's strategic economic concepts. To dramatize this approach and completely exclude Stalin's "patriarchal-peasant" leftism from the revolutionary working-class movement, Klyamkin deliberately converges the economic strategies of the left and the right wings, trying to prove that Trotsky and Bukharin did not differ at all in their attitude to Stalin.* He says, addressing the reader,

If you all of a sudden find in the documents of the thirties that two adjectives with the opposite meaning "right" and "left" were used to coin a single one "right-Trotskist," i.e, "right-leftist," do not regard it as some specific political ingenuity or, on the contrary, political naivety. The "right-leftists" are an indisputable fact rather than the verbal fruit of Stalin's imagination: since in terms of their attitude to the political regime that took shape and consolidated after collectivization the former "leftists" became "rightists." Neither the former nor the latter regarded the socialism built in the thirties as socialism. And they did not consider it to be such because it differed from their concepts of the new society.[2]

Psychologically, the wish to accept such an interpretation is understandable. It is difficult to put up with the thought that there are inherent

---

* Lev Davidovich Trotsky (1879–1940) was one of the leaders of Russian Social Democrats. In July 1917, he joined the Bolshevik faction of the Russian Socialist Democratic Workers' Party. Together with V. I. Lenin, he prepared and carried out the October Revolution. Later he was the people's commissar for military and naval affairs and took an active part in organizing the Red Army. He was also chair of the Revolutionary Military Council and made a major contribution to the Bolshevik victory in the Civil War. In 1929, Trotsky was accused of anti-Soviet activities and expelled from the Soviet Union. He was killed by Stalin's agent in Mexico in 1940.

Nikolai Ivanovich Bukharin (1888–1940), V. I. Lenin's close associate, was known as one of the most talented theoreticians of the Bolshevik party. As a member of the Politburo of the Central Committee of the All-Russia Communist Party (Bolshevik), Bukharin took an active part in the struggle against left-wing opposition. In 1929, he led a group of Politburo members who opposed Stalin and insisted that Lenin's policy of a union between the working class and all farmers be continued. The group also opposed the policy of the accelerated industrialization and forced collectivization. In 1921, Bukharin was expelled from the Central Committee of the All-Russia Communist Party (Bolshevik). In the course of the "right-wing and centrist anti-Soviet bloc" trial, he was sentenced to death by firing squad in 1938. He was rehabilitated posthumously.

reasons for the failures of the movement with which one's life is associated, that the causes of the failures lie in the revolutionary movement per
se, its own errors and miscalculations. It would be so much more comfortable to blame its enemies—some external, casual circumstances—for
everything that happened. You may observe that such psychological self-
defense back in the twenties contributed to the habit of always, under any
circumstances, looking for "wreckers" and "saboteurs." I think that it was
this tradition of our political thinking that resulted in the "Thermidor
phenomenon." Zinaida Nemtsova, a party veteran who lived through all
the atrocities of Stalinist concentration camps, tries to convince us in her
interview in the magazine *Ogonyok* that the repressions of 1937–38 were
organized by the white guards and the gendarmes who had penetrated
into the NKVD bodies in Moscow and Leningrad.* The journalist
O. Lazebnikov writes that Stalin from the very outset was a stool pigeon
and an agent of the tsarist secret police.[3] According to Professor of Philosophy A. Butenko, the political system of the cult-of-personality period
can hardly be called the political rule of the working class and its allies.
It would be sacrilege to assert that the working-class government could
do something like that. It would be much more correct to say that Soviet
history witnessed an usurpation by Stalin and his cronies of the class
dominance with all its perversions, deformations, and Bonapartist profiteering from the differences in the interests of the workers, peasants, and
office employees.[4]

The temptation to separate Stalinism from our socialist construction is
great, but we should, nevertheless, take into account the results of such
"separation." And, besides, we should take into account the historical
facts.

If, for example, we agree with Klyamkin that the left and the right
wing, Trotsky and Bukharin, basically shared the same views on socialism and the ways of socialist construction, we shall rob ourselves of the
chance to understand the substance of the ideological struggle of the
twenties, to identify the inherent, revolutionary sources of Stalinism,
and to get an insight into the meaning of the global alternative that the
new government born in October 1917 has always faced. The assertion
that all cats of the revolution are gray in the darkness of Stalin's night-
mare does not add anything to the understanding of our historical fortunes, to say nothing of the fact that we have absolutely no reasons to
believe that Lev Trotsky backed up the NEP† or shared Lenin's idea

---

* The People's Commissariat for Internal Affairs.
† The adoption of the New Economic Policy (NEP) was proclaimed at the 10th Congress of
    the All-Russia Communist Party (Bolshevik) in 1921. It marked the end of forced labor,

of socialism as a system of civilized cooperators. On the contrary, both Trotsky and the leaders of the other leftist opposition, Zinoviev and Kamenev, in their works written in the midtwenties did their best to instigate the party to eliminate private family farming. The antagonism between Trotsky and Bukharin in their attitudes toward the NEP and the understanding of the ways of building socialism could never be settled.

Clearly, the version of the Thermidor at once dramatically allays the researcher's and public's concern for all other possible causes (or, to be more exact, prerequisites) of Stalinism—primarily, the doctrinal ones. The more indignant we are with the vices of this "traitor to the cause of the revolution," the less we think about the revolution itself and its inherent objective contradictions, about the internal inconsistency of leftist radicalism, about the dialectic of revolutionary violence, etc. By no coincidence, most authors writing about Stalinism (with the exception of, probably, V. Selyunin, A. Nuikin, and L. Saraskina) prefer to ignore all these difficult and completely forgotten problems of our revolution. The talk begun by Yuri Trifonov in his *Old Man*, unfortunately, had no continuation.* The dialectic of revolution, the translation of social knowledge into a historical process, the change from theory to practice, the dialectic of centralization, the socialization of the means of production— that is, the deep contradictions of the process initiated by us in 1917— have not yet been thoroughly and dependably analyzed. This fact in itself hinders the development of a realistic philosophy, the philosophy of perestroika.

Here lies one of the paradoxes of glasnost characteristic of our current spiritual situation. The reduction in the number of zones closed to criticism has not entailed any measurable expansion of the territory open to free philosophical thought.† There is a kind of invisible line that cannot be overstepped by the vast majority of writers, publicists, and sociologists who write about the thirties. This invisible line demarcates the secondary

---

prodrazvyorstka (the surplus grain tax), the ban on free commerce, which had been introduced during War Communism from 1918 up to 1920. The NEP reinstated personal economic interest as the driving force of economic progress. It also helped to promote cooperation and called for a durable political union between the working class and laboring farmers.

* Yury Trifonov is a prominent Soviet author. He was particularly popular during the 1970s, when he published his novel *The Building on the Embankment*. His novel *The Old Man* is a poignant critique of the ruthlessness of the Civil War and a denunciation of revolution for the sake of revolution.

Selyunin, Nuykin, and Saraskina are prominent Soviet publicists.

† This phrase is a product of the Brezhnev era. "Zones closed for criticism" is another name for leaders of the party and the state, ministers and first secretaries of regional party organizations.

causes of this period's tragedies and our revolution's failures from their basic causes, which we have not yet started to contemplate.

Most complicated historical processes have so far been studied as points in isolation. Thus, the alternative of 1929, the option of the scope and the methods of industrialization at that time, is in no way harmonized with the basic alternative of Russia's development or with the substance of the socioeconomic and political choice made by revolutionary workers and peasants in October 1917. The idea of collective farming is very seldom associated with the closely related idea of *prodrazvyorstka* (the requisition of surplus grain in the first postrevolutionary years) or the practices and the ideology of War Communism.*

We have actually identified all Stalin's miscalculations and blunders. We have said everything about all his crimes and the harm done to the people by his political adventurism. But we have yet said nothing about the miscalculations and the errors for which he personally is not to blame. We have kept silent about the tragedies and the mistakes of the revolutionary working-class movement. We have drawn the veil over the delusions of the epoch, the structures of political government, the principles of inner-party life organization used by Stalin for his selfish, mercenary motives. We have said nothing about the moral and spiritual conditions that favored the whipping up of animosity, hatred, and suspicion. We have been until now unwilling to recognize that a society that has lived through the atrocities of a civil war is ill for a long time afterward, that for a long time it cannot recover from this shock.

Simply placing Stalin's crimes in the broad context of other senseless cruelties and in the terror of all other great revolutions will not, of course, help us to make headway toward truth. Such an approach would result in the loss of historical specifics and the loss of truth. But, on the other hand, there are no grounds to isolate Stalin's creation—the thirties—from the general logic of our revolution's development, just as there are no reasons to distinguish the terror of 1937 from that of 1929.

Our publicists seem to have for some reason forgotten that Stalin was not simply building his kingdom and consolidating his autocracy. He was transforming the social structure of society and peoples' life-styles. He was building socialism in keeping with the theoretical provisions. He was doing his best to speed up Russia's advancement toward communism, since he was deeply convinced of its feasibility and vital necessity. Just remember what he thought as he lay at death's door. As demonstrated by

---

* The economic strategy of War Communism relied on forced labor and equal distribution of basic consumer goods.

his work *Economic Problems of Socialism in the USSR,* Stalin to his last days opposed the attempts to underestimate the importance of revolutionary struggle against, as he believed, dying capitalism that had exhausted itself. "To eliminate the inevitability of war," he taught, "it is necessary to abolish imperialism."[5] Stalin remained the spokesperson for uncompromising Marxist opposition to the market, fiscal-commodity relationship, and to all that bore the stamp of capitalism and, in his view, hindered speedy advancement toward a Communist economy free from considerations of profit making and producers' autonomy. For instance, he regarded as unacceptable even such indulgence to cooperative property as the permission to sell to collective farms machinery such as tractors and harvesters, since, as he wrote, "it would turn back the wheel of history, it would not bring us any nearer to communism, but, on the contrary, remove us farther from it."[6]

While reading Stalin's piece, *Economic Problems of Socialism in the USSR,* I had the feeling that he was still continuing the polemics with Bukharin, started a quarter of a century before. He was arguing against the latter's idea of harmonizing socialism with the fiscal-commodity relations, which from Stalin's point of view was opportunist. Read the section on the NEP and the market relationship from his speech "The Right Deviation in the CPSU(B)" at the April 1929 joint Plenary Session of the party's Central Committee and Central Control Commission. Nearly twenty-five years later in his last theoretical work, published a few months before his death, he repeats the same ideas and just as passionately presses for the speedy elimination of the remains of commodity circulation, which in his view, are the main obstacle to the rapid development of productive forces providing the material and technical facilities for building communism.

Why should we deceive ourselves? Why foster myths about Stalin and his case? Both he and his activities were engendered by the revolutionary movement that had taken shape long before Stalin came to power. In the beginning was the word (i.e., theory), the urge to build communism in Russia. Therefore, we simply ought to correlate this theory, scientific socialism, with Stalin's own ideas of a collectivist society and only then compare things done by him with Marx's, Engels's, and Lenin's concepts of socialism.

How does a serious commission set out to determine the causes of cracks in a newly constructed building? With what does it start? It starts, of course, with the examination of the design. And only on making sure there are no mistakes in the master plan does it start checking the quality of work and materials used and the skills of the construction workers.

This is exactly what Lenin did when he analyzed the causes of the political and economic crisis that broke out in the newly established Soviet Republic at the beginning of 1921. He neither blamed the peasants for their wish to remain the owners of their land and to possess things they produced nor condemned the workers for the demands to be paid for their work. Lenin mentally went back to the sources, that is, to the philosophy of the economic strategy of War Communism, which had led the country to the crisis. He recognized the flaws in the original plan of socialist construction that leaned, above all, on enthusiasm and class-consciousness. He recognized the flaws in his own ideas of communizing production and everyday life.

In contrast, how do Soviet publicists and sociologists reason and act when they research the causes of the 1929 disaster and the following tragedies of the 1930s? They start with the end rather than the beginning. They completely ignore the problem of the socialist construction plan. It simply does not exist for them at all. They talk only about bad executors who allegedly did not want to and could not do what they were supposed to do.

One can hardly call it a serious and responsible approach to the subject. We are, of course, justified in our grief and indignation with the Russian Apocalypse—the tragedy of the thirties. We should not forget that only one hundred years ago Russia was a country of slaves, that slavery has for centuries dominated our national psychology, and, frankly speaking, we have still failed to eliminate it completely. In this context L. Ionin and I. Klyamkin have given us a timely reminder about the historical roots of our society. Even today many Soviet people are appalled at free speech and independent judgment. But as we are really challenging the heights of civilization, as we are willing to improve our society and to understand what has happened to it, we should set out to analyze these events from the very beginning, from the "word," from our theoretical foundations. This is because socialism is the only society in human history that is built deliberately, relying on a theoretical plan.

In this case, as never before, top priority is given to the accuracy of calculations. People should be both able and willing to get an insight into the doctrine on which they have entrusted the destiny of their country and their children.

In this case it is much more important to know the plan than the percentage of workers and peasants in the party by the end of the twenties or the number of horseless peasants by the time of Stalin's Great

Change.* Then why do our publicists dedicate hundreds of pages to stories about the insufficient zeal of the Russian peasants in erecting the socialist building but say nothing to stimulate reader's interest in the "word" per se (i.e., the original plan)?

I have read in this context a great deal of articles, particularly those of O. Latsis, L. Ionin, I. Klyamkin, L. Gordon, E. V. Klopov, and V. Kozhinov. These writings abound in interesting ideas, considerations, historical materials, and testimonies. But, unfortunately, none of these authors mentions the original positions and the very designs of our socialist construction, the doctrinal causes of socialism's deformations. However, they, to all appearances, understand that these are not trifles or minor philosophical niceties. These are the ideas that, once they are adopted by the ruling Communist party, become an enormous material force and determine the life and fortunes of hundreds of millions of people. Never before has humanity paid so high a price for its fondness for illusions as in the twentieth century and, above all, in the countries that are building socialism.

It is, of course, impossible to avoid mistakes in predicting the future, in particular, in forecasting the design of the socialist construction. A theorist always knows for sure only the things that have already happened. Hence, the theorist's knowledge is always incomplete. He or she cannot be aware of possible future human experience. But, nevertheless, it's a theorists's job to make judgments about the future, completing in his or her mind the economic and political processes that have not yet fully revealed themselves in life.

More important, a theorist, even though lacking some necessary expertise, has to take risks, to go beyond the frame of what has already existed, to subordinate life and production to his or her model of the future. This is because, as shown by our revolution, the impatience of the masses often precipitates events. The situation when "it is no longer possible to live in the old way" sometimes precedes precise knowledge of how to live in a new way, where and how to go. In this case, as Lenin wrote, we have to start acting and then see what happens. Lenin never concealed that we had to "engage in a serious battle in October 1917, and then saw such details of development [from the standpoint of world history they were certainly details] as the Brest peace, the New Economic Policy, and so forth."[7]

---

* According to Stalin, the transition to accelerated industrialization and collectivization marked "a great watershed" in the history of our revolution.

Is Economy without Trade Feasible?

Being aware of all this and actually getting down to building a socialist society unparalleled in history, we should pay prime attention to
avoiding mistakes in the theory of socialism, to improving and deepening our dependable knowledge of the future and finding new "details of
development."

We currently have a unique chance for this. The plaster put up by our
former propaganda has fallen off, and, as well as revealing all the basic
elements of the frame, this has given us an opportunity to examine the
foundation of a socialism built in battle. And obviously, right now, the
defects of the construction are not limited to Stalin's deviations from the
original design of socialism. (We should, most probably, say that he has
perverted the values of Marxism and misinterpreted the idea and aims of
socialist social transformations.) They also result from the deviation of
theoretical thought from realities, its arrogance, and its underestimation
of the complex and fundamental nature of social structures created by a
commodity civilization.

For example, it has become general practice to criticize the deformed,
barracklike, leveled-off socialism built in the thirties. But this criticism
painstakingly passes over the structural reasons why socialism was barracklike. And it shies away from the key question of whether we can
feasibly build nonbarrack, democratic socialism on a noncommodity,
nonmarket foundation.

This is really the million-dollar question, both for those who think
about the future and for those who try to understand the past. Why has
the antimarket and fiscal-commodity relationship campaign in all cases,
without any exception, in all countries—today's Iran of the Ayatollahs
included—always entailed autocracy, infringement on human rights and
personal dignity, and the omnipotence of administration and the bureaucratic apparatus? Why is even terror helpless against trade? Why have all
known historical attempts to eliminate free circulation and the producer's
economic autonomy, ours included, ended in failure that ultimately
urged a retreat?

Marx did not see this difficult question, as in his time there was no
respective historical experience for its statement. Therefore, he never
tried to go to the roots of the internal contradictions inherent in the methods he suggested for treating the evils of capitalism. This problem was
identified by Lenin in the last years of his life when he was studying the
reasons for the failures of War Communism's economic strategy.

A similar deficit of conceptual thinking is also characteristic of Soviet publications criticizing Stalin's policies of coercive collectivization. The authors writing on this topic (with the exception of articles by G. Shmelev and V. Bashmachnikov published in the magazine *Octyabr*) unwittingly foster the illusion that the problem is reduced to the dilemma, Should collective farms be set up by cavalry or noncavalry methods? As if our destiny would have been absolutely different had Stalin obeyed Engels and given an individual farmer a chance "to think on his little plot of land."

But today, in the context of all our (and not only our) experience of socialist transformations in agriculture, this dilemma clearly does not itself reflect the real depth of the problems we face and which we have started expertly to resolve since the June 1988 Plenum of the CPSU Central Committee. One should not foster the illusion that we can remedy the situation by simply going back to what Engels wrote about collective agriculture and acting strictly in keeping with his prescriptions.

The substance of the problem that urges us to look for the truth, concrete reality, is quite different: Should we without fail seek production cooperation in agriculture? Do we really make a major breakthrough when we transform a peasant into a worker laboring according to a single plan on one large national factory?

Was the peasants' labor organization, wedding the way of life, production, and the family into a single entity, really an anachronism? To what extent was the plan of nationwide farming organization scientifically grounded? Is land nationalization really a necessity in all cases?

Besides the problem of collectivization, dozens of other "difficult questions"—not directly related to Stalin's personality—crop up when we contemplate his epoch.

I shall list just a few of them to give the reader a better idea of the closed zones that up till now neither our scholars nor even publicists touch upon under any pretext.

Can there be reliable guarantees of democracy and an individual's freedoms when all members of society are employed by the proletarian state and have no autonomous sources of existence? Was it possible to avoid coercive pressure on the peasantry in the context of the Marxist theory that socialized work and collective farming are an economic necessity? Has not the teaching on the revolutionary vanguard of society entailed new forms of social inequality? Are "pure," direct forms of harmonizing an individual's interests with the interests of society always more efficient than the "impure," indirect ones? Does the experience of humanity's development in the twentieth century give us grounds to persist with our belief in the feasibility of complete elimination of ideological pluralism and religious consciousness and in the possibility of doing away with the multiplicity of social and economic forms? Is it generally worthwhile to seek the elimination of all traditional mechanisms of human life, organization, and encouragement, including those that we call patriarchal?

These are, of course, difficult questions. They are impossible to answer at once. But we should neither put off their discussion till tomorrow nor go on sacrificing the interests of our state, our people, our offspring in order to foster the illusion that the working class, as L. Kamenev asserted, "could not be wrong." We often say today that history has given us a last chance and is giving us extremely little time to correct our mistakes. But why then, even under these circumstances, do we still lack courage to attempt to identify the essential mistakes, to tell ourselves the fundamental truth?

I believe that our movement toward this fundamental truth should start with ascertaining the already known and not at all frightful truth that Stalin's reasoning and his views of socialism as a whole were quite typical of Marxists at that time. At least we must screw up the courage we had thirty years ago after the 20th CPSU Congress and initiate serious research into the philosophical and social ideas and stereotypes of thinking that underlay political and economic practices at the turn of the thirties.

It has become somewhat difficult today even to say that Stalin as a personality took shape in Marxist surroundings, that he mastered to the best of his capacities and background the theoretical heritage of the classics and generally never went beyond the frame of Marxist truisms in his writings and speeches.

When, how, and why was it possible to deform Marxism and turn it into the formulas of the Stalinist epoch? What are the inherent prerequisites for such deformities in Marxism per se?

It is, naturally, easier to write about Stalin's petty bourgeois degradation and the patriarchal sources of his consciousness than to ask oneself difficult questions and to answer them. But now it is already impossible to avoid these difficult questions. They will crop up by themselves as soon as the grass-roots readership can get hold of the writings by the leaders of the October Revolution.

Then the myth that Stalinism is peculiar, a myth that is neither of the Right nor of the Left but is a third interpretation of Stalinism's aims, will immediately collapse on its own. Suffice it to compare, for instance, the criticism of Bukharin's economic ideas in the co-report by G. Zinoviev at the 14th CPSU(B) Congress with Stalin's attacks on the views of the "right wing" at the joint April 1929 Plenum of CC and Central Control Commission of the CPSU(B) to see the same leftist line, the same leftist revision of Lenin's political will.

This line essentially consists of attacks on the key elements of the NEP, trade, and the free exchange of produce. To be truthful, the party leaders who handed to Stalin the baton of radicalism, for example, the above-mentioned Zinoviev, were even more devoted to left-wing dogmata than the author of the Great Change of 1929.

No, Stalin was only an epigone of the uncompromising Communist opposition to the old and of the impatience that dominated the old Politburo after Lenin's death. Stalin and his methods of controlling the market and free trade even lacked in leftism compared to the co-report of the Leningrad opposition. That is what actually happened. And we hardly have a right to ascribe to Stalin, as I. Klyamkin does, the laurels of the most leftist of all left-wing leaders of our revolution. He was a pupil in everything. But a diligent pupil, one cannot deny that.

Stalin maintained continuity with all our left-wing oppositions along all lines. He shared G. Zinoviev's negative attitude toward the market and free trade, whereas his etatistic and technocratic feeling, his mechanistic attitude to social life, and his belief that the strength of socialism and its gains depend on the power of its administrative bodies related him to Trotsky and all the ideologists of Trotskyism. All the ideologists of Trotskyism could only dream of the powerful administrative socialism that Stalin managed to build. Did not E. Preobrazhensky, the main theorist and the brain of the Trotskyist opposition, call for the marriage of political and economic power, the absolute omnipotence of administrative bodies, the establishment of large grain factories in agriculture—the ones that were later built by Stalin on corpses? I do not know. Why should I deceive myself and other people and convince the reader that Trotsky and his comrades-in-arms dreamt of a different, non-Stalinist socialism?

But the point is that, despite Klyamkin's assertions, Stalin did not break with the left wing in 1929. On the contrary, he returned to their ideas and concepts, their views on the ways of socialist construction in Russia. The year 1929 did not see any Thermidorian coup or any degradation of our revolutionary spirit. Our tragedy was that Stalin attempted to hold Russia artificially on the revolutionary wave by coercive methods. He tried, in keeping with the prescriptions of the left-wing oppositions, to revive in the country the political climate of the Civil War epoch, the atmosphere of uncompromising antagonism to everything that was associated with private property and a fiscal-commodity relationship.

As for the key question of all Russian revolutions—that of attitude to the peasantry—Stalin was a typical leftist, a typical peasant-hater. I think that the deep, hidden essence of Stalinism and *Stalinschina*, as a variety of Russian left extremism, was precisely the hostile attitude to peasants and the rural way of life as a whole.* The methods of politically discrediting the individual farmer-proprietor and, above all, politically discrediting the middle peasants were also borrowed by Stalin from the leaders of the left wing. Back in 1925 none other than Zinoviev openly came out against Lenin's idea of the popular alliance. He said that "now the middle peasants can and should be called petty bourgeois." "Those who fail to see it," denounced the leader of the Leningrad opposition, "impudently idealize the middle peasant."[8] None other than Zinoviev urged the 14th CPSU(B) Congress to show "much greater resoluteness in our attitude to the peasant than we had shown before."[9]

The same methods were used by Stalin to intimidate the dissenters—Bukharin, Rykov, and Tomsky—who "stumbled" in their weakness for the peasantry. He blamed them for underestimating the middle peasant's proprietary nature that draws him nearer to the village rich—the kulak. In his view, they underestimated that "the peasants as long as they remained individual farmers involved in a petty goods economy indirectly and continuously engendered capitalists amidst them and could not do otherwise."

It is beyond my understanding how some Soviet publicists have managed to find something peculiar, Russian, patriarchal, and national in Stalin's conceptions of socialism. Everything he wrote in the late twenties and in the thirties bears such a strong resemblance to our socialist antipeasant sentiment, leftist impatience, and biased attitudes of the Civil War period as well as to the impatience shown later by Trotsky, Zinoviev, and Kamenev. To me there is nothing unexpected even in Stalin's thesis on the feasibility of the victory of socialism in one country. Just remember that as early as mid-1918 the party started the direct, immediate transition from capitalist to Communist Russia. I doubt that someone will risk blaming that Politburo for a liking for the Russian idea or for patriarchal conservatism.

Moreover, I cannot see in Stalin's worldview anything that distinguished him from the European Marxists of the twenties either. For example, Karl Kautsky, the antithesis of Stalin and Russian revolutionary

---

* The Russian word *Stalinschina* is used to refer to Stalin's policies of reprisals during the 1930s, the extermination of the well-to-do and middle farmers, and political trials in the USSR in the late 1930s. *Stalinschina* also implies arbitrary and illegal actions of the secret police.

leftism, had a conception that was absolutely similar to Stalin's idea of the substance of socialism. Resolutely opposing Stalin's coercive collectivization, Karl Kautsky, nevertheless, also believed in the feasibility of non-market, noncommodity (i.e., from his point of view, genuinely socialist) production. "Socialism means," Karl Kautsky wrote in a book devoted to the criticism of Stalinism, "that an enterprise should no longer be the source of profit it was in the capitalist's hands. It should rather be the means of meeting consumer requirements to the utmost and building up workers' standards of living. The capitalists will be no longer satisfied with the results of its work but consumers and workers should be satisfied with them without fail."[10]

Compare this quotation from Karl Kautsky with Stalin's writings on socialism in such works as, for instance, "The Agrarian Policies in the USSR" (1929) or especially *Economic Problems of Socialism in the USSR* (1952), and you will see for yourself that these two authors shared the same concepts of the ultimate aims of the future system. In terms of the substance of Marxism, there were actually no differences between a Marxist Stalin and a Marxist Kautsky.

The fundamental economic law of socialism formulated by Stalin repeats nearly word for word Kautsky's view on the objective of collectivist production. It basically boils down, as our social science has repeated ever since Stalin, to "the securing of the maximum satisfaction of the constantly rising material and cultural requirements of the whole of society by means of continuous expansion and perfection of socialist production on the basis of higher techniques."[11]

Note that Kautsky's suggestion that workers, in contrast to capitalists, can be satisfied with minimum profit or disregard it altogether was also proclaimed by Stalin as one of the basic laws of the socialist economy. He gave special priority to this "law" in the collectivization period when the economic efficiency of socialized agriculture dramatically decreased. "Large grain factories do not take hold in capitalist countries," he said at that time.

In capitalist countries large grain factories cannot be organized for there private ownership of land exists and the organization of such grain factories would entail the purchase of quite a number of plots of land, or the payment of absolute ground rent, which could not but impose a heavy burden on production. In our country neither absolute ground rent, nor the sale and purchase of land exist, for in our country there is no private ownership of land, and this cannot but create favorable conditions for the development of large grain farms. In capitalist countries the purpose of large-scale farming is to extract the maximum of profit. In our country, on the contrary, the large grain farms need neither a maximum of profit, nor the average rate of profit for their development; they can limit themselves to a minimum of profit, and sometimes even forego profit altogether, which again creates favorable conditions for the development of large grain farms.[12]

Note too that the above-mentioned E. Preobrazhensky, an international authority on the theory of socialism and the planned economy, also said that socialism could be satisfied for a long time with minimum profit. He, for example, wrote in his central work, "The Fundamental Law of Socialist Accumulation," that whereas capitalism did not and by its very structure could not endure any period of making losses instead of profit (i.e., a period when from the capitalist point of view its work was wasted), that kind of performance was characteristic of the War Communist economy. Preobrazhensky insisted that "whereas the capitalist economy is motivated by seeking maximum profit, the period of War Communism featured aspiration for the largest possible produce even at the cost of greatest losses."[13]

If Preobrazhensky's works are republished, it will be clear to all that Stalin repeated his ideas even in minor details. Even the idea of accelerated industrialization belongs to Preobrazhensky. He wrote, "To get through this period as fast as possible, to reach as soon as possible the moment when the socialist system will display all its natural advantages over capitalism—this is the question of life and death for the socialist state."[14]

Stalin's views of socialism and its major aims could not measurably differ from the ideas of other Marxists of that time as they relied on the same social and philosophical doctrines. This was conclusively demonstrated by Adam Szaff, a distinguished Polish philosopher and a veteran of the Polish workers' movement, in his recent interview to the Krakow magazine *Zdane*. This scholar believes that the essence of Stalinism had been expressed long before Stalin became the omnipotent ruler of Russia. It lies in the conviction, characteristic of many Marxists at that time, that the author formulates in the following way: "It is not really important what people actually think. The important thing is what they must think." According to Szaff, this philosophical substance of Stalinism was most fully and precisely expressed by the Hungarian Communist D. Lukacs in his world-famous book *History and Class Consciousness*. And, Szaff adds, it went without saying that only the party of the proletariat knew what the people had to think, only this party knew the truths of Marxism.

The mere fact of distinguishing scientific consciousness—"what people must think"—from everyday consciousness—"what they think"—or opposing the "advanced" ideology of the working class to the "backward" worldview of the peasant masses does not, of course, automatically lead to any abuse or repression. Everything depends on society's sense of justice and on the moral and spiritual standards of those people who can influence the course of events. But the conviction of some people that they know better, that they are aware of something that is beyond others' understanding, this conviction alone can become the reason for justifying any violence, especially in extreme political circumstances.

By elevating theoretical consciousness, the consciousness of the revolutionary vanguard, the Marxists of that time unwittingly elevated to the extreme the power of the revolutionary leaders over the ordinary people. They elevated those who spoke on behalf of the laws of history. In the context of such an uncritical attitude to everything that was said in the name of Marxism—the science of the laws of social development—there was a dramatic increase in both the threat of a subjective and arbitrary attitude to everything that differed from the theoretical forecasts of the future and the threat of political tyranny.

Most dangerous in this respect are the decades of stormy upheaval, as an atmosphere of mass hysteria provides neither the spiritual nor political conditions for doubts and self-verification of the projections of future events. Doubters are doomed at this time to the lot of counterrevolutionaries, antagonists of progress and of the great cause of the world proletarian revolution.

We may agree with Szaff that the gnosiological sources of Stalin's disdain for what people actually thought and felt lie even deeper and are rooted most deeply in Hegelian gnosiology. Hegel pioneered the idea that "class in itself" differed from "class for itself." Our present habit of opposing the true, fundamental interests of the class to the so-called false, empiric interests of some of its representatives derives precisely from Hegel's belief that one should not give credence to what people think about themselves since they are presently unable to realize their true, essential interests.

The dichotomy, "class in itself"–"class for itself," was itself imbued with the latent possibility of tyranny over this class. Where can one find the criteria for distinguishing true thoughts from false ones, genuine interests from imaginary ones? What gave Stalin grounds to believe, for instance, that industrial farming corresponded to peasants' true interests whereas their love for their own plot of land reflected their sham, imaginary interests?

Stalin, like Trotsky, appealed to the "great historical challenge," to the idea of building a society without peasants. But the very concept of such a great aim is merely a possibility, a hypothetical phenomenon.

The so-called sham interests, despite all their inevitable limitations (as actual things are always limited by what exists), have the self-evident advantage of being real. We are risking a lot when we regard them as inferior to the interests that people, in our view, should ultimately realize. It's acceptable if theorists and politicians do not err but find and formulate for workers and peasants their true fundamental interests (these classes cannot, as we know, rise to scientific ideology).

And if not? If the theorists make a mistake? And if there are no absolutely dependable criteria for distinguishing the genuine interests of the class from sham ones? Then how shall we distinguish rascals who exploit peoples' faith in the possibility of a different and happier life from those who came to assume the sufferings of the miserable?

It is true that Stalin, in Szaff's view, was so artful that, in contrast to Lukacs, he never admitted his "golden rule" aloud. Things he wrote, with the exception of his thesis on the aggravation of the class struggle with the development of socialism, never contradicted Marxist-Leninism. This is the opinion of many Marxists in the socialist countries. This is the opinion of those who listened to Stalin and remember his epoch. At least none of them agrees to compare Stalin's Great Change to the Thermidor of the French Revolution.

D. Zatonsky, a member-by-correspondence of the Ukrainian Academy of Sciences and the son of the distinguished Ukrainian Communist leader V. P. Zatonsky—a victim of the 1937 repressions—writes,

What Napoleon, the first Consul and then the Emperor, suggested to the French bore no resemblance to the kingdom of reason of which the Enlighteners had dreamt. In contrast, the version of socialism that Stalin presented to us looked on the face of it very much like the designs drafted by Marx, Engels and Lenin. We became especially confused because these were virtually nothing but draft designs. Lenin had, of course, a general theoretical idea of socialism, but we had to build it in one isolated country, and what's more, the country was Russia.[15]

"As for Stalin," Zatonsky writes, he tried "to be true to the letter." He knew his job well. The concept of the party as the "Order of Sword-Bearers," the reduction of the role of common people to the function of "mere cogs of the wheel," and the thesis on the aggravation of the class struggle with advancement to the heights of socialism—these are actually

Stalin's only evident deviations from the spirit of Marxism. At least these are the only examples one comes across while reading about his revision of scientific communism."[16]

NOTES

1. I. Klyamkin, "Which Street Leads to the Church?" *Novyi Mir*, 1987, no. 11.
2. I. Klyamkin, *Novyi Mir*, 1988, no. 11:178.
3. O. Lazebnikov, "The Fortune's Lines," *Sovetskaya Cultura*, June 16, 1988.
4. See *Moscow News*, 1987, no. 43.
5. J. Stalin, *Economic Problems of Socialism in the USSR* (Moscow: Gospolitizdat, 1952), 41.
6. Stalin, *Economic Problems*, 101.
7. Lenin, *Collected Works*, 33:480.
8. Shorthand record of the 14th VKP(B) Congress (in Russian), 121.
9. Ibid., 128.
10. K. Kautsky, *Bolshevism in the Deadlock* (in Russian) (Berlin: Granat, 1930), 51.
11. Stalin, *Economic Problems*, 86.
12. J. Stalin, *Problems of Leninism* (Moscow: Gospolitizdat, 1947), 296.
13. E. Preobrazhensky, "The Fundamental Law of Socialist Accumulation" (in Russian), *Vestnik Communisticheskoy Academyi* 8 (1924):99–100.
14. Ibid., 81.
15. D. Zatonsky, "Why Did They Give False Testimony Against Themselves and Others," *Nedelya*, 1988, no. 28.
16. Ibid.

CHAPTER 2

The Kingdom of Marxist Truisms

It is difficult to prove that after 1929 only "Marxist phraseology" and "the theoretical guise" were left of Stalin's Marxist views and his devotion to the ideals of the socialist revolution. Generally speaking, separating Stalin's ideas and concepts from their political and economic substance is impossible. The philosophical and socioeconomic content of ideas is always and without fail greatly determined by the ideological means of their realization and, above all, by the spiritual atmosphere, the sociopsychological environment of their existence and reproduction. Stalin maintained a firm belief in objective, unavoidable laws of historical development, in the imminent breakup of the capitalist production mode, and in the feasibility of all the theoretical forecasts of the Communist future developed in the classic works. He was a staunch atheist who did not care a straw about any Christian moral values. Stalin was a deadly enemy of private property.

Note that the fundamental difference between traditional Russian conservatism and today's anti-perestroika conservatism, which rejects glasnost and radical economic reform, lies precisely in the attitude toward religion, private property, and peasants. Hence, Stalinism can hardly be regarded as the Renaissance of Russian patriarchal tradition.

Russian patriarchal conservatism has sins of its own. But at least it was not obsessed, as our Marxist dogmatists are, with repeated attempts to build a society on the principles of Robert Owen's utopian commune, dismantling in passing the cultural heritage of world civilization. This is also a kind of conservatism—to persist in a state of fragmentation, disintegration, and destruction.

In contrast, our present-day conservatism comes out in favor of a peculiar immobility. It urges the retention of the former basic line that undermines cooperation, family work, and the market. It looks forward to a continuous sequence of crises but only insofar as they do not affect the conservatives' top priorities; that is, they should maintain the conditions for retaining power and controlling the lives and thoughts of other people.

The current situation is so complicated precisely because it is difficult to find in the works and the slogans of our conservatives anything that clashes with the habitual, conventional views of Marxism and even Marx's texts. In fact, this is equally true of Stalin's works and slogans: He was fond of harmonizing everything with the classics, and if he deviated from their fundamentals, he always explained why he did so.

For instance, Stalin was well aware of Engels's words that Communists should side with "the small peasant" and "should make it possible for him to remain on his little plot of land for a protracted length of time to think the matter over." He cited this quotation from Engels's "The Peasant Question" in his report "Concerning Questions of Agrarian Policy in the USSR." But he simply believed that in Russia, in contrast to Europe, it was unnecessary to give the peasant "a protracted length of time," as in Russia the Communists were dealing with a totally different type of peasant. Stalin's arguments in favor of accelerated industrialization bear, by the way, a strong resemblance to the arguments given today by some publicists attempting to prove that Russian patriarchal peasants had to "reconcile themselves" to collective farms. "How are we to explain this circumspection displayed by Engels, which at first sight seems exaggerated? What did he proceed from?" asked Stalin, as usual employing a few rhetorical questions. And he answered them:

Obviously he proceeded from the existence of private ownership of land, from the fact that the peasant has [his little plot of land] which he will find it hard to part with. Such is the peasantry in the West. . . . Can it be said that such a situation exists in our country, in the USSR? No, it cannot. It cannot be said because here we have no private ownership of land chaining the peasant to his individual farm. It cannot be said because in our country the land is nationalized, and this facilitates the transition of the individual peasant to collectivist lines.[1]

Let us at least recognize today, when we are trying to tell the truth, that it was this thesis on the idiocy of rural life and the disharmony between socialism and small farming (i.e., farming on the peasant's own plot of land) that lay the foundation of Stalin's arguments in favor of collectivization. Had he failed to substantiate expropriation in agriculture by

Marxist ideas, he would have hardly won the support of the party. Stalin's speech on right-wing deviation in the CPSU(B) at the April 1929 joint
Plenary Session of the CC and CCC of the CPSU(B) relied on a Marxist
interpretation of the peasantry as the last capitalist class.

I for one generally cannot understand why many Soviet social scientists and publicists are so unwilling to recognize the Marxist inheritance
of our revolution and our socialism. Still they try to press home to the
reader that everything that has happened to us has nothing to do with
original, true Marxism. I'd wager that those who attempt to build an
insurmountable wall between Marx and the Stalinist socialism of our
revolution know neither the theoretical heritage of the founding fathers
of scientific socialism nor the history of our party. Marx was the one to
pioneer the idea of the feasibility of building socialism on the foundation
of the Russian commune–provided, of course, timely political and technological assistance from the victorious proletariat in developed capitalist
countries arrived to support the revolution in Russia! In the last years of
his life, Marx, in contrast to everything he had written earlier on the
prerequisites of socialist revolution, urged his followers "not to be too
afraid of the word *archaic.*"[2] Who was the man who wrote to Vera
Zasulich,* "Special research conducted on the basis of the materials I got
from the original documents convinced me that the commune was the
foothold of Russia's social renaissance"?[3] Was it not Marx? If it was
Marx, then what is the essence of the so-called differences between him
and the Russian Bolsheviks? The latter, while storming the Winter Palace,
also hoped most of all for any political and other assistance they would
get after the imminent and, it seemed to them, speedy victory of the
proletarian revolution in the West.

Even more absurd are the recently more frequent attempts to portray
the authors of the *Communist Manifesto* as zealots of private property and
the fiscal-commodity relationship and in every way opposed to the
expropriatory sentiments of the Bolsheviks, including Joseph Stalin.
None other than Karl Marx and Frederick Engels firmly linked the concept of "communism" to the process of "abolition of private property."[4]
And none other than Karl Marx related humanity's historical and economic progress with the replacement of capitalist property by "the
highest form of the archaic property type, i.e., by communist property."[5]

No, in terms of their attitude toward property, to the nationalization
and socialization of the means of production, and to the campaign against

---

* Vera Ivanovna Zasulich (1849–1919) was an active participant in the revolutionary movement in Russia at the end of the eighteenth century. She was one of the organizers of the
Social Democratic movement called the "Liberation of Labor" (1883).

the market and the fiscal-commodity relationship, the Bolsheviks, including Stalin, were highly consistent and orthodox Marxists. Even with the best will in the world one cannot deny that. The idea of nationalizing all land, of making it the property of the entire people, was taken by the Bolsheviks from Karl Marx. They were more orthodox in this respect than George Plekhanov and his Menshiviks,* who were more inclined to municipalize arable land.

Stalin, of course, attempted to realize the model of socialism that took shape under War Communism. But the economic strategy of War Communism had been directly influenced by Marx's teaching on producers' association and general work organization on a national scale. This teaching rules out small private production and the free exchange of produce, in short, trade.

In keeping with the letter of Marxism, "within the cooperative society based on common ownership of the means of production, the producers do not exchange their products; just as little does the labor employed on the products appear here as the value of these products."[6] Marx's idea was to organize production along the lines of a large factory where everything is subordinated to the manager's iron will and the shops do not trade with one another but simply supply the necessary products to one another. That is why Lenin's conception of socialism as a society, "all citizens of which become employees of a single country-wide state 'syndicate,' work equally, do their share of work and get equal pay,"[7] described in his book *The State and Revolution*, can be regarded as a reproduction of the essence of Marxist teaching on the collectivist society. Even our practice of eliminating the former division of power is in line with the ideals of the classics of Marxism. Indeed, the early writers on Marxism believed that one of the advantages of the Paris Commune was that, as a form of political organization, it wedded executive and legislative functions.

By studying the doctrinal, theoretical sources of the practices of the thirties we may gain a clearer understanding of what has happened to us. We also provide the conditions for the self-verification of Marxism and its creative development. A theory is alive until it can be correlated with practice, with the results of its practical implementation. Then to look after itself and mature in a healthy condition, it should examine itself in the mirror of historical practice.

Our dramatic history has taught us that reference to Marx, even when

---

* Georgy Valentinovich Plekhanov (1857–1918) was the founder of the Russian Social Democratic Party. At the 2d Congress of the Russian Socialist Democratic Workers' Party in 1903, the party split. The hard-line revolutionary majority, led by V. I. Lenin, broke away from the moderate minority reformers, led by G. V. Plekhanov.

the quotation is just, is not always a sufficient and exhaustive argument. We should not forget that Stalin's, and Trotsky's, belief in the need for complete elimination of small goods production and individual worker's isolation took root in Marxism.

That is why I think that the standpoint of truth is the only possible one in this dispute about the origin of our real socialism. At least, it allows the researcher to preserve a scientific, materialist approach to Marxism and our socialist practices.

We can and, indeed, should ask ourselves, Which elements of Marxism have been corroborated and to what in it should we adhere? Which aspects of Marx's teaching were true only of his epoch, the nineteenth century? In what were Marx and Engels mistaken?

We are no longer afraid of all these questions since such a rational attitude to scientific socialism was bequeathed to us, their Communist followers, by the founding fathers of Marxism themselves. They considered themselves to be scholars, no more and no less. We ourselves turned them into prophets who could foresee centuries ahead. In contrast, they believed that their views on the differences between the future non-capitalist and the then existing society were "accurate conclusions from historical facts and development processes and . . . of no academic or practical value outside their context."[8]

We shall never "squeeze slavery out of our system" until we develop within ourselves a healthy doubt about, among other things, the conclusions of Marxism. The question about the mistakes of the founding fathers of Marxism is justified since they were human beings, they had their own preferences, and, like all true revolutionaries, their preferences were considerably strong ones. Just remember Engels's idea that parents should be liberated from the duty to support and educate their children or his thoughts on the elimination of the family home and inheritance or his declaration that there will be neither wheelbarrow pushers nor architects in the future society!

We badly need today Marx's materialism, his dialectic, his flexibility of mind, and his ability to think in concrete historical terms as well as his critical attitude to reality. But it is difficult to agree with the view that all the truths of socialism have been long found, all the designs long developed, that there is no need to "reinvent the wheel" and our job is limited simply to the honest and thorough execution of what was conceived by the classics. I am deeply convinced that this position is devoid of even declared dedication to Marxism, to say nothing of a scientific, responsible attitude to the future of our country and a serious attitude toward science.

The theory of a Communist society developed in the middle of the nineteenth century cannot remain absolutely invariable at the end of the twentieth. What passes for "loyalty to Marxism" in our everyday political life is frequently nothing but servility and may be even another manifestation of our traditional idleness.

Our former conviction that everything written by Marx is the ultimate truth can hardly be useful today. Just imagine what would become of our country if we once again, for the third time after War Communism and Stalin's onslaught on the market, attempted to model our economy on Marx's pattern, that is, to rely on the direct exchange of production and to impose absolute, comprehensive planning from above.

If today you hang onto faith when the ground is slipping from under your feet, you demonstrate your infantilism, your spiritual and intellectual underdevelopment. To believe, to dream, and to hate is, of course, easier than to reason, to doubt, and to analyze. It is easier to give up dogmatic illusions than the style of thinking resulting from them, to say nothing of the dogmata on which one's political career or living standards and amenities depend.

All this urges us today to examine seriously and openly Marxist doctrine on the economic foundations of the future society and the correlation of his theoretical forecasts with the actual results of their practical implementation. This is important not only in order to do away with all the concepts of socialism that have long hindered our progress but also to improve the spiritual atmosphere both in the party and society. We must revive active theoretical studies, get rid of sloganlike Marxism, and encourage concern for independent thinking. The light shed on Stalin should at the same time promote our concern for ourselves. This concern is necessary since, if our original structures of thinking are similar to his and take root in the same truisms, we are not, therefore, guaranteed against the fall into the abyss of violence and crimes once experienced by Koba—a revolutionary who fought underground against tsarism and capitalism. Nobody will manage to convince me that this man was preordained to become the worst criminal in history.

The historian M. Hefter warns us in one of his articles, "We should not be afraid of our spiritual kinship with Stalin, we must see and realize it in order to eliminate all that is of Stalin in us." In my view, he is right because "if we fail to understand it we may even today grow dangerous" by chance. "Dangerous to ourselves and, hence, to other people, since the mental paralysis of the past activates the worst prejudices, with all their attendant, servile lies, and probably most dangerous of all, blocks historical consciousness from politics."[9]

I think these are not futile apprehensions. Our social scientists grew unaccustomed to considering the moral content and sociopolitical effects of their ideas. We have generally developed a firm belief that before entering the temple of social science we must sell our souls to the devil and elevate ourselves above good and evil. Many people are still convinced today that they should above all love the laws of history and that law and goodness are incompatible.

These motives persist even in the recent philosophical and historical journals published in the perestroika period. We are still no better than Stalin when we show indifference to the deaths of people unconnected to us, which is strange for a sane person. The magazine *Novyi Mir* asserts that neither economic nor technical progress can come about in Russia without "a massacre" and, hence, we should love and understand this history of "massacres."

Whereas the authors of this magazine try to bring home to the public that collectivization and mass deaths from starvation in the early thirties were the punishment for peasants' folly and laziness, the magazine *Nash Sovremennik* tries to prove that the party intellectuals deserved their lot, and we, once again, deal with punishment rather than repressions. In both cases we witness a Stalinist, fatalistic understanding of historical law as providence, an irresistible elemental force. Both examples demonstrate the firm belief that class cannot be harmonized with morality, that certain classes and social strata are worthy of approval whereas certain other classes simply should not be regarded as people.

True, under perestroika it is also imperative to remember Marxist truisms and to keep in mind that, as the historian L. Ovrootsky noted in the popular newspaper *Sovetskaya Cultura*, Stalin's adventurism and cult "resulted from the lack of political culture among the numerically dominant peasant masses and their psychology of petty-bourgeois revolutionism which essentially boils down to a continuous change of heart from extreme anarchism to passionate longing for 'a strong hand.'"[10]

But shall we profit much today from the mechanical repetition of these truisms? Will this kind of analysis promote the enrichment of thought, the advancement of our society as a whole? Will it help to do away with the stockpiled deformations? What is the political and practical aim of all these persistent discourses on the political and social inferiority of peasantry, on the petty-bourgeois regeneration of the party, on the leftism and adventurism of a patriarchal peasant?

And, finally, the most important question to ask: Can we overcome Stalinism if we agree with its doctrine that peasants posed the greatest threat to socialism? If we agree with this thesis and want to be consistent, we should recognize that Stalin was correct in his attempts to annihilate a class that allegedly stood in the way of building a new society in Russia.

If all the misfortunes of our revolution result from our peasant origins, from a peasant way of thinking and living, we should be consistent and exterminate the remnants of the rural roots in ourselves, destroy completely our peasant traditions, and conclude the task of turning a peasant into an agrarian worker and building large grain-producing factories. Rationally speaking, the biased and one-sided analysis of such complicated phenomena as leftist failures of our revolution will do us no good.

If, for example, some publicists derive their political charges against former individual farmers—men of property—from their faith in the absolute political stability and economic realism of the working class, then why cannot Nina Andreyeva, the author of the notorious anti-perestroika manifesto, derive from the same source her dislike for the intelligentsia, for instance, the descendants of the Russian liberals and Social Democrats?* Mikhail Hefter is right: Stalin with his cruel understanding of the class approach is not yet dead; he lives in us.† We go on mechanically repeating the so-called Marxist truisms without bothering to think about the now considerable experience of their practical implementation.

Many people must be unwilling to go deep into the truth about Stalin because they are afraid to learn the truth about themselves. They are afraid to realize what they really are when they fail to step beyond their ideological past.

By now, hundreds of people of culture and science have officially expressed their disagreement with Nina Andreyeva's so-called letter, this anti-perestroika manifesto. But please bear in mind that everyone is criticizing her political views without seriously discussing their ideological sources, the understanding of the class struggle and the class approach to which she appeals. Nina Andreyeva said nothing new. She simply reminded society of the philosophical and political truths that had been rammed into people's consciousness for decades. Her letter is a sample of our traditional opposition of the public interest to the individual's interest, of the future to the present and the past, of consciousness

---

* Nina Andreyeva is the author of a letter entitled "I Cannot Sacrifice My Principles," published by the newspaper *Sovetskaya Rossia* in March 1988. Reflecting the sentiments of the opponents of perestroika, this letter represented an attempt to defend Stalin; it put in question Gorbachev's economic and political reforms and his foreign policy.

† Mikhail Yakovlevich Hefter is a prominent Soviet historian who came under strong criticism during the Brezhnev period.

to elemental forces, scientific thinking to everyday and religious thinking, collectivism to individualism, a political approach to an economic one, class ethics to human morality. And, finally, we are dealing with the tradition of dogmatists contrasting the social and political integrity of the industrial working class and its nucleus with the social and political flaws of all other nonproletarian classes, above all, the peasantry and intelligentsia.

The unwillingness to debate these principles with the apologists of Stalinism turned out to be equivalent to capitulation without fighting. This is the road toward that very half-truth that is worse than a lie. If you agree, for instance, that the "collective farm system" (i.e., labor organization in agriculture with the help of warrants and constant instructions)— "go there . . . do this . . ."—is generally in line with peasants' interests and that "not collectivization per se was bad but the perverted methods of carrying it through," you are thus robbing yourself of the chance to substantiate current reforms in agriculture: namely, the need for a family lease, for contractual forms of labor organization, and the revival of the peasants' economic autonomy that was taken away from them. If the collective farms in the form they were conceived by their creators virtually correspond to peasants' interests, then for what do we need Gorbachev's present-day agrarian revolution?*

For the case of reforms to be undermined, it is enough to agree with only one of the Stalinist dogmata that has been revealed to us. Any opponent of perestroika will drive us into the corner and knock us down.

And it is especially difficult to understand a champion of perestroika who is ready to accept the dogma of Stalin's epoch that bourgeois culture should be "thrown away" without fail. How can one then defend the right of the people and the individual to enjoy national culture in all its wealth without exception? And what counter-arguments can then be given to those who believe that this "proletarian half" of culture is enough to bring up a spiritually rich personality able to think for itself?

In my view, establishing the rule of law is impossible if we persevere in the old conviction that certain classes and people cannot themselves, on their own, realize their true interests and should therefore be drawn to happiness by force. It is impossible to revive our service sector, to live a normal comfortable life if we persist with our former hostile attitude toward the artisan, if we go on threatening society with the specter of the petty bourgeoisie and continue to believe in the possibility of a "pure" proletarian culture. It is impossible to have freedom of creativity,

---

* Transition to lease-contract and family-run farms.

discussions, and thought, and to protect intellectuals from the attacks of such "critics" as, for example, Nina Andreyeva while at the same time agreeing that culture of the past should be thrown away.

Generally speaking, it is probably impossible to create anything worthwhile if we are still convinced that humanity can achieve happiness only through the destruction of the old. The rule of law is also part of the heritage of bourgeois culture. Bourgeois culture gave birth to the freedom of conscience, too. If culture is culture (i.e., the mechanism of controlling humanity's savage instincts and the forces of destruction), then humankind needs a strong united culture, and we should not weaken it.

NOTES

1. I. V. Stalin, *Works*, 12:159.
2. K. Marx and F. Engels, *Selected Works* (Moscow, 1973), 3:154.
3. K. Marx and F. Engels, *Werke*, bd. 19, s. 243.
4. Marx and Engels, *Selected Works*, 1:120.
5. See Marx and Engels, *Werke*, bd. 19, s. 398.
6. Marx and Engels, *Selected Works*, 3:17.
7. Lenin, *Collected Works*, 25:478.
8. Marx and Engels, *Werke*, bd. 36, s. 429.
9. M. Hefter, "Rabochyi class i sovremenyi mir," 1987, no. 1:122.
10. *Sovetskaya Cultura*, February 4, 1988.

CHAPTER 3

The Vicissitudes of "Pure Socialism"

The Dead Hold Onto the Living

Ironically, a close look will show that the opponents and proponents of Stalinism do not really differ in their outlook on central issues. The initial matrix of social thought is the same and based on the same blueprint. Both the opponents and proponents believe that the movement to socialism represents a process whereby all alien elements "break off," as it were. Both the opponents and proponents of Stalinism believe, in particular, that socialism means doing away with the many modes of production that existed before the revolution and, primarily, eliminating small peasant production. Also, they think that it is impossible to strengthen the planned economy of socialism without diktat* and the subordination of all economic activity in the country to central administrative bodies; that the only way to prevent the introduction of petit-bourgeois ideology in a socialist society is by its proletarization; and that the imposition of atheism brings unquestioned good.

Having accepted these as their postulates, the opponents of Stalinism in their ideological approach cannot break away from the ideology of its proponents, and, incidentally, cannot take an active and assertive stand in the debate on the future of the country.

It would seem that the partisans of perestroika have one important advantage in the struggle with conservatism. They can rely on the experience of socialist transformations in socialist history, which have long disproved the previous linear and mechanistic notions about the stages in

---

* Diktat refers to the pressure that ministries put on enterprises and their interference in all aspects of economic activity.

the building of socialism, the transitional periods. The Stalinist definitions of socialism have been discredited. The socialist countries that proved to have the greatest vitality are those that did not encourage the "breaking off" of old structures, refrained from the attempts to speed up the final solution of the problems of the transitional period and the elimination of different modes of production. They are open to new ideas and enjoy high living standards. In contrast, all attempts to move further down the road to only one mode of production and the Communist "purity" of socialism, as a general rule, have brought about a decline in both living standards and production and ultimately ended up in crisis.

It would seem that those who can muster enough courage to write about the destiny of the new society in our country must always remember this most important lesson of the history of the building of socialism. Today, in the eighth decade of the history of real socialism we have no right to judge Stalin without criticizing the principles he was guided by. We have no right to limit ourselves to a denunciation of Stalinism and its crimes yet ignore the ideology that underlies them.

But contrary to logic and the interests of the truth, the majority of those writers who condemn Stalin do not dare or cannot resolve the dual task: to pronounce their moral and political condemnation of Stalin's adventurist policies and to overcome the philosophy of his epoch. Without this, the only thing they can do is criticize the 1930s from the ideological position of the 1930s and the level of social knowledge characteristic of the time. But we have come a long way from that. Whether we like it or not, their analysis pulls us back to the narrow-minded notions about the objectives of socialism that were equally typical of all the leaders of the party who fought for power after Lenin's death.

All of them were guilty of the crudest application of sociology; they regarded the function of human society as the operation of an ingenious machine, overestimated the significance of technology, and ignored the human factor. They linked the progress of society with greater uniformity and the total expulsion of spontaneity from the economy and human existence itself. In short, all those leaders, with the exception of Bukharin, were guilty of underestimating the richness and complexity of human life.

At that time, the majority of the Communists did not and could not foresee all the consequences of the revolutionary renewal of life. Only a few people were prepared to consider the consequences of the situation when all those who thought differently from the revolutionaries were barred from active social participation. The prerevolutionary intelligentsia, in particular, could not engage in their professional activities. After

Lenin's death, the leaders of the revolution involved in the power struggle did not realize, as a general rule, the negative consequences of a policy aimed at both making the economy subordinate to politics and
selecting the cadres on the basis of class identity. They did not foresee all
the possible consequences of a situation in which the party apparatus
was all powerful, because they sought absolute power themselves. They
also overestimated the role of prohibition as a means of resolving economic and social problems. It was a time when a scornful attitude to the
law and the traditions of justice generally prevailed. The 1920s and the
1930s were the epoch of the crudest and most simplistic notions about
the role of religion in human history and the possibilities and methods of
replacing religious idealistic philosophy with scientific and materialist
philosophy.

All those notions are reflected in the party documents of that epoch,
including those that were the most realistic and scientifically grounded,
such as the decisions of the 15th Congress of the All-Russia Communist
Party (Bolshevik).* The present-day critics of Stalinism take those decisions as some sort of a starting point, believing as they do that all the
troubles began after those decisions had been abandoned, particularly,
after the decision to speed up the rate of industrialization and collectivization. But is it right to take this as a starting point? Is it right to take
something for the absolute truth when it stands in need of a profound
analysis in comparison with previous experience?

By asserting that the decisions of the 15th Congress contained all
the necessary prerequisites for creating in the USSR a humane socialist
society that could exist for a long time, we impose constraints on our own
thinking and have no possibility of taking a broader look at the objectives and problems of the revolution in Russian than that of its direct
participants.

It is quite clear that one important question is how fast we should have
moved toward the destruction of the old life-style and its principles and
modes of production, something that lies at the heart of the polemics
between the proponents and the opponents of Stalinism. But we also
have the question of how expedient the "rejection" of certain elements of
the capitalist legacy was, what the limits were for the old society's transformation, and whether humanity should in principle accept certain
innovations. If the notions about the objectives of socialist transforma-

---

* The 15th Congress of the All-Russia Communist Party (Bolshevik) sealed the defeat of the
left-wing opposition, led by Trotsky and Zinoviev (the so-called Trotsky-Zinoviev bloc),
which was destroyed organizationally and ideologically. The congress adopted a program
of the building of socialism in the USSR on a stage-by-stage basis.

tions were erroneous, unrealistic, and incompatible with the laws of the preservation of society, there is no point in arguing about the rates and methods of the movement toward those objectives.

No matter how you approach an unrealistic problem, whether to resolve it by cavalry attack tactics or by a prolonged siege, the result will be always the same. In any case, the movement to something that is impossible and contradicts the objective laws of social organization and human nature will result in self-destruction and a waste of effort, energy, natural and material resources, as well as senseless human suffering. The cavalry attack tactic may seem preferable because it very soon revealed that the maximalists indulged in wishful thinking, and it has shown both to the leadership engaged in experiments and to the rest of humanity what they should not do and what objectives they should not formulate. Unfortunately, nations seldom draw lessons from their mistakes and learn from them.

I believe, therefore, that the current controversy surrounding Stalinist implementation of the concept of the collective farm economy is utter nonsense. My reasoning is simply that "the *kolkhoz* economy" (the implantation of collective farms and state farms, that is, state-controlled organization of agricultural production in Russia) is just as utopian as the noncommodity economy.

Since the critics of Stalinism usually ignore the realities of present-day socialism, the best they can do is to go back to the social philosophy of the 1920s. This distracts our attention from the analysis of the structural preconditions of Stalin's unlimited power and his adventurist policies. It also strengthens the illusions of those past times when it was allegedly possible to prevent the country from sliding into the abyss of tyranny and an orgy of self-destruction on a national scale without radical changes in the political system that had evolved during the Civil War and the restoration of the rule-of-law state. It was alleged that all that was really needed to prevent those dreadful developments was to show greater concern for the party's old guard and increase the number of people working in the Central Committee.

As a result of this, our contemporary intellectuals "reject" not only the social philosophy we have created but also Russian non-Marxist sociology with its wealth of ideas about nature, the contradictions of revolutionary power, and the role of science in social development.

It is revealing that a careful student may find that Russian prerevolutionary philosophy gives better insights into the origins of Stalinism than some of the dogmas of the 1920s and the 1930s. Dostoyevsky and many other Russian philosophers pointed to the dangers facing any society that tried to make all its life subordinate to social science. Another example, Bakunin, warned that a democratic socialist republic, particularly in Russia, could result in a new type of "military-bureaucratic centralization." "In no other situation can government despotism be more terrible and powerful as when it relies on the alleged representation of the alleged people's will. . . . Particularly terrible is the despotism of the enlightened and therefore privileged minority which alleges to understand the interests of the people better than the people themselves," he wrote. First, the representatives of this minority will endeavor to put the life of future generations on the "Procrustean bed" of their ideals; second, these twenty or thirty enlightened scientists "will cut each other's throats."

Bakunin wrote:

To be a slave of the pedants—what a destiny for humanity! Give them a free hand, and they will experiment on human society just as now they experiment on rabbits, cats and dogs for the benefit of science. . . . Woe betide humanity, if thought ever became the source and the only guiding principle in life; if the sciences and the scientists stood at the helm of public administration. The source of life would dry up, and human society would turn into a dumb and slavish herd. The administration of life by science would achieve no more than to make all humanity the sillier.[1]

The philosopher P. L. Lavrov, one of the ideologues of the Narodniks,* gave a similar warning. It is true, though, that in comparison with the tempestuous Bakunin, who harbored a personal enmity to Marx and his philosophy, Lavrov was more balanced in his assessment.

Addressing the Russian revolutionary intelligentsia, Lavrov wrote,

History proves and psychology convinces us that any unlimited power and any dictatorship corrupts even the best people. Even people of genius, who want to do good to the people by their decrees, cannot escape this fact. Every dictatorship must surround itself with a coercive force and blindly obedient instruments; every dictatorship has to exert violent pressure not only on reactionaries, but simply on people who do not agree with its methods; every dictatorship instituted by force has to spend more time, effort and energy in the struggle for power with its enemies than in the implementation of any programme employing that power. That the dictatorship established by any party by force will be abandoned voluntarily, that is, that the dictatorship will serve only as a "starting point of revolution," is a dream that can be nurtured only until it is actually established. In the struggle of the party for power and the interplay of open and secret intrigues,

---

* *Narodnichestvo* was the idology and the policy opposing capitalist development in Russia that emerged in the wake of the peasant liberation from surfdom in 1861. It can be regarded as a variety of a peasant socialist utopia.

every minute creates a new necessity for preserving power and shows again and again that it is impossible to abandon power. Dictatorship can only be snatched from the hands of the dictators by a new revolution.[2]

Apart from everything else, this analysis helps identify the psychological origins of Stalinism with much greater precision than the oft-repeated assertion in our publicistic pieces that Stalinism was simply a petit-bourgeois reaction to the October Revolution. This idea was put forward by Trotsky, and it is easy to understand him: The label of petite bourgeoisie in a Communist environment was an effective means of disposing of a political opponent. But taking into account his way of thinking and his set of social axioms, Trotsky, no matter how hard he tried, could give no other explanation for his defeat. For him, all the major problems of social life boiled down to the interaction of classes, and in postrevolutionary Russia it was the interaction of the "pure" and advanced consciousness of the proletariat, on the one hand, and, the "impure" consciousness of the predominant reactionary peasant masses, on the other. Trotsky believed that the relics of the past and philistine ideology were to blame. This is what he wrote:

To realize a certain world view in flesh and blood, subordinate all aspects of your own consciousness to it and coordinate the world of your emotions with it—this is something that not everyone can do, rather, few people can do it. The working mass substitutes its class instinct for it, and it attains great sophistication in critical epochs. However, in the party and the state there is a large section of revolutionaries who, although they come predominantly from the mass, have long since separated from it and are opposed to it by virtue of their position. *The class instinct has already evaporated from them.* On the other hand, they lack theoretical stability and the broad outlook required to be able to embrace the process as a whole. In their psychology many unblind spots still remain, through which—in a changed situation—alien and hostile ideological influences freely penetrate. During the times of clandestine struggle, insurrections and the Civil War such elements were the soldiers of the party. Only one chord resonated in their consciousness, and it resonated on the same frequency as the tuning fork of the party. But once the tension has subsided, and the nomads of the revolution settled down, the philistine features have reawakened and developed in them. . . ."[3]

Today we know only too well that the dangers facing the socialist revolution are much more numerous than originally believed by the leaders of the left opposition parties. The new society has developed not only the philistine features but has also provoked starvation, loss of love for the land, lack of interest in work, apathy, complacency, drunkenness, mismanagement, indolence, hypocrisy, double standards, and the atrophy of such basic social feelings as sympathy, solidarity, and compassion. Today we know what price the ruling Community party has to pay for its right to control all the phenomena of life without exception and all the aspects of social existence. This kind of unlimited power undermines the thrift of the population, breeds general apathy toward independent decision making, and promotes irresponsibility. It puts the leaders of the party outside the people's control and creates the possibility of the feudalization of society and the degeneration of ruling bodies. In all the socialist countries, the selection of cadres was based on the rigid principles of class identity, which made mandatory that all the cadres should belong to the party and come from a proletarian background. This ultimately turned into a policy of antiselection. It made the leadership increasingly incompetent and undermined the socialist foundations of new power.

Just think! What can be achieved using such ingenious instruments of thought as the theory of petit-bourgeois survivals?* Little, if anything. The only thing left for those who embraced that theory was to expose ingenuity and passion as the ills of the petit-bourgeois ideology and to denounce the patriarchal peasant collectivism embodied in the pronoun *we* that had already been exposed in the classics of Marxism. They can do no more than add to the sins committed against the progress of reason and democracy by the petite bourgeoisie and, particularly, the individual peasant producer. Many present-day opponents of Stalinism can do no more than limit their criticism to the condemnation of the innocent, and without sufficient grounds they add Stalin's crimes to the list of "sins" of the peasant. As a result, people are conditioned to be scared by the survivals of "petit-bourgeois ideology," and our analysis has come full circle. Whether we want it or not, we come back to where we began our movement in the late 1920s, when the first appeals to preserve the purity of the "revolutionary conscience" were made.

At the same time we have been unable to prove it a crime to enforce collectivization, to liquidate the industrious and civilized peasant, and to destroy the national intelligentsia, which did not abandon its people in times of trouble. We have failed to prove the criminal nature of the repressions carried out against the party and state apparatus in the second half of the 1930s and to condemn the rotten Stalinist ideology, because we began our dispute with Stalinism bypassing the central issue. We failed to criticize the principles and the political ideas that Stalin used to justify his domestic policy. At the heart of this dispute lies the problem of

---

* According to this theory, it is the customs and the consciousness of petite bourgeoisie (traders, farmers, and artisans accustomed to economic independence and motivated by profit, etc.) that represent the major obstacle to the building of communism.

determining the ways and means of preserving the stability of the party's political leadership in the wake of a victorious revolution—and the price to be paid. The real problem is whether it was justified to use preventive measures and preemptive violence against possible candidates for power and what action was justified in relation to those who refused to think along the lines of the majority in the Politburo organized by Stalin.

The Mechanism that Destroys Compassion

To understand all that happened, we must first take into account the type of political thinking characteristic of those who fought for domination in the party after Lenin's death. Without doing this, it is impossible to understand how the party was morally disarmed, enabling a sadist to exterminate millions of people with impunity. It is also impossible to understand the mechanism of the total destruction of compassion that he created.

The calls for repression against the defeated leaders of various opposition movements had been made long before the victory of "the most powerful." As early as 1924, Kamenev* insisted on the need to liquidate the leaders of the Trotskyist opposition, a move that was quite in keeping with the prevailing spirit of the time. Let us recall that only a few years before, the anarchist sailor Zheleznyakov, chief of the guard of the Constituent Assembly, made a translation of the bloodthirsty speeches of his leaders into the vernacular of the masses. He said that for the well-being of the Russian people it was quite possible to kill one million people. And the Communist economist Kritsman wrote a book entitled *A Heroic Period of the Great Russian Revolution* in which he was singing the praises of revolutionary violence. He suggested the moral level of the revolution should be measured by the number of victims and the social destruction that had evolved in the course of its history and by the elimination of the nonproletarian classes. In particular, he asserted that "the merciless class exclusiveness and the social destruction of the classes of exploiters was both the source of a high moral upsurge and the passionate enthusiasm of the proletariat and all the exploited." He wrote further: "The brand of the class of the exploiters could open up the road only to a concentration camp or a prison or, under favorable conditions, to the hovels abandoned by the proletariat who had moved to better homes."[4]

This explains why many members of the Bolshevik old guard were prepared to tolerate Stalin's crimes. No one is trying to justify the tyrant,

---

* Lev Borisovich Kamenev (1883–1936) was one of the closest associates of V. I. Lenin.

of course, but the principle that says "in the name of" must be blamed first and foremost. The root cause of all our tragedies resides in the conviction that the happiness of future generations justifies the terror and violence inflicted on the current generation.

Nothing is new in this statement. In the years of the Civil War, the writer Vladimir Korolenko warned People's Commissar A. V. Lunacharsky it was a mistake to believe executions by firing squad were justified in the name of the people's good. "I believe that not all means can, in fact, be excused by the people's good, and I have no doubt in my mind that the administrative executions which had become systematic and continued for the second year running do not belong to their number."[5]

During the 1960s this idea was expressed by the poet Naum Korzhavin in "Little Tanya."[6] "How could you allow such woe to take place?" he asked his heroine. But as she remained silent, the poet said:

> How could it happen despite your deeds?
> In what damned year or month
> Was the road open to the enemy—
> That sly little phrase "In the name of"
> Meaning that everything is allowable
> If, in theory, it leads to the good.
> Evil in the name of good!
> Who could invent such nonsense!
> Even in the darkest day!
> Even in the bloodiest struggle!
> If evil is encouraged,
> It triumphs on earth—
> Not in the name of something,
> but in itself.

The tragedy of 1937 was that the executioners and the victims thought in the same terms and were afflicted with one and the same disease—the thirst for power and the desire to cement the foundation of the victorious revolution with blood. It is stunning to read the book *Portraits and Pamphlets* by Karl Radek, who was Trotsky's comrade-in-arms. Radek called for children's participation in the trials of specialists, that is, bourgeois intellectuals working at Soviet plants. He was overjoyed that children, just like their parents, wanted executions by firing squad to continue. "Try to isolate the children from such events and the saboteurs trial," exclaimed that pedagogue of the young generation. He further argued that "when the saboteurs were granted pardon, it provoked a storm of indignation among the children I know. How could it be that those who betrayed their country and wanted to cause starvation among the peasants and workers were not shot by firing squad?" How was it possible to sing the praises of violence and death? How was it possible to think that way and instill hatred in children?

There is no question that the level of morality among the many victims of Stalin was just as catastrophically low as that of the executioner himself. But this does not justify his crimes and the reprisals of 1937 and 1938. Nevertheless, this fact alone reveals the genuine and profound causes of the orgy of self-destruction the country went through during the 1930s. This could do no good in the end, and the journalist Medvedev, who interviewed Sonya Radek, was quite right to condemn her father. Some of Karl Berngardovich Radek's thoughts are simply monstrous. Probably, in no other country in the history of humanity were children consciously called upon to be ruthless and encouraged to show their indignation when certain people were not executed.

Today we are trying to reassess many things and develop a more serious attitude toward Stalinism as a terrible manifestation of the deep-running contradictions of revolutionary violence. Which of the things that happened to us were inevitably due to the dialectics of progress, and which of them were due to the bestial nature of vicious and embittered people? I can find no other words to assess the outlook of Stalin or Radek. But it would be wrong not to heed the words of Radek's daughter when she recalls that it was not only her father and Stalin who thought in that manner but also many writers of the period. They condoned and were overjoyed with the mass shootings. There was some kind of universal insanity.

Evidently, the analysis of the dialectics of revolution should begin with a closer look at the conviction that the interests of the revolution are paramount, that it makes its own laws and rules, and that the interests of a future classless society are primary.

It is appropriate to recall at this point that, long before Stalin's time, Russian Social Democrats placed the interests of the revolution and its defense above the traditional notions of legality, democracy, and morality. For example, the founding father of the Russian Social Democratic movement, Plekhanov, wrote,

Every given democratic principle must be regarded not in itself and in the abstract, but in its relation to the principle which can be called the basic principle of democracy: Salus populi suprema lex. Translated into the language of the revolutionary, this means that the success of the revolution is the highest law. If for the sake of the success of the revolution, it were necessary to restrict temporarily the application of this or that democratic principle, then it would be criminal to stop short of such a restriction. . . . The revolutionary proletariat could restrict the political rights of the higher classes in the same manner as the higher classes previously restricted its political rights. . . . If in a surge of revolutionary enthusiasm the people elected a very good parliament, then we should try to make it a long parliament; and if the elections proved unsuccessful, then we should try to break it up not in two years' time, but in two weeks, if possible.[7]

Thus, early in the century, special revolutionary legality and morality were proclaimed that placed the success of the revolution above all.

Trotsky took just one step further and placed the success of the revolution not only above the sovereignty of the majority of people but above the principles of universal human morality, or normative morality, to use his own phrase. Guided by this principle, namely, "the success of the revolution is paramount," he argued in favor of the legitimacy of repression in relation to political opponents who refused to withdraw from the power struggle, and he justified the preventive and preemptive defense of the political regime that had been set up.

In 1918, Trotsky applied those principles for the first time. Speaking on the question of the repression of the members of what we would now call "a coalition party," which wanted to come to power, he explained his motives for insisting on the execution of the leaders of the left Social Revolutionaries. Despite the appeals of Clara Zetkin and other European Communists to grant them pardon, he said,

The question of this repression in the revolutionary epoch acquired an altogether special character which humanitarian platitudes could not pierce. The struggle that is waged directly for power, and the struggle of life and death—this is what revolution is all about. In these conditions what significance can imprisonment have for the people who hope in the next few weeks to seize power and put in prison or eliminate those who stand at the helm. From the point of view of the so-called absolute value of the individual human, the revolution must be "condemned" along with war and, for that matter, all the history of humanity as a whole. However, in order for the concept of person to become real and in order for the half-scorned concept of "the mass" to cease to be the antithesis to the philosophically privileged concept of "person" it is necessary that the mass itself use the crane of the revolution, or, to be more precise, arteries of revolutions, to raise itself to a new historical level. I don't know whether this road is good or bad from the point of view of normative philosophy and must admit I am not interested in that. But I know full well that this is the only road that was known to humanity until this time.[8]

It is now difficult to understand that the new step taken by Trotsky brought social consciousness closer to the acceptance of reprisals against defeated political opponents, and reprisals were then regarded as an absolutely justified measure. But if reprisals were justified against children who had the ill luck to be born heirs to the throne, why were they not justified against former comrades in the struggle against tsarism who then posed a threat to the revolution? If repression could be used against Social Revolutionaries, who had their own ideas about the October Revolution, why was it not possible to use such reprisals against Bolshevik revolutionaries who also had their own ideas about the building of socialism? How can it be proved that the unlimited power of Trotsky or Zinoviev was more or less justified than Stalin's unlimited power? The revolution had destroyed the former mechanism of the succession and now created a new and more democratic one. Can this be the root cause of all our tragedies?

These are not simple problems for historians. Without question, it is much easier for them to turn their backs on them and instead give themselves over to the study of the ratio between the workers and the peasants in the party at different stages of the revolution. But if historians do not ponder over the essential questions of the revolution, namely, its internal contradictions and its drama, then they should not pretend they are engaged in the search for the root cause of what was described as the Russian Apocalypse. It may be right to say that we have not yet become mature enough to regard the Civil War as a tragedy of people who could not find a different and less bloody way of overcoming their internal conflicts, who had no option but to break away from a life they could no longer endure and then had to pay a terrible price for their actions. If this is so, we should not pretend that we have become different and think differently from those who approved of the orgy of self-destruction of the 1930s.

Let me be quite frank and say that a person's attitude to the tragedy of the Civil War shows how civilized that person really is. The butcher of the class struggle and the Civil War is just as repulsive as the butcher of Stalin's repression, and there is nothing to celebrate and nothing to admire. No moral is learned from the fact that one class was enthusiastically exterminating another and that brother was fighting against brother. The drama of this situation is not something that we have discovered in our time. The true tragedy is that every one of the opposing parties believed it was right, defending its own sacred truth. By no coincidence, the novel Leo Tolstoy wanted to write about the revolution and the revolutionaries was to be entitled *No One to Blame*.

Essentially, what we are talking about is not the struggle of classes or political parties, as its participants believed, but the struggle between different states of one and the same people, between its past and its future. Thus, in Russia the old regime was not only the power of the tsar and the landowners but also the past of the people of the country. The drama essentially consisted in that the truth was being established by the force of arms. The terror of Stalinism cannot be justified, just as it is impossible to justify the terror of the Civil War that preceded it. Any kind of terror means not only the ruthlessness that can somehow be justified toward an enemy who has taken up arms. Terror is not just an eye for an eye and a tooth for a tooth. Red terror, as unleashed by Stalin and Zinoviev in St. Petersburg, consisted in mass shootings of hostages and the introduction of the principle of the collective responsibility of a class or a social group, as well as the wholesale slaughter of those who did not belong to the proletariat. Officers of the tsarist army were killed for the simple reason that they were officers, and priests were killed because they were priests. Former students of military colleges who were still in their teens were killed because they walked in the streets with their peaked student caps on. If we condemn the terror organized by Stalin in the 1937–38 period, then it is impossible to justify the terror of 1918 and 1919. In both the period of the Civil War and in the period when he consolidated his power, Stalin was guided by the same principles and the strong belief that the cause of strengthening revolutionary power was above any dissertations on normative morality. If it was possible to execute the Socialist Revolutionaries who had encroached on the Bolsheviks' power, then why not execute the revolutionaries of the Bolshevik minority who encroached on the power of the Bolshevik majority? Terror is always insanity, like a dam that has burst. It is the beast in humanity that has been set free. Morality cannot be defined merely as a function of revolution. On the contrary, revolution is only justified when it asserts morality and serves to defend its interests and the interests of humanity.

All our ills stem from our inability to combine the dictates of human morality with the dictates of the class struggle. This inability forces us to make decisions about the least of all the evils with which life inexorably faces us. Many people were wrong to embrace the dictum that says, in effect, you can't make omelets without breaking eggs. They were wrong to believe that human suffering did not matter and that the old dictum "Thou shalt not kill" could be ignored when the destiny of revolution and human history was at stake. People were sentenced to death because one of them did not want to give his horse to a Red Army soldier. Another was shot because he was a priest's relative. Seldom did those who passed sentence realize that the condemned were also part of our country and part of Russian history. It follows that no justice can exist in a future earthly paradise if built recklessly, without regard for the misfortune and suffering of a priest's relative. Many people were prepared to listen to the commissars, like Shigontsev, who drove home the message, "The republic won only because it knew no mercy. What difference does it make whether Bychin killed eighteen people or Braslavsky killed one hundred and fifty? People are frightened by figures, as if arithmetic had any significance."* And then the contradiction between morality and "world revolution" was resolved in the simple phrase, "There is no morality, but there are the interests of the building of communism." We're sweating our own guts out in the name of "the great result," they thought, and there is no reason why we should spare anyone else. If Commissar Shigontsev had not had any followers, then Stalin's ultraleftism of the 1930s would have been impossible. For the architects of complete collectivization, figures did not matter either, whether it was 3 percent of kulakst dispossessed or 15 percent. It is only too logical, therefore, that in 1937 no one was surprised at the vast number of spies and enemies of the people uncovered among the leaders of the party. What mattered was not the number of people subjected to repression but the stronger unity of the party and the development of socialism at any price. There is no such thing as a low price or a high price in history. Not surprisingly, therefore, even at this late date, five decades on, many people still embrace the ideas of Commissar Shigontsev. They simply cannot think differently. No alternative was left open to Stalin, they say. How could it be otherwise? "Could suffering be avoided, when the world bourgeoisie was literally assailing our country?"⁹ This is the mode of thinking of some of the representatives of contemporary socialist intelligentsia. A short time ago Professor A. Z. Seleznev wrote, "It must be understood that under the conditions of a capitalist siege and continuous hostile actions against the USSR, and later owing to the extraordinary threat of the fascist invasion, there could be no alternative. The dictatorship of the proletariat, to use Lenin's own words, excludes a jelly-like state. . . . Like any other man, Stalin could not avoid making mistakes."¹⁰

Let us ignore the implications of the sociological absurdity in the statement quoted above. Never before in history has a massive increase in the number of people who were wronged, trampled upon, and purged by

---

* This is a reference to the hero of Y. Trifonov's novel *The Old Man*.

† In Russia, a kulak was a well-to-do farmer who hired laborers and opposed the collectivization of farms. The Bolsheviks regarded the kulaks as exploiters and the most dangerous enemies of Soviet power. The kulaks had their property confiscated and were practically exterminated as a class.

the government contributed to social unity. We are no exception to that rule. I don't think we need evidence to confirm that.

Let us try to expose the morality underlying such statements, if the word *morality* is at all appropriate in this context. First of all, this morality is revealingly opposed to any attempt to pass moral judgment on the historical events in our historical development. It alleges that the notion of crime cannot be applied to the leader of a country engaged in the building of socialism and even less so to the political events taking place in it. According to the latter-day commissars of Shigontsev's type, we can only speak about "mistakes." They further argue that if there is no alternative, there is no crime. Moreover, they are unaware of the unique value of every human being and the sacred right of every person to his or her one and only life. In accordance with their logic, the right of humanity to life is subsidiary to the situation in the country and the historical period. The really important thing is your social status and how it relates to current priorities. For example, if you are an industrious and well-to-do farmer who was given your plot of land by the revolution, then you and your children can feel that you are full-fledged citizens enjoying all rights to the land, including the right to your home—but only so long as the period of the restoration lasts. There is a place where you may labor in peace. But once the priorities change, you, my dear "proprietor," lose all your rights. Now you are no longer an industrious farmer but a kulak, a representative of the last class of proprietors, and the last obstacle on the road of the country's progressive development. And it does not really matter what your views are or whether you abided by Soviet laws or how many children you have. The important thing is that your previous economic situation is contrary to the requirements of the current priorities. And therefore, you and your children must step aside from the road to the future and not interfere in the life of the pure proletarian classes. I wish Andrey Platonov, who described this monstrous logic in his novel *The Foundation Pit*, were wrong! But, no, all this is true. After Lenin's death, voluntarism was particularly manifest in the definition of the so-called current priorities. Every new faction opposing the NEP introduced a new interpretation of the current priorities aimed at denying the peasantry basic human rights.

And finally, those who believe that the notion of crime is not applicable to these historical events severely limit the number of people who are subject to moral judgment. They believe it is not necessary to be concerned about the moral rectitude of such people or whether they were guided by the principle "Thou shalt not kill." Even the representative of their own party, not to mention the representatives of all the other defeated parties, fell out of the narrow circle of untouched people if they found themselves in the minority during those tragic moments of transition from one set of political priorities to another. As a rule, those former comrades-in-arms were subjected to administrative reprisals in the most harsh and systematic manner. This is something that has stuck in people's minds, and even now many of them are convinced that the reprisals against former deviationists were justified, although nobody will now question the role of Trotsky and Bukharin, for instance, in the preparation of the October Revolution and its defense. I believe that this is the key to the mystery of this ultrarevolutionary way of thinking. The more a person's life, behavior, and views are seen in relation to the interests of the world revolution, the fewer chances that person has of being treated as a human, as a being with a right to life. In this respect, of course, the meaning implied in those suprahuman interests and the concrete notions about a universal paradise are not important.

One more striking detail must be pondered very carefully. A former landowner or a general of the tsarist army could hope for mercy, but a former member of the Russian Communist Party did not really have a chance. A former factory owner who did not flee the country had many more rights than a former Red Army man who became right tilling his plot of land. The former at least had the possibility of living in the place where he was born and of traveling around the country. The dispossessed kulaks did not enjoy those rights for a very long time. But these are just minor details. The essential quality of the ultrarevolutionaries' way of thinking is their absolute scorn toward the people in whose name they are trying hard to succeed. Ultrarevolutionaries are incapable of thinking about, accounting for, and comparing the interests and happiness of people currently alive. Their sole concern is the interests of so-called historical necessity. To them, historical necessity is something vague that exists all by itself, independent of those who are living today and those who will live tomorrow. Ultrarevolutionaries do not serve people but a mystical law of history.

But they would never admit that "arithmetic does matter" and that attempts to build progress on suffering have always been in vain.

An objective assessment of Stalin's actions is possible only from the position of unequivocal repugnance toward violence, proceeding from the assumption that no one has the right to encroach upon the life of another. There is nothing to argue about in this respect. The trouble is that many of those people who condemn Stalinism are not prepared to make general conclusions of principle and not just particular conclusions from everything that has happened to us. The trouble is that the people who stand in defense of humanity and common sense are surprisingly inconsistent. Perhaps my last statement is too categorical, but I am profoundly convinced that it is illogical to think the way many of our present-day writers do when they write about our revolution and the 1930s. It is illogical to defend the Narodniks' idea of a "socialist instinct of the Russian peasantry" and in the same breath argue that there are no guarantees against a return of Stalinism until we overcome the Russian peasant collectivism embodied in the pronoun *we*.* It is illogical to call for the development of the democratic and civilized individualism embodied in the pronoun *I* and in the same breath blame people for their desire to condemn a crime and cleanse their souls from the vileness of the Stalinist epoch. It is illogical to enthuse about the workers and the peasants whose spiritual vigor gave rise to the idea of a world proletarian revolution and at the same time try to prove that the very same people could not do without a "butcher" to resolve their problems and force them to grow wheat and make steel.

On the one hand is the growing realization that the party and many of its ideologues took a nihilistic attitude toward bourgeois culture, in particular, toward legal culture and professional lawyers, and this was one of the root causes of the party's sins, manifested as Stalinist repression. But on the other hand, some writers mechanically repeat the thesis that "rejecting" bourgeois culture is necessary.

Antipeasant Hysteria

Let us begin by discussing various claims about the so-called bourgeois character of the peasantry.

Some claim the peasantry is necessarily "petit bourgeois" under any historical circumstances. Metaphorically speaking, this is a thorn in our side, even today. In fact, this attitude springs from the Stalinist element in us all. We continue to harbor antipeasant feelings, and we suspect everything that comes from individualized rural labor. And this blurs the difference between the critics and the apologists of Stalinism. Today, Stalin's thesis that "kulaks posed a threat to the country" is still used by contemporary opponents of perestroika to justify the arbitrary and violent actions that Stalin look in the countryside. Similarly, another thesis says that, in a country with a predominantly peasant population, the party is faced with the threat of petit-bourgeois ideology winning over the membership. But the latter thesis is still accepted by many critics of Stalinism.

---

* According to I. Klyamkin, *we* means the communal element and the spirit of collectivism that constrains the development of entrepreneurship.

Total mistrust of the individual peasant producer is wrong, not because it was characteristic of Stalin, but because it runs contrary to common sense and is unnatural. It is no more than an illusory desire for another world where those rude and uneducated peasants will exist in pastoral bliss. This Stalinist suspicion is the product of a pipe dream of socialism that dates back to when progress was linked with growing uniformity and the simplification of the class structure. That was when everybody lived in expectation of a historical miracle and the attainment of a state of society when total and ideal equality would ultimately triumph. The negative attitude toward the peasant, who was regarded as a small farmer-producer and an individualist, was born of the belief in pure non-commodity socialism. When this time came, everything that was transitional and transient was to die off and large-scale production through public ownership of the means of production was to dominate and oust all other forms of property and labor organization. This was an example of social primitivism and intolerance, if you will, and a naive desire to remove everything that did not correspond to an ideal of urbanized people. As the writer Karpinsky correctly observes, Stalinism is based on the belief that the peasantry is "petit bourgeois" in their identity. This dogmatic belief is closely linked with Stalin's major theses, including his assertion that the class struggle will necessarily become more acute in the cause of successful socialist development, his insistence on the "bourgeois nature" of the market and the law of value, and his faith in the superiority of a state structure over collective structures and the primacy of class interests over universal human values.

Today we understand that the approach based on class identity is essentially one-sided. It places a heavy emphasis on those qualities of humans that are necessary for achieving the objectives of the revolution, and at the same time it inevitably obscures those qualities that are necessary for creative work. When the approach based on class identity is adopted, it is more important that a person should be ready for revolutionary struggle, rather than effective and intelligent work.

In the conditions of a revolutionary rising, a person is judged first and foremost by his or her social background and commitment to the ideal of a kingdom of workers and peasants. That person's worth lies in his or her sense of Communist equality and determination to serve in the name of a cherished objective. Sometimes such external features as clothes or even a cap were enough to distinguish a doomed person from one destined to live in the happy future. The result of this is a loss of interest in the internal and profound structures of the human personality and the most complex problems of human existence, such as sin and conscience, life and death, love and hatred, crime and repentance.

Now let us imagine the monstrous tension created by the approach based on class identity, where 80 percent of the population was regarded as an impediment on the road to this ideal. Because of this, in the 1920s the leaders of the party must have felt they were besieged in a fortress. They were alarmed, not so much because they were surrounded by capitalist nations, but rather because they found themselves in the world of the NEP, markets, commodities, and peasants. They realized that the predominant social majority could not and would not accept a new order. Stalin was not a naive person, and he did not believe in the fairy tale of the "socialist instinct" of the Russian peasantry. In contrast with certain present-day friends of progress and democracy, he did not underestimate the mental abilities of the people living in the countryside, despite all his hatred for them. He realized that the peasantry would not submit to the yoke of productive cooperation voluntarily and that the peasants would never give up their freedom. That is why he insisted on the need to "implant" collective and state farms. The Bolsheviks of late October 1917, who believed that the revolutionary proletariat of the world would immediately follow in their path, are one thing. The Bolsheviks of 1929, who came face-to-face with people who differed from their long-held beliefs, are quite another thing.

Surprisingly, even before Yezhov's terror, people were prepared to believe unthinkingly in the guilt of those who had been considered true Communists. It is stunning that, on the one hand, people took an unemotional attitude to death, just as in the days of the Civil War, but, on the other hand, they were prepared to do anything so that the cup would pass from them. What did Blukher think at the moment when he was signing Tukhachevsky's death warrant? Did Bukharin have any premonition of violent death at the time he led a patrol to Trotsky's flat to supervise the latter's expulsion from Moscow?* But all this relates to the psychology of the people at the top, those who lived in the famous gray building on the embankment. And what about the people at the bottom?

They lived in communal flats that were very similar to the homes of the prerevolutionary Russian poor, where one's shame was evident to all.

---

* A. Yezhov headed the People's Commissariat for Internal Affairs (NKVD) during the period of reprisals in 1937–38. The Russian people refer to those terrible times as *Yezhovschina* (cf. *Stalinschina*).

Vassilli Konstantinovich Blukher was a hero of the Civil War and marshal of the Soviet Union. He was shot by a firing squad in 1938.

Mikhail Nikolayevich Tukhachevsky, one of the most talented Red Army commanders, a hero of the Civil War, and marshal of the Soviet Union, was liquidated in 1937.

No question, the people living in such communal flats were, on the whole, closer to one another than those living in modern apartment buildings. But not everyone can stand overcrowded flats and constant deprivation for a long time. Don't forget that in the 1930s and the 1940s the city dwellers were worse off than in the 1920s, and in some cases their life was even worse than before the revolution. Medical services were available to far greater numbers of people, but their standards were largely inadequate. Though children were born in maternity centers, the infant mortality rate did not really change compared with the 1920s: In 1940 it was even higher than in 1926. According to the sociologists L. A. Gordon and E. V. Klopov, the most acute contradiction of social development in the 1930s and the 1940s was that, despite the unquestioned and impressive progress in education, medicine, and social services, the standard of living did not increase and very frequently people were badly hit by inflation, food shortages, and a prolonged housing crisis.

Our Russian peasantry has committed enough sins and mistakes, but it is unjust to add other people's sins to their list. The peasant could never have come up with such wild ideas as state-owned grain factories in the countryside and measures to standardize and unify agricultural techniques of wheat production. People who were accustomed to making plans and calculating all their lives and who, unlike the intelligentsia, were in constant touch with the basics of life, land, and material things would never have believed it possible to change the world overnight. Peasants would never have imagined that land put in the harness of state decrees would bear fruit without respite and without rest, like a wild cat bears her kittens year in and year out. I cannot agree with the opinion that peasants do not understand the law of nature. Yes, they probably did not understand the law as necessity breaking through spontaneity, as a force, a mechanism that controls the development of commodity production. But the laws of the market that Marx discovered exhaust neither the many different laws at work in real life nor the essential notion of "law." It is much more important to understand the law as the objective limit: something that cannot be infringed upon by anybody, not even by God. This profound understanding of the law, I think, is typical of the peasantry. Working on land, peasants cannot fail to understand the objectivity and complexity of nature. Incidentally, it is this kind of understanding of the law that we have been developing in recent times under perestroika, when we try to reassess the lessons of the past.

This is why the peasant has always been suspicious of different innovations. And this must be regarded not so much as a manifestation of natural conservatism, which frequently let down the peasantry, but as a manifestation of a profound belief in the objective nature of work on the land and the primeval earthly nature of all human deeds. The peasant cannot believe that any mortal can breath life into dust and create heaven and earth in just one day. That is why the peasants themselves have never taken seriously quack agronomists like Lysenko. The peasant Ignashka Sapronov was not guilty of the extreme leftism and ultra-radicalism of the 1930s.* It is only a socialist intellectual, such as Stalin, brought up to respect "historical regularities" that invisibly move the wheel of history, who could believe and promise that large-scale collective-farm and state-farm agriculture "would display miracles of growth" and that the "experience" of collective farms and state farms would disprove the scientific arguments against the effectiveness of large-scale grain factories of 100,000 to 125,000 acres. It was Stalin who said that if "the development of collective farms and state farms proceeds at an accelerated rate . . . then our country will become one of the richest, if not the richest, country in the world, producing wheat, in something like three years' time."[11]

Even if Ignashka helped to build those grain factories, it does not mean that he genuinely believed in the promises of miracles. He had a concrete job to do, and, unlike the city dweller, he knew what those factories were really worth and how his fellow peasants were working there. He knew, too, how hated he was by those peasants because he had gotten involved in that hellish business they thought would do no good.

The Russian peasant has always disliked state interference in agriculture, and I believe this is one more fact proving that the peasant could not have initiated ultraleftism and ultra-etatism. Yes, it is true that peasants in Russia have always been in need of strong state power because they regarded it as their defender. The books analyzing the Asiatic methods of production are quite correct in this respect. Despotism inevitably emerged because small peasant producers were disunited. But this is only one side of the coin. The other side, which is just as important, is that prosperous and industrious peasants did not like to take part in organizing state-controlled business and liked even less the extension of state power into their economy. That was always the case over many centuries of Russian history. In some places such sentiments have been pre-

---

* Trofim Denisovich Lysenko was the ill-famed advocate of an ideological approach to biology. He was an active opponent of genetics and scientific methods of analysis of living nature. Lysenko prompted the arrest and subsequent death of Nikolai Ivanovich Vavilov, the founder of modern biological theory of selection and the theory of the centers of origin of agricultural plants.

Sapronov is a character in Vassilli Belov's novel *Thresholds*, a man without principles and an active proponent of collectivization.

served even today. The ancient instinct of opposition to the city and its power is at work.

Unfortunately, our contemporary writers do not take into account the dialectics of this kind of attitude toward state power on the part of the peasant. But even today, it is difficult to understand this kind of attitude. Indeed, Fyodor Abramov believed he was a Russian author who knew a thing or two about rural life; still he could not understand why his fellow peasants from Verkholtsy refused to work on a state farm. He could not imagine why they shunned work and why not a single able peasant agreed to take up an administrative job. To support the administration was to strengthen the power of the city over the countryside and to contribute to an unjust cause. That was the opinion of all able peasants who no longer believed that city folk could do any good for the countryside. This was something that Russian authors, writing about the developments in the countryside after the revolution, understood. For example, Ivan Sokolov-Mikitov's letter to Konstantin Fedin, reproduced in A. Strelyany's article "Two Conclusions," exposes many mysteries of our socialist history. This is what the author of that letter wrote:

I don't know whether you have noticed or not, but until now not a single able and "genuine" peasant could muster enough courage to go and see the authorities. And, moreover, there is no way that a "real" peasant can be persuaded to take up an administrative job. "I won't have any peace of mind doing this job; I'd be better off tilling my plot of land!" This situation is well known to the "centre," but there is nothing they can do about it. That was the case in the past, and it has remained so today. In the past it was a drunkard, a knave or a good-for-nothing that wanted to become the village chief, but now things have changed, and today there is no way that you can get Ivan Osipov to take up a post on the executive council. He does not know how to "go about it"; he just won't take it. Even if he is forced to accept the job, he would break down and languish as if he were imprisoned, and rather, would hang himself above the table in his office. . . . Now I have walked across all our region from one end to the other, and in all the executive council offices there are only young people conditioned by city life and hardened by the war; not infrequently they are honest, have strong convictions, and are set on their work, but nevertheless, almost all of them are "city folk."[12]

So any way you look at it, the central question in this history of the extreme leftism of the 1930s and Stalin's dictatorship is this: Who was it that gave power to Ignashka Sapronov? Today, we have to trust something that was for all to see, something that everybody had a sense of, something that many still believe in. Why use the mystical and elusive peasant *we* to smoke-screen the real architects and practitioners of atrocity? Yes, it is true that its soldiers were recruited from among the country folk. But they were just soldiers. It was city people who most of the time served as officers. Yes, it is true that those soldiers conducted the dwellers of the gray apartment building on the embankment of the Moskva River to the Lubyanka prison of the OGPU.* But note a very revealing observation by the author Yuri Trifonov, who said that they treated the situation as somebody else's business. They were present there, yet at the same time totally absent. This is largely explained, of course, by lack of spiritual development. But they were also unconcerned about something that did not depend on them. They did not start it all. It was impossible to find out who was right and who was wrong. That was none of their business. Everybody was scared to death.

The question of which was first—the fear or the cult—is just as pointless as the question of the chicken and the egg. The cult of the leader and the mass psychosis of adoration could not have emerged without subconscious fear, and the cult could not but trample upon and denigrate humanity. The first to break down were those people who stood closer to the authorities, with whom they were in constant touch, namely, the city folk. Fear extended from the center to the periphery, spreading the psychosis of mistrust, suspicion, and spy paranoia. The city mores sharply deteriorated during the 1930s when the peasants, who remained in the countryside, were isolated and the links between them and the city were maintained through the activist Ignashka.

At that time people were embittered, and it was the heyday of people who were aggressive, vengeful, or just plain sick. They were sick because they were full of hatred and envy. They hated everyone who had talent and individual identity. From the early 1920s, any manifestation of natural, moral feeling toward those who suffered was politically punished. With the elevation of Stalin, compassion and humanity declined. And this was no coincidence. According to Soviet author Daniil Granin, during the time when the kulaks were dispossessed and mass reprisals were carried out, people were not allowed to give help to their kith and kin or the neighbors and families of victims. Giving shelter to the children of those who had been arrested and sent into internal exile was not permitted. People were forced to show their approval of harsh sentences. Even compassion toward the innocent victims of the purges was banned. Feelings that even hinted at compassion were looked upon as suspicious or even criminal; they allegedly

---

* The house on the embankment of the Moskva River is an apartment building built in the early 1930s for the top echelon of the party and the state. Whenever any of its dwellers were arrested, the usual procedure was to take them to the prison on Lubyanka Street, which in 1937–38 was operated by the Ministry of Internal Affairs.

bred political apathy, were not based on class identity, and made people lax and defenseless in times of struggle.

The serious scholar would say, of course, that it is not easy to destroy a person spiritually and that the psychopathology of suspicion could not have spread to any great extent among spiritually healthy people. All true, but observe again that, as a rule, serious scholars link such cases of mass hypnosis first and foremost with the accelerated and superficial urbanization stimulated by rapid industrialization. In this case we are talking about the snowball phenomenon. During the 1930s, urbanization brought about a rapid and unjustifiable break with the past. In that situation the destruction of the old traditions and institutions proceeded at a far greater pace than the emergence of new mores and life-styles. As a result, a kind of cultural and moral vacuum was created, and the overall moral level of everyday life actually dropped in certain respects. The significance of the massive renunciation of religion is not at all clear. People who forsake their faith become spiritually free, but very frequently this leaves them without spiritual support. In the past, a sadistic and envious Ignashka was nevertheless a God-fearing person. But then there was no God, and communism was a far-off dream, and, consequently, everything was allowed. Generally speaking, even a convinced atheist and Marxist should not be overjoyed when his people reject their old beliefs and centuries-old traditions. Is there any guarantee they will not abandon their newly found Marxist convictions just as easily and unthinkingly? The adoration of Stalin can be regarded as a surrogate belief characteristic of a superficial atheist. He has abandoned his God but has not achieved any dignity or freedom of personality. He has stopped halfway and become an idolator.

And again, the peasants, and most frequently the peasant women, were in a more favorable situation. It was far less risky for them and their children to perform their religious rites, and I think, therefore, compared with the city, the countryside had fewer cases of spiritual emasculation caused by the unrestrained love for the leader of all nations.

I believe that it is naive to think, as some of our writers do, that the peasant, who was the carrier of the collectivist spirit embodied in *we*, was unable to see the connection between the violence and ruthlessness of a Borzov, administrator of the party's regional committee, and the "superior thought," that is, Stalinism. Indeed, these were not the peasants of ancient China, who hated the tax collector but, at the same time, revered the supreme authority.

In the spring of 1950, peasants sawed down their apple trees and prune trees in their gardens during the night and cursed, not the tax collector who was to come in the morning, but the "mustachioed villain" who tormented them with his senseless notions. I can testify to this under oath. And they sacrificed their lives in the struggle with the Germans not because their social inferiority blinded them to the senselessness of many "superior thoughts" but because patriotism runs in the blood of the peasantry. It may not be true today, but in the past some sort of umbilical cord linked the peasants to their land and their native place. We are speaking, of course, about a typical Russian peasant. There was no dearth of traitors, in other words, untypical peasants, too. Let's take the interviewee of Kozlovich's essay "Gain and Give." Did she not understand where a Borzov was to blame and where the responsibility of those who invented the inane collective farms lay? She did not therefore exclude herself and her children from the notion of the "country." Just ponder over what she is saying to the author:

There was misery all round, not a collective farm. At work you sweated your brow until the soil was damp, and then you thought: "What shall I have for supper? What shall I feed my children with?" There was no justice on that collective farm. In the spring we would be mowing, and the chairman would say: "Once we are through with this, I'll give you two kilos of grain and three potatoes for every work day." In the fall we would bring in the harvest, and the chairman would say: "I'll give you two hundred grammes of grain and three hundred grammes of potatoes for every work day. It is necessary to feed the country, comrades." And I would come to my hut, hug my little children and just weep and weep: "My good children, my golden children! Are you not the people? Why is there nothing left for you to sow? Is our collective farm not part of our country?

We have suffered not because of the peasant *we* but because of the general aberration of the mind caused by the slavish admiration for and fear of the dictator Stalin and his satraps. Let us be quite frank and admit that we admired all the dictators, both big and small. Only a few years ago, many young Communists went to pay their respects to the last living dictator, Molotov, who was one of the main culprits responsible for the "success of collectivization that made our heads spin." What we need now is not just the memory of our history but elementary human repentance for the sin of idolatry.

The Price of Diabolical Ideas

I don't understand why some of our writers are so critical of the central idea of Abuladze's film *Repentance*, which, I think, gave the initial impetus to the process of the expurgation of Stalinism. In my opinion, Abuladze is quite right. We had to begin with an intellectual protest against the crimes perpetrated by dictators and, with unconscious effort, restore the respect for the innocent sufferers. This is not a childish approach to history, as the writer Klyamkin believes, but it is a very wise adult approach. If the people, that is, the Georgians, Russians, Ukrainians, Uzbeks, workers, farmers, and intellectuals, do not repent of this terrible sin, love for the criminal, and if they do not feel utter shame for adoring those idols, no significant truth can help us. Generally speaking, the truth can only have significance if it finds its way into a healthy soul, particularly if it is a social truth. Today, we have no more important task than to make the souls of people morally healthier. I am not speaking about any lack of enthusiasm or self-denial. Generally, I do not regard the readiness to sacrifice either oneself or one's kith and kin as necessarily a virtue. A negligent attitude to life will always remain negligent, even if directed at oneself. It is a totally different matter if one sacrifices one's life and its comforts in the name of the preservation of human dignity. But objective limits must be taken into account, too. All of us committing suicide together in protest against conditions of life unworthy of humans would not be reasonable. But ruthlessness toward oneself nonetheless remains ruthlessness in relation to other people's consciousness and the human race. A person comes into this world to preserve humanity and keep the chain of generations intact. Violence in all its forms and ruthlessness even in the name of humane ideals always bring some kind of destruction with them and undermine the spiritual foundations of life. As the experience of all revolutions has shown, their victories were achieved at a very dear price. All must be blamed for the habit of killing acquired during the Civil War and the conviction that, in the name of a great objective, it is necessary to be able to step over cold corpses. By killing a murderer, a person commits a mortal sin. This is the price of retribution. As the prominent Soviet author Andrey Platonov correctly observed, you cannot put anything together without taking your soul apart. Therefore, as a rule, it was the real villains and murderers who were killed first. And then it was the turn of those who were alleged to be villains and murderers. Finally, it was the turn of those who were wholeheartedly dedicated to the cause of the revolution. People who insist on the need for an "adult" approach to our history and the 1930s should ponder this. Their attempts to preach moral relativism are totally uncalled for.

I don't see any particular danger that people today are not ready to make sacrifices. Far more dangerous, I believe, is the lack of elementary moral feeling. There is no need to scare people out of their wits and mislead them. As to the evil of the 1930s and the causes of left-wing extrem-

ism and ultrarevolutionary attitudes of those years, they are now exposed. Dictatorship was born not of the peasant *we* and Russian patriarchal life but as the consequence of their destruction.

Some writers believe that Stalinism can be essentially reduced to the
idea of the "cut off" past and the "rejection" of bourgeois culture, in particular. They are not far from the truth. Nothing gives greater freedom to
a radical politician than this kind of theoretically justified nihilism toward
everything previously created. This historical nihilism makes it unnecessary to consider the policy of total destruction pursued by such a politician. What is the point of thinking about something that is doomed? That
is why such a politician provokes a conflict between generations, a spiritual row between fathers and sons, and nihilistic attitudes toward the
past, its achievements, and the memory of his or her people. This position
engenders a scornful attitude to the traditions of economic philosophy,
rationalism, social organization, consistent thinking, self-administration,
and the culture of choice, including spiritual choice and its responsibilities.

The philosophy and politics of the "rejection" of bourgeois culture is
responsible for the deep-rooted desire to ban everything. It has given rise
to the long-standing illusion that everything "impure" must be prevented
and that the destruction of the relics of the old culture represents a simul-
taneous act of creation and must be regarded as a great and useful
endeavor.

What is a negative attitude toward the past? It inevitably accompanies
the conviction that pure socialism is feasible, the belief that history advances
toward an ideal and nonantagonistic state, completely free of the evils of
the past, in which human beings will be perfect physically and morally. Utopia is a world in which everything will be new and different from the old.

In my view, there is nothing inconsistent in the fact that Soviet society,
although brought up on a belief in humanity's purity and on ideas put
forward by the most noble people of genius, nevertheless, generally
blessed a group of maniacs possessed by the craving for power to commit
the most serious crimes against the people.

To look at it in a different way, the belief in the pure person let our people down and resulted in the policies of self-destruction. The hell in
which our people lived in the thirties could be justified by something
extraordinary—for instance, the temptation to create something absolutely new. If the writer Alexey Prokhanov and the professor of chemistry
Nina Andreyeva believe even today that our poverty, our uncomfortable
life, the absence of goods in shops, our bad hospitals and computers are
an inevitable and reasonable price for our "nontrivial economy" and say
so in all earnestness, then why should people who did a fantastic job—

overthrew the centuries-long rule of landlords and capitalists—not believe in the miracle of the unique economy and the pure and perfect human being? Here lies the catch prepared for us by history. We came to believe sincerely that we were a unique country and a chosen people preordained to work wonders, to do things that cannot be done, and to rise to the most fantastic challenges. And Stalin skillfully capitalized on this belief, this arrogance of the people who had worked the wonder of revolution.

Stalinism must be difficult to spy out and fight exactly because its very nature is linked with the deepest motives of political activity characteristic of the revolutionary socialist intelligentsia. Why did our intellectuals, and not only revolutionary-oriented ones, so easily put up with Stalin's violence to peasants? Why did they not respond to the horrors of the dispossession of the kulaks and the famine of the early thirties? Why were they so convinced that people were happy with their life? I think they regarded it as an inevitable price to pay for the purity of future society and sincerely believed that our history was moving in the only correct direction. Stalin was congenial to these people because of his aspiration for the new, his belief in the feasibility of building a unique society in which would be neither trade nor peasant nor merchant.

I'll risk the claim that at the turn of the thirties Stalin was closer to most party activists than Lenin, who urged them to learn to trade and to make profits. In his last years, Lenin gave up his naive faith in pure socialism, to the great disappointment of most party theorists. It was Lenin who described this most abstract yearning for the new, "which should be so new that there should be absolutely nothing old in it," as a typical error of the revolutionary consciousness.

In contrast, Stalin carried their original ideas to their logical conclusion and rejected all compromises. He called for a fierce class struggle, a struggle to the end, a struggle to determine "who will have the upper hand." Lenin's criticism of naive and romantic conceptions of pure socialism struck no chord with most party members, and the idea of a "popular alliance," an alliance of the proletariat with the cooperated peasantry, failed to persuade party activists. This most probably explains Stalin's surprisingly easy victory over the party favorite, Bukharin. The personal tragedy of the latter was that he was one of the few (Rykov, Tomsky, Dzerzhinsky, and Bukharin) who in all earnestness responded to Lenin's urge to "build communism by non-Communist hands."

But is it strange after all that at that time many people wanted their pure and radiant future built only with clean hands? Even today—after the dream of a pure proletarian socialism free from bourgeois philistinism, trade, and market has turned into the Apocalypse of the thirties—

many of our intellectuals proclaim their dedication to Marxist traditions, still convinced no democratic socialism can exist in this country until we completely destroy the remains of the peasant *we* in us.

Nothing is new about this faith in the pure person and the dislike for people who bear on their shoulders the routine of everyday life, its drudgeries and chores; who have settled down (with the emphasis on "down") and are interested in nothing but making more money. The writer Fyodor Abramov has noted repeatedly that our habit of judging a Soviet person, a peasant, from the heights of the ideal Communist personality quite often turns into injustice. Instead of glorifying them, we deliberately humiliate those people who support the country and stubbornly do a difficult job.

In his day, the Russian philosopher S. N. Bulgakov warned that faith in the transformation of the world and humanity's soul could result in "a specific kind of spiritual aristocratism which arrogantly looks down on the man in the street." This thinker wrote:

Intellectuals who have set themselves the task of serving their people continuously and inevitably fluctuate between two extremes—people worship and spiritual aristocratism. The need for people worship (whether in the form of old populism taking root in Herzen's doctrine, and relying on the belief in the socialist instinct of the Russian people, or in the latest Marxist form which ascribes the same features to some stratum rather than the whole nation) arises from the very foundations of the intellectuals' faith. But it simultaneously entails its opposition—a haughty attitude to the people as an object in need of salvation, as if it were under age and needed a nurse to develop its "consciousness" and were undereducated in the intellectuals' meaning of the word.[13]

If society and, principally, the party and its activists, old and young, had not shared the widespread belief in the pure human being, Stalin would have never managed to carry through his coercive, indiscriminate collectivization and to destroy the peasant (i.e., Russian folk traditions) so quickly. The thing is that the more our society, especially the youth, had been educated in romantic conceptions of the human being (which were, by the way, in harmony with Rousseau's ideas) and on utopian concepts of the future and socialism, the better were the conditions provided for Stalin's economic adventurism, and the easier it was to justify violence to this underdeveloped and still "impure" people.

The belief in a new harmonious personality, which entailed the growing dislike for everything traditional and, therefore, national, simply promoted leftist extremes, the abuse of common sense, and, consequently, the violation of reality.

This belief, relying on policy concepts formulated by the most lucid minds in history, only aggravated the situation—it built up the already rhapsodical and, therefore, uncritical attitude to Stalin's experiments, to the cause of building a nontrivial, "unique" society.

For example, it is difficult to say whether we profited or suffered from the basic idea of the Enlightenment—Rousseau's conception of humanity's natural kindness; his view that we are all born angels, like Jesus Christ; that all evil comes from social circumstances and, above all, from private property, mercantilism, and exchange. Rousseau's basic thesis, no doubt, strengthened the faith in humanity's creative potential of those who came out first against medieval obscurantism and then against the ideology of bourgeois values and profit making at any cost.

But today from the heights of our experience of collectivist transformations of society and the realities of modern socialism and modern civilization, we can also see serious flaws in such an uncritical attitude to human nature.

In keeping with Rousseau's logic, the less people are involved in the mire of unfavorable conditions, the higher are their chances of preserving the natural purity of their souls and of resisting the inevitably corrupting influence of civilization. This logic, carried over to the world of Communist concepts and values, should have inevitably led to dramatic contrasts. The social features of the classes and social strata, as a result of their place in the social labor division, were out of direct contact with market and marketing (the working class and the revolutionary intelligentsia). These social features were contrasted with the social features of those classes and social strata that, again as the result of their place in the social production process, came into direct contact with market forces (the bourgeoisie, craft workers, merchants, peasants, etc.).

At the same time, these ideas promoted the development of an active dislike for the market, money, and exchange and provoked a campaign against them. Robespierre, who was, of course, a Rousseauist, fought against profiteering and free trade just as fiercely as the Communists, equally inspired by faith in pure humanity, fought against petty profiteers in 1918–20.

It is generally difficult to explain why the Rousseauist rather than the Marxist view on human nature found so many followers among the Communists, and not only in this country. Marx and Engels, brought up on the ideas of Enlightenment, nevertheless remained dialecticians. In contrast to Rousseau, they did not idealize humanity. They saw humanity as contradictory, with conflicting humors, passions, and desires. None of them made a secret out of what is obvious to a naked eye: There are many animal impulses in every person. According to Engels, people originated in the animal kingdom, and clearly they will never be able to do away with savage elements altogether. We may speak only about quantitative differences in the expression of their beastly and human features.

Such a view of human nature did not repeat the concept of Original Sin, but, nevertheless, like Christianity, it favored a rational assessment of human nature and spotlighted the urgency of moral education problems. It urged people to appreciate the achievements of civilization in controlling natural human selfishness. This explains a different, more serious approach to human ethics than our dogmatic one and helps appreciate the basic standards of morality and the terrible consequences of, as Marx and Engels put it, the effect of elemental forces in the field of morality.

In contrast, we ignored human nature, humanity's conflicting essence, and as a result deprived ourselves of the chance to resolve seriously and with due understanding of the human factor the issues of labor organization and encouragement. We thus robbed ourselves of the insight into the nature of any government. The idealization of human nature contributed to the worsening of the moral climate in society instead of its consolidation, as it favored neglect above natural control mechanisms and allowed demagogues and bigots to tamper with the simple biblical truths and to mock those who reminded society of the value of a clear conscience, decency, and the rules of propriety. For example, at the beginning of the sixties, the writer G. Markov wrote this in the *Literaturnaya Gazeta:* "To discredit socialist values, to disparage them in relation to general human values in the old limited meaning of this word is tantamount to sliding towards undervaluation of the human being." One should keep in mind that besides the Stalin era, the years of stagnation also witnessed a very "high" appreciation of human nature. Stalinists' revenge at the end of the sixties manifested itself in philosophy by unbridled attacks on general human values. It was marked, among other things, by the ideological "denunciation" of those who proclaimed the primacy of conscience and good in their works on ethics. By no coincidence, the attack on perestroika on the pretext of unwillingness "to betray one's principles" was once again accompanied by attacks on the so-called scholasticism of ethical categories.[14]

The pseudo-Communist interpretation of Rousseauism at the same time drastically narrowed the understanding of vital social issues, fostered the illusion that absolutely all human problems can be solved with the help of two such master keys as greater socialization and increased ideological impact on the masses. Hence, our still persistent belief that presocialist society had many "redundant elements" without which our social mechanism can do perfectly well. Market, competition, the rule of law, the principle of division of prerogatives, and religious feeling were all classed as such redundant elements. Rousseau's nihilistic attitude to civilization was paralleled by our theory of "throwing bourgeois culture away."

This was virtually true of the ideals of progressive Western thinkers, too. Orientation toward idealized conceptions of the human being and the new society entailed rigorism and maximalism and completely deprived us of the possibility and the wish to think in flexible, alternative terms. From these springs our longing for absurdly simple solutions.

It must still be so difficult to eliminate the Stalinist paradigm, the ideology of "throwing the past away," because it leans on ideals extremely deep-seated in our consciousness: the ideals of the Enlightenment and the dream about a pure person and pure socialism. A lot depended then on faith in the unlimited potential of knowledge and science and humanity's boundless capabilities. The thinking of Stalinism is similar to that of people who do not recognize the limits of their claims in this world and who are convinced they can meet any challenge and conquer the world, nature, space, and time.

This faith in the limitless possibilities of human knowledge explains, first of all, the belief in the feasibility of the complete ousting of chance by necessity, element by consciousness; the belief that it is feasible to subordinate completely all economic relationships in society to planning, and to control by the state all manifestations of labor activity.

All those who write today about Stalin's interrelations with the world of science draw their readers' attention to the ease with which he could be tempted by an insane and, therefore, from the very outset, unfeasible idea. This reveals, besides insufficient expertise and incompetence, his deep belief that science can do everything and his lack of any healthy skepticism in anything sanctified by science.

But we must be fair to Stalin in this respect. A politician, a professional revolutionary, who generally had no opportunity for methodical daily scientific research could hardly be expected to gain insight into the relative nature of all knowledge, to develop the instinct of doubting and the need to verify even the most plausible truth. Only true scholars, by building up and deepening their knowledge and by penetrating into the sophisticated nature of society, can develop an insight into the abyss of their own ignorance, which gradually opens up to them. But researchers who have become familiar with the intensity of social contradictions and have in-depth knowledge of national history, who realize to what extent their attained level of expertise is questionable, will never be able to make radically thinking politicians, true revolutionaries, or active participants in changing the world.

I think that Marx could never himself lead the masses in storming the barricades or in attacking the old world. He was much too afraid that the onslaught on the old world could turn into, as he wrote about the first days of the Paris Commune, "the storming of the sky." It is no mere chance that he to his last days doubted whether his research into self-devitalization of capital was conclusive and accurate enough, and he returned to this problem over and over again.

By no coincidence, Plekhanov ultimately turned into a typical reformer. It would be naive to think he was less courageous or less compassionate to the sufferings of the working class and the oppressed than Lenin and his followers who took power in October 1917. There is some historical intricacy in this. Everyone has his own destiny.

After Lenin's death, socialist construction was headed by brave and active people. Moreover, they disliked scholars who did not believe in working wonders and who reminded them of the complexity and the limits of scientific research. In the epoch of general enthusiasm when fairy tales were to become true, *Lysenkovschina* had much higher chances of success. It was in line with the unlimited claims of an omnipotent epoch. This explains the reasons for Vavylov's tragedy. It was imminent in the context of the widespread opinion that the proletarian dictatorship was incompatible with the autonomy of a scientist, of science and independent opinion.

One should not forget that Lysenko was not only Stalin's, but also Khrushchev's, favorite and for the same reason. He promised to work a miracle—to save by nontrivial methods our nontrivial agriculture that was in a state of crisis.

Lysenkovschina flourished in other branches of knowledge, too. Lev Razgon, for instance, tells in his memoirs about the prospering leaders of the National Institute of Experimental Medicine. Its organizers were not, of course, swindlers. But their scientific ideas were so much in keeping with the aspirations and ambitions of the country's leadership that an enormous current of patronage was rapidly carrying them upward. Their theories enchanted prominent Russian author Maxim Gorky and then Stalin himself.

These physicians believed they would very soon manage to find "something special" in the human organism and be able to influence it, and thus they would quickly eradicate all disease, including the most unpleasant of all—old age. This objective, besides being extremely seductive, was in absolute harmony with the spirit of the epoch: conquering space and time was not enough; controlling all that was still unknown and intractable was imperative. "This," concludes Razgon in his story, "fully coincided with Stalin's ambitions as he could not put up with the existence of anything beyond his power."[15]

I believe that Stalinism as an ideology has to do not only with the history of socialism and that of Russia. It is part of European history and in many respects the child of its expansionist culture. Therefore, even the errors and the tragedies of our revolution are of paramount importance to humanity. They reveal the true substance of many once-attractive social ideas. They disclose the depth of spiritual degradation to which faith in "a pure person" and "pure society" may lead.

This universal significance of our experience of socialist construction was evident at once. Immediately after War Communism, we find the first attempt, as Bukharin put it in his speech to the Constituent Assembly in January 1918, to "at once," "right now" translate into reality the best ideals of humankind. Even our liberal intellectuals, who generally refused to accept the October Revolution but considered it their duty to share the fortune of their motherland, recognized the universal importance of its lessons. Professor A. Izgoyev wrote in January 1922,

No matter what the results of the present revolution will be for the Russian people, it is of great and universal significance as it gave mankind a chance to test on Russia's flesh the basic ideas that have inspired European revolutionary thought for already more than a century. There is only one sure method of putting them to the test: to try and realize the given idea in practice. Before 1917 all foreign and Russian revolutionaries only spoke about socialism and communism. Russian Bolsheviks were brave enough to start translating these concepts into practice."[16]

But does this mean that humanity could not have tested all these doctrines of the pure human being, the rule of consciousness and consistency, otherwise than by Stalin's practices, his unnecessary perversions and losses? Could we not have otherwise realized that elemental forces are not always a synonym for evil, that a peasant should not be turned into a worker, that the fight against exploitation should not spill over into a fight against initiative and resourcefulness, and, finally, that not everything new is better than the old?

NOTES

1. A. M. Bakunin, *Selected Works* (St. Petersburg, 1919), 1:236–37.
2. Quoted in V. G. Plekhanov, *Selected Philosophical Works* (in Russian) (Moscow, 1956), 1:311–12. Lev Trotsky, *My Life* (in Russian) (Berlin: Granat, 1930), 2:89.

3. Trotsky, *My Life*, 211.
4. L. Kritsman. *A Heroic Period of the Great Russian Revolution* (Moscow, 1926), 80.
5. See V. Korolenko, "Letters to Lunacharsky" (in Russian), *Novyi Mir*, 1988, no. 10:199–200.
6. Naum Korzhavin, "Little Tanya," *Znamya*, 1988, no. 12:89–90.
7. *The 2nd Congress of the All-Russia Socialist Democratic Workers' Party: Protocols* (in Russian) (Moscow, 1959), 181–82.
8. Lev Trotsky, *My Life* (in Russian) (Berlin: Granat, 1930), 2:101.
9. P. Petrov, *Literatunaya Gazeta*, August 19, 1987.
10. A. Z. Seleznev, "Common Means Ours!" *Sobesednik*, 1987, no. 29:10.
11. Stalin, *Works*, 12:126, 129, 132.
12. A. Strelyany, "Two Conclusions," *Novyi Mir*, 1987, no. 2:240.
13. Vekhi, *Collected Articles on Russian Intelligentsia* (in Russian) (Moscow, 1909), 49.
14. "I Cannot Betray My Principles" is the title of the above-mentioned notorious letter by Nina Andreyeva published in *Sovetskaya Rossiya*.
15. See *Yunost*, 1988, no. 5:10.
16. A. Izgoyev, "Vekhi" and "Smena Vekh," in *On Smena Vekh* (Moscow: Izdanie Svobodnykh Literatorov [Free Writers Publishers], 1922), chap. 4.

CHAPTER 4

The Russia of Dreamers

The Enigma of History Lies in the Rule of Chance

It is difficult to say exactly what a person wants more: the truth or a soothing lie. Life is filled with deception. But that is only half the truth—and not the most important truth at that. What we must acknowledge is that we very often long for self-deceit and stubbornly refuse to face reality. We fix our attention on those aspects of life that offer us comfort.

There are numerous reasons why people avoid the truth about themselves. It is difficult for us to accept that we are weak, that we have worshiped false idols, and that we have been champions of the wrong cause. People must be very strong and courageous to overcome their illusions and tell the whole truth about their country, ancestors, and the political movement to which they belong. But sooner or later the day comes when the aspiration for the truth prevails.

Most people of my generation (and I have not yet met a single devoted Stalinist among those born in 1941) who were thunderstruck in their youth by the revelations about the atrocities of the Stalin era, and especially those who could acknowledge this truth in their hearts, have been tormented by the question of whether it was possible to avoid the Russian Apocalypse.

Later, when I had entered the philosophy department of Moscow University and studied Russian philosophy of the early twentieth century I came to realize that this urgent question should be reformulated: Was it possible to preclude leftist leaps and experiments that so characterize our post-October history? After all, the essence of Stalinism lies in extreme radicalism. Was there an alternative to coercive collectivization, Stalin's total state socialism, and his policies that destroyed the life-style of the Russian people?

Theoretically, I believe that in history in general and in Russia's history in particular there is no such thing as an inevitable event. True, necessity as a historical tendency sooner or later manifests itself; sooner or later the ugly tsarist regime had to perish. But when and in what form? A lot depended on chance, on the unpredictable. The Russian philosopher Alexander Hertzen wrote, "History improvises, she rarely repeats herself. . . . She uses every chance, every coincidence. She knocks simultaneously at a thousand gates. . . . Who knows which may open?"[1]

This is probably a typically Russian perception of history based on a deeply hidden hope that we might have had a different destiny, but we accidentally let it loose. Russian intellectuals are inherently opposed to fatalism. Nevertheless, it is difficult to argue with Hertzen's idea that "the future does not exist; it is created by the combination of a thousand causes, some necessary, some accidental plus human will which adds unexpected dramatic denouements and coup de theatre."[2] The conviction that a development results from the struggle of "elemental forces and the will," the consequences of which cannot be predicted, that "Nature simply hinted in most general terms at its intentions and left all the details to human will and the circumstance," was characteristic of Hegel and later of his disciples Karl Marx and Frederick Engels. Interestingly, whenever the inveterate materialists Marx and Engels write about chance, they always mention the "will," which is absolutely immaterial and unpredictable, as well as the eternal interaction of matter with the spirit and that of economic determinants with psychology.

The unpredictable, accidental, avoidable appears in history due to variability in the very process of reflecting people's living conditions and their interests.

If it is true that every person was initially provided with several variations of life, at any rate many more than he or she could realize during the time alloted by God, and if it is true that we underuse our mental and physical potentialities, then why should we believe that history as it happened was the only possible alternative, that only things that happened were necessary, and that nothing else could ever happen? It would make more sense to acknowledge, as Frederick Engels did, that one-sided evolution "excluded the possibility of evolution in many other directions."[3]

The enigma and tragedy of human history, in my view, lie in the great power of chance, which may intervene in the course of events and dramatically change it. Some historical events were totally accidental and cannot be justified even by the slightest necessity. But they have had a measurable impact on the course of what has followed. How and when would World War II have ended if the attempt on Hitler's life in August

1944 had succeeded, that is, if the raised table had not shielded his body from the explosion? It is clear that, had Hitler been killed, the war could have ended earlier and the postwar history of Europe would have been quite different.

What would have been the history of Russia and that of the February revolution in 1917 if Lenin's fantastic revolutionary will and his insistence on the need for an immediate military uprising against the Provisional Government had not prevailed over the more moderate and conciliatory views of most Central Committee members? Trotsky marked time; Zinoviev, Kamenev, and Rykov were categorically opposed to the seizure of power and pressed for an alliance with the Menshiviks and the Socialist Revolutionaries in order to save the gains of the February revolution. Even Stalin restrained to the best of his capacities revolutionary pressure from below, especially in the first months after the overthrow of the tsarist autocracy.

We need not even guess what would have happened if Lenin had failed to crush the resistance of the majority in the Central Committee or if he had lost heart. There simply would not have been an October Revolution in Russia, with all the ensuing consequences. I am deeply convinced, as proven by revolutions in Germany and Hungary, that it was impossible to avoid a proletarian revolution in Europe at that time. But there is no evidence of fatal inevitability of the Bolshevik victory in Russia. Only a few months before, in February 1917, the Bolsheviks were supported by an insignificant minority of the population. In this particular case, as Lenin wrote, everything actually depended on the art and political flair of the party leadership, its ability to profit politically from the discontent of the working masses with the absurd policies of the Provisional Government. Lenin himself said on the eve of the October Revolution that all ultimately depended on the day of the action. He wrote, "History will not forgive revolutionaries for procrastination when they could be victorious today (and they certainly will be victorious today), while they risk losing much tomorrow, in fact, they risk loosing everything."[4]

An eyewitness to the October Revolution, American journalist Albert Rhys Williams, in his book *Journey into Revolution*, specially stressed the decisive impact of Lenin's persistence and will on the tactics and the decision of the Bolsheviks at this historic moment of Russian history. In his view, but for the courage and insight of Lenin, who was not afraid to turn to the party's judgment on his differences with the Central Committee, the October Revolution might never have taken place.[5]

Granted, if for some reason a personality and leader such as Lenin is taken out of the political game, the need for the leader remains, and with time a more or less successful substitute will be found. But time for history-making decisions does not wait. The elements and factors capable of forming the critical mass of explosion converge and may merge for perhaps just a fraction of a moment. The conditions conducive to a revolution, to an upheaval of established structures, can take a very long period, sometimes decades, to mature. But after they do, they favor the positive outcome of the revolution for one very short instant. And if at such favorable moments, no one can perceive that disagreeing elements have agreed just for a fraction of an instant (for example, peasants dreaming of private ownership on land are ready to support workers and socialist-minded intellectuals opposing private ownership), if no one can trigger off the explosion, the opportunity will be missed and the events will develop in a different direction. Sociopsychological strain will diminish, existing forces will regroup, and new political combinations will emerge. Life proceeds quickly, especially at the time of revolution.

I am treating chance as something mystical, as history's mystery, simply because people capable of changing the course of events in the necessary direction very often mark time when it is imperative to make decisions and show striking persistence and will, though they have absolutely no possibility of succeeding. Everything would be quite simple in history, as Holbach put it, if people sought self-perservation and loved themselves, if everybody sought what was profitable and felt aversion for everything that could be harmful.[6] But in every complicated situation fraught with historical consequences, people are not guided by their intellect alone. All their being is involved in decision making. Fyodor Dostoyevsky wrote, "Human nature acts as a whole, and with all that is contained in it. So that whether conscious or unconscious, sane or mad, it is always human nature."[7]

How can one explain the episode from the history of the Bolshevik party when Trotsky remained passive in 1924–25, though he still had a chance to win power by forming an alliance with G. Zinoviev and L. Kamenev, who were ideologically close to him? Instead, he entered into this alliance in 1926, after the 14th CPSU(B) Congress, when Stalin already had the majority in the Politburo.*

I could list many more arguments that reject the fatalist view of history and give us every reason to believe that not all the events in our history were inevitable and that we had a chance to avoid Stalin's genocide

---

* In his article "On Stalin and Stalinism," Soviet historian Roy Medvedev observes that at the time of struggle between Kamenev and Zinoviev, on the one hand, and Stalin and Bukharin, on the other, Trotsky sometimes came to Politburo meetings with a French novel and ignored the discussions, lost in reading.

against his own people. But the major argument, in my view, is the nature of the human being—a spiritual being with the freedom of choice. If we recognize the freedom of will, we must, consequently, recognize the varied nature of human behavior and the varied character of human history.

It is telling that recent CPSU official documents do not discuss the October 1917 revolution in Russia as something inevitable and unavoidable. Today we increasingly employ the word *choice* for describing this turning point in Russian history. In my view, this approach to what happened in 1917 is closer to reality not only philosophically but in practice. The events of the thirties were essentially instigated by the choices made in 1917, by the future victors of the Civil War. Therefore, I believe that we must look for the sources of the tragedies of the thirties in the people who made their choices back in 1917 and ultimately lost control over the events and in the ideas that incited them. I think that only such analysis of the sources of Stalinism can lead us to the truth.

Who Could Be and Was the Subject of Leftist Leaps?

V. Loginov, a popular Soviet historian, commented on a recent television program, "The mystery of Stalinism lies in faces." Talking about a newsreel of the thirties on mass enrollments into the party, Loginov drew his audience's attention to the characteristic face representing this new, already Stalinist guard. It is true that these faces—broad, plain, and, frankly speaking, void of any thought—the faces of the people who joined the party in those years, could hardly win the sympathy of the spectators. Suffice it to remember other faces, to compare the appearance of Stalin's guard with that of the Leninist one. Suffice it to remember those Russian intellectuals who followed Lenin's coffin in January 1924, and the enemy image involuntarily took shape. The audience began to believe the historian who was arguing that all our misfortunes had resulted from changes in faces and that all these politically illiterate, uneducated people who flooded into the party at the turn of the thirties were guilty of all the atrocities of Stalinism.

But we should not believe such interpretation of our historical fortunes. It is not that the predominant part of the population is different nor is it because the original Russian peasantry has been replaced today by something else.

And if we are deceived in this respect, the deception is insignificant and purely technical. Simply put, the less numerous but equally typical Russian peasants—smart, thrifty, and reliable, keen on cooperation and engaged in trade with Europe—had been killed before the reporter had time to film them. These Russian peasants simply disappeared in the vast regions of snow-covered Siberia during the period of the dispossession of the kulaks. This is what some of our publicists and historians who like to claim the social inferiority of Russian peasantry tend to forget.

As for the typical Russian villager's face, generally speaking, Loginov and other authors who describe patriarchal, illiterate, and uncultured Russia are telling the truth. This face type, unfortunately, remains, revealing the individual's lack of independence and self-respect. Such people are not yet trained to think unaided and make independent decisions. Recall the haggard, almost hopeless faces of the inhabitants of a small town near Krasnoyarsk. These people practically implored Mikhail Gorbachev, when he visited their town in November 1987, to help them and improve their living standards. This reveals the persistent lack of some people's spiritual independence, their eternal belief that a benevolent tsar will come, establish justice, and help the miserable. But where can self-respect and spiritual training come from if these people have had no responsibility for six decades, if, as distinguished Soviet surgeon N. Amosov wrote in *Literaturnaya Gazeta*, the virus of "general untraining" has long contaminated our society?

This deception is more than twisting facts; it has to do with the interpretation of the truth about peasants' faces. The deception is about attempts to convince readers and spectators that the former peasants provoked leftist leaps into the future, and that all our misfortunes have resulted from the political instability and inherent anarchism of the individual farmer. The deception is about the attempt to convince my fellow Soviets that they could not be different, that they have received their just deserts. They are being told there is no use complaining of the destiny they have chosen for themselves, that all the atrocities and outrages of Stalin's epoch are rooted in Russian patriarchy, and that Russia's misanthropic history made Stalin's dominance inevitable.

We are deceived because our attention is diverted from the true subject and creator of our socialist destiny and drawn to the imaginary subject of our historical drama—the peasants, whose only fault is that they are numerous and bearded. This numerous class, the peasants of all nationalities inhabiting this country, are guilty of nothing that happened here in the thirties. It was not their fault; it was their great misfortune.

They did not choose Stalin to lead them, and, if the truth be known, they never liked this tyrant and oppressor.

The moment you present history as it is, that is, as a chain of decisions and actions of people seeking their own interests, everything fits and becomes self-evident. It was the Bolshevik old guard that was insufficiently particular about people they involved in their revolutionary struggle. They overlooked Stalin's criminal inclinations. The young Bolshevik Joseph Dzhugashvili did not start carrying out the so-called exes (expropriation of capitalist property) for the party masses on his own accord.*

It was the old guard that placed the country on a path of development that, contrary to all its forecasts and expectations, led to the self-annihilation of the people and the party.

It was the old guard that created the political mechanism, the instrument of absolute omnipotence, Stalin later used for his own selfish needs, assassinating those who saw him for the beast he was and were more intellectual than he. The old guard failed to reform the system that portended totalitarian dictatorship; it failed to revert to legal norms of life.

And, after all, it was no one but the old guard who voluntarily, before Lenin's death, gave Stalin the enormous power created by the revolution and later, after 1924, impatiently urged the country to take the leftist leaps that turned into a national tragedy. This was the way it was, and nothing can alter it.

Certainly, no one who stood then on the captain's bridge of our revolution and actively participated in the development of the party's policies could have ever predicted the future course of events. These were people seeking to eliminate the evil—the Russian order that had given rise to the revolution and the protests of the working class. They believed there could not be a worse evil than the massacre unleashed by the European bourgeoisie. They were not prepared to oppose the new evil born by their own movement. The tragic aspects of their revolution, they saw only later. Hence, the old Bolsheviks erred unintentionally. At any rate, we should try to distinguish the mistakes of revolutionaries who failed to predict the consequences of their decisions and the crimes of extremists who used political struggle to realize their own inherent aggressiveness and ambitions.

---

* Roy Medvedev writes, "The revolution of 1905–1907 gave Stalin a chance to display some of his other abilities. He was entrusted with carrying out a number of large-scale raids or, 'exes.' Those were mostly armed bank burglaries, hold-ups of post coaches and steamers. At that time the Bolsheviks allowed for such 'exes' as a means of improving the financial situation of the party. The money went into buying weapons. It was also believed that the exes would frighten the tsarist administration. The best known of all was the armed raid on the Tiflis Treasury which gave 300,000 rubles to the Bolshevist cash fund. This 'ex' was carried out by a group of militants including Kamo (S. S. Ter-Petrosyan), but Stalin and A. B. Krasin, the leader of the 'military-technical group under the Central Committee,' took an active part in its preparation and planning" (*Znamya*, 1989, no. 1:160).

It is no use trying to explain events by claiming the weakness of some individuals or difficulty in predicting secondary and tertiary consequences of the revolution, its tragic outcome. In my opinion, these consequences primarily occurred as the result of our social structures. This is the fundamental evil of human life: It takes many years and the efforts of thousands of talented and skillful people to create something significant, whereas the dreadful ingenuity of one mediocre person who had greedily grasped power is enough to destroy everything created with such difficulty.

Stalinism is a dreadful lesson for our people, for all of humanity. But it is nevertheless a lesson: We must all learn to be wary of those who rush headlong into events and tempt people with easy solutions and prompt results, and we must learn to be cautious of those who believe that destruction can promote human life. To learn to be vigilant, we should thoroughly and seriously study Stalinism as a variety of left-wing extremism.

Stalinism emerged within the framework of the left-wing school of social thought. Hence, we should first of all study the nature of leftist radicalism and its programs; we should identify its weak points, which, as we know now, in an unfavorable set of circumstances could result in total destruction. Clearly, the discussion of Stalinism and *Stalinischina* should start with a review of the principles of the party's organization, its rules and beliefs, that directly or indirectly promoted the development of these principles.

Tsarist feeling, patriarchal sentiment, illiteracy, and lack of culture among the bearded peasants ultimately contributed to the consolidation of Stalin's dictatorship. But this was only the soil; the seed itself came from a different, leftist field. The peasant alone would never have been able to bring about the events of the thirties. Patriarchal sentiment and patriarchal illiteracy in themselves inspire no revolutions. They might lead to a riot or to plunder. Under different circumstances they might nurture belief in the tsar or in God, in private property or the eternal order and the Russian Orthodox church. But they could never be the source of revolutionary structural transformations or the force that disrupts people's lives.

All nations have outgrown patriarchal feeling and peasants' conservatism. But why were we the only country to have Stalinism? Let us take a better look at the social physiology of Stalin's power. Such methods of government are not feasible in a society with persistent patriarchal principles of life. Why did Japan, which in the nineteenth century was a more traditional and patriarchal state than Russia, manage nevertheless to avoid something akin to Stalinism?

The evil of patriarchal underdevelopment, however, in no way reduces the responsibility of the left-wing intelligentsia for the consequences of their choice. On the contrary, the lower the cultural and educational level of the country's population, the more careful and well considered should be their actions. Under such circumstances, full responsibility without any reservations rests with those who proposed the idea of revolutionizing society, led the uncultured people into the unknown, and urged them to destroy their old world.

I think that since we interpret Stalinism as leftist impatience or left-wing extremism we have absolutely no right to shift the blame onto the bearded peasant. He had nothing to do with it.

Our great leaps were initiated not by former peasants but by the revolutionary proletariat and socialist intelligentsia, who were both of urban origin. Long before Stalin emerged victorious in 1929, back in the years of War Communism, they attempted to leap on the bandwagon of revolutionary enthusiasm and take Russia from capitalism right into socialism. Let us use our common sense and intellect. A peasant, a villager was simply unable to think up such fantasies and utopia; only the intellectual could do this. One needs a developed imagination and much leisure to imagine and dream. Peasants have neither the former nor the latter. They must work hard all their lives earning their living by the sweat of their brows. They should make their daily bread and provide for themselves and unpractical urban dreamers.

Now that we have touched upon the social sources of our left-wing leaps, we should note that, at all the stages of our revolution, workers were much more contaminated by this virus than peasants. This is quite understandable; a worker has nothing to lose but his or her chains.

Do not forget that peasants never supported the Bolshevik radical agrarian program—the idea of organizing farming on a national level on socialized land and in accordance with a single plan. If Russian peasants really had had an inherent socialist instinct they would have come in droves to the Bolshevik faction of the Russian Social Democratic Party, which inscribed on its banner "Common Work on Common Land." But that was not, of course, the case either before or after October 1917. Stalin had to organize collective and state farms by force.

One should keep in mind that the workers of St. Petersburg, not the peasants, were ardent admirers of Trotsky's leftist radical talents and his theories. Twice, in the revolution of 1905 and that of 1917, they shared the

dreams of this most radical leader of Russian socialist democracy, prefer-
ring his theory of permanent revolution and continuous upheaval. It was
probably not coincidental that very few former peasants were in the left-
wing oppositions.

The working class actively supported the most radical out of all our
revolution's leftist policies (I mean the policy of Poor Peasants' Committees—the Combeds*). This policy was pursued under its direct supervision. The most fantastic of all our revolution's fantastic programs—that
of the immediate transition from capitalist to Communist Russia, setting
up a single network of production and consumption communes that
should compete with one another, the replacement of market and money
exchange by bartering—was adopted by the party in 1919 under pressure
of revolutionary-minded workers and socialist intelligentsia. And, finally,
none other than the growing new socialist proletariat and the new growing socialist bureaucracy represented the most militant opponents of the
New Economic Policy (NEP) in the second half of the twenties.

No reasoning is needed here. Long before Stalin, with the help of his
cronies, managed to dissolve the "pure" proletarian nucleus of the party
among the numerous newly adopted members who were "sullied" by
their peasant origin, the vast majority of the CPSU(B) membership had
visions of leaping into a kingdom of pure socialism free from kulaks or
individual farmers.

One should refer in this respect to Stalin's declaration in his political
report to the 14th CPSU(B) Congress in December 1925 that the party
was prepared to do away with kulaks. "If we were to ask Communists
what the party is better prepared for—to strip the kulaks, or not to do
that, but enter into alliance with the middle peasants—I think that 99 out
of 100 Communists would say that the Party is best prepared for the
slogan: "Beat the kulaks! Just let them—they would strip the kulaks in a
jiffy."[8]

This is what happened. So let us tell the truth rather than fan hatred
against the innocent.

As for what the prevailing type of prerevolutionary Russian could or
could not choose or what Russian peasantry as a class could or could not
do, this is pure conjecture.

One well-known fact from Russian history at the beginning of the
twentieth century is familiar even to schoolchildren, though denouncers

---

* Combeds, or village committees of the poor, were set up by Lenin and Trotsky in the
summer of 1918 to dispossess well-to-do farmers of grain and to intensify the class
struggle in the countryside. The idea behind it was to carry over the October Revolution
from the city to the countryside. This measure made the Civil War even more ruthless.

of the Russian patriarchal system and underdevelopment somehow tend
to forget about it. The incident occurred in October 1917. When Russian
peasants actually had the chance to choose, they chose, of course, the
Decree on Land, which distributed the lands of landlords among peasants who were thus able to expand their individual plots by several des-
siatinas (approximately an acre) and cultivate them. Peasants voted at
that time for the Socialist Revolutionaries' *chornyi peredel* (redistribution
of all lands held by landlords), for private family farming, and for the
bourgeois way of development.

One can, of course, complain that the peasants, as Marxists used to
put it, had believed in "reactionary utopia," that it was possible to preserve small family farming under capitalism. And one might be correct in
saying that the peasants lacked both the knowledge and political culture
to realize the advantages of collective farming. But regardless of what we
believe, the countryside remains the countryside, and peasants remain
peasants. They were quite willing to grow rich at someone else's expense
and to rob the landlords. And in the vast majority of cases, our Russian
peasants most probably had enough reasons for that. But they could
never imagine anything like Stalin's collective farms in their most frightening nightmares.

These bearded peasants, the rural population in general, should never
be connected with the choice made by the urban revolutionary proletariat and socialist intelligentsia. The basic contradiction of the October
Revolution is that, though there was a single revolution in the country,
the choices were different. In the urban areas, the choice was mainly in
favor of socialism, whereas in the rural areas (i.e., on the predominant
part of the national territory) the people favored capitalism and private
ownership.

This is an open secret, as a perusal of Lenin's works of the Civil War
period will reveal. In that initial phase of the revolution, Lenin paid particular attention to the basically bourgeois character of the revolution,
stressing that it would be a bourgeois revolution "as long as we march
with the peasants as a whole." From his point of view, only the Combeds
started the spread of socialist revolution in the rural areas. And even in
this case, as Lenin explained, the subject of the new policy, of transferring the class struggle from town to the countryside, was, above all, the
proletarian state itself. This is what actually happened.

However, sober reasoning reveals that it should not have been unexpected that the Russian peasants did not voluntarily join collective
organizations in agriculture. On the contrary, it would have been a miracle if it had been otherwise, if peasants on their own accord, without

coercion, had preferred to join a collective farm and give up their individual plots of land, something they had dreamt of for centuries. Would any normal person, to say nothing of a patriarchal conservative, give up something he or she has grown accustomed to in exchange for something unusual? Only a poor peasant who has nothing to lose or an irresponsible youth could take such a rash step.

After all, even industrial workers, to say nothing of peasants, did not choose socialism of their own accord.

Having dulled our consciousness with hackneyed propaganda clichés and however accustomed we have grown to hearing the praises of the spiritually and politically perfect working class as opposed to the evil petite bourgeoisie, we somehow seem to have forgotten this truth about the proletariat.

As Lenin, the creator of the Bolshevik faction in the Socialist Democratic party, put it himself, workers must be encouraged to accept socialist democratic ideology. They can neither form scientific concepts of reality nor determine the substance and the objectives of a socialist transformation of social life. Developing this thesis in "What Is To Be Done," Lenin wrote,

The history of all countries shows that the working class, exclusively by its own effort, is able to develop only trade-union consciousness, i.e., the conviction that it is necessary to combine in unions, fight the employers, and strive to compel the government to pass necessary labor legislation, etc. The theory of socialism, however, grew out of philosophic, historical, and economic theories elaborated by educated representatives of the propertied classes, by intellectuals. By their social status, the founders of modern scientific socialism, Marx and Engels, themselves belonged to the bourgeois intelligentsia. In the very same way, in Russia, the theoretical doctrine of Social-Democracy arose altogether independently of the spontaneous growth of the working-class movement; it arose as a natural and inevitable outcome of the development of thought among the revolutionary socialist intelligentsia.[9]

The basic truth about our revolution (about all Russian revolutions: in 1905 and in February and October of 1917) is that they all were organized by the intelligentsia and were carried through under its direct guidance. As the American Albert Williams writes, "all major parties with the exception of the Constitutional Democrats and, particularly, the Socialist-Democratic party—Menshiviks and Bolsheviks—actively participated in preparing the workers of the Vyborg district—this smoke-filled and trembling heart of the revolution—for the ongoing changes. Selfless and passionate propagandists had for many years sown the seeds of socialism in this fertile soil using all legal and clandestine means. (Nadezhda Krupskaya, Lenin's wife, was one of them. She resumed teaching at a night school for workers in this Petrograd district.) Low wages and long working hours, tiny closets instead of decent housing, and police spies and stool-pigeons poking their noses into everything, speed-up work system and fines, and finally the growing hatred for war did the rest."[10]

I think that if Soviet publicists who write about the petit-bourgeois roots of Stalin's leftism just for a moment imagined in the flesh those people whom they blame for everything, they would think again. Judge for yourself. Why does a peasant need large-scale industrial farming? Even a poor peasant, the former Combed member, who was prepared at any time to divest his prospering neighbor, thought about the chance of getting a horse rather than about the possibility of collective farming. Envy per se never leads to collective work organization.

For the urban petite bourgeoisie—the same Russian shopkeepers, artisans, and traders who had managed to grow rich during the NEP period—any social radicalism was out of the question. Their blood froze at the mere mention of collectivization or of a possible speedup of the rate of socialist transformation. Nothing could frighten them more than the return to the methods of War Communism. To them, Stalin's attack on the NEP was the equivalent of doomsday.

Even the sentiments and the expectations of the vast majority of the working class were not so "red" as is generally believed. It is true that the working class of Russia and, above all, that of Petrograd was the locomotive of our revolution and the uncompromising opponent of the capitalist system and private property. But what was a worker's idea of socialism? It would not be difficult to prove that it differed from that of Karl Marx and socialist intellectuals. The proletariat understood literally the slogan of the October Revolution, "Factories to the Workers!" They interpreted it as alienation of capitalist property in their favor. They thought that the plant would become, as we would say today, the possession of its collective. At the time of nationalization, Lenin and the party leadership had to oppose anarcho-syndicalist feelings and the workers' aspiration to make plants their collective property.

Which conclusion can we draw from this? It follows that only the socialist intelligentsia, the social stratum that had a scientific abstract concept of the future and was convinced that neither family farming nor group property could be compatible with modern technical progress, was the basic source of leftist urges and the aspiration to speed up the transition to a system that went beyond workers' and peasants' expectations. To be fair, there is nothing to debate here. Immediately after the revolution it became clear that a revolution in Russia could be nothing but an intellectual's revolution. Yu. V. Kluchnikov, a political emigrant and one of the authors of *Smena Vekh*, asked back in 1921,

Could any revolution in Russia be anything but an intellectual's revolution? The Russian intelligentsia is doomed to play the starring part in any revolution, is it not? We, the intellectuals, represented the major revolutionary force out of those that pressed on our motherland and finally exploded it as the result of the war. So the great historical process started in March 1917 was simply administering justice over us.[11]

People cannot seek something they are unable to conceive. But those who have let into their hearts and minds the image of a world differing from the one currently existing immediately become the source of radicalism. Therefore, I insist that people having theoretical knowledge of the future have always been the main source of leftist extremism.

The teaching of the need for and inevitability of complete and direct socialization of labor on a national scale per se does not, of course, entail leftist impatience, to say nothing of violence. It all depends on the cleverness, common sense, and the sense of responsibility of those who have undertaken to reorganize the national economy along new lines. But Marxism lacked expertise as to how and in what forms to socialize production. Hence, it was fraught with the dangers of experimentation.

The First Cavalry Charge on the Market

In my view, since the major instigators and organizers of the socialist revolution in Russia were the intellectuals, people engaged in scientific work and giving top priority to scientific knowledge, the first attempt at least to achieve pure communism was inevitable. By this I mean the so-called policy of War Communism. We should take into account that the Bolsheviks, at that time including Lenin, piously believed in the possibility of realizing Marxist teaching of socialism as a society absolutely free of trade, market, and small private production in its pure form. In the prerevolutionary and Civil War years, Lenin's original ideas of socialism in conceptual terms were in complete harmony with Marx's vision of the lower phase of the Communist formation as described in his work "Critique of the Gotha Program."

Lenin guided the party's assault on the old world, planning for a socialist society completely free of everything inherited from the previous formations. It simply could not be otherwise. Marx interpreted socialism as the negation of market, money, and classes, as production organization, farming included, on a national scale, according to a single plan under the direct guidance of society's central bodies. Marx's idea was to organize social production like a large factory where everything is subordinated to the manager's iron will and the shops exchange their produce instead of marketing it. Lenin's concept of socialism as described in his book *The State and Revolution*, written a few months before the October Revolution, is a direct reflection of Marx's views on the would-be socialist society.

Hence, in my view, the attempts of Soviet historical science to explain by extreme circumstances alone the system of imposed commands in production management established during the Civil War, and generally the entire economic system of War Communism, are unjustified. They were conceived like that from the very outset. Socialism was interpreted, above all, as strict management of all material resources by means of instructions, as the elimination of economic autonomy of enterprise, trade circulation, and the law of value.

Many party members both then and later, in the twenties, were convinced that the economy of War Communism reflected the general regularities of building socialism. In their opinion, it was the practical realization of Marxism rather than a deviation from it. This idea ran through the works by L. Kritsman, an economist and a party theorist who devoted a whole book to proving this thesis. He, inter alia, wrote that "coercive suppression of all capitalist and market relations first eliminated all overt resistance and then allowed us to implant inherent trends of the proletarian revolution. Due to this, 1918–1920 saw the establishment of a very peculiar system of proletarian subsistence economy." He insisted that it was not "a delusion of a person or a class." In his view, it was rather "the foresight of the future, the breakthrough of the future into the present."[12] This author went on to say that so-called War Communism was actually "the first great experience of proletarian subsistence economy, the experience of the initial steps toward transition to socialism."[13]

At least then, in 1918–20, nobody in the Bolshevik party doubted that "the proletarian subsistence economy" was socialism par excellence or that it was impossible to proceed into the future without suppressing free trade circulation, all manifestations of the economic autonomy of former capitalists, traders, artisans, and especially peasants. Historical truth is also distorted by the current attempts of some Soviet historians to present the organization of Poor Peasants' Committees and the requisition of surplus grain as an imposed measure resulting exclusively from the consequences of the Civil War and economic dislocation in the country. The reality was much more complicated.

Requisition of surplus grain (with the active participation of Poor Peasants' Committees), apart from giving bread vitally needed to the town and the army, should have laid the foundations of a collectivist way of life. The Combeds were also regarded as a necessary measure designed to consolidate the socialist character of the October Revolution and as a step toward communization of the entire social production. The conceptual, strategic origin of the Poor Peasants' Committees is proved by Lenin's appraisal of their setup. In the conditions of the Civil War, he regarded their creation as a political event whose "significance is incomparably deeper and greater than that of the October Revolution."[14]

His logic was simple and consistent. Lenin thus explained the essence of his position: "In October 1917 we seized power together with the peasants as a whole. This was a bourgeois revolution, inasmuch as the class struggle in the rural districts had not yet developed." In the country where the proletariat had to seize power with the peasants' help and had to play the part of the petit-bourgeois revolution agent, our revolution was, prior to the setup of the Poor Peasants' Committees (i.e., till the summer or even the autumn of 1918), to a measurable extent a bourgeois revolution. Poor Peasants' Committees emerge in keeping with this logic to encourage the working class "to go with the poor peasants, with the semi-proletarians, with all the exploited against capitalism, including the rural rich, the kulaks, the profiteers." It was only then, according to Lenin, that "the revolution becomes a socialist one." The Combeds were set up, as he wrote, for "the urban October revolution to become a real rural October revolution."[15] At that time nobody tried to conceal that revolution in the rural areas, coercive pressure of the poorest peasants on the affluent ones, had been imposed from above and that none other than the socialist state had assumed the role of the organizer and the catalyst of the class struggle there. Lenin said, "We decided to split the peasants."* It went without saying that broad strata of peasants, including the middle peasants,[16] would resist socialization in agriculture. It was impossible to harmonize the interests of the urban and rural proletariat with those of the peasants. Therefore, Lenin insisted that "a difficult period of struggle—a struggle against the peasantry" was unavoidable. Otherwise, in his view, we would fail to meet the challenge, that is, to organize "the productive labor of millions employing large-scale machine industry in accordance with a previously established plan."†

---

* "We were compelled within the framework of the state organization to start the class struggle in the countryside, to establish Committees of Poor Peasants, of semi-proletarians, in every village and to carry on a methodical fight against the rural bourgeoisie." (Lenin, *Collected Works*, 28:473.)

† "The middle peasants are peasant proprietors, and although they have no land as yet, although private property in land has been abolished, they remain proprietors, primarily

Requisition of surplus grain was the instrument of realizing in practice the idea of "control, supervision, accounting, regulation by the state, introduction of the proper distribution of labor-power in the production and distribution of goods,"[17] with which Lenin associated socialism back in his article "The Impending Catastrophe and How to Combat It,"[18] written on the eve of the October Revolution. In this piece he substantiated the thesis that the victory of socialism in Russia was feasible.

However, at first this policy was not regarded as anything unusual. Since socialism means control and accounting, the proletarian state is entitled to possess everything produced within the frame of a single national plant, including the foodstuffs produced by the peasants. This idea was reflected in the Bill on the Grain Monopoly. Addressing the 4th Conference of Trade Unions and Factory Committees in Moscow, June 27, 1918, Lenin spelled out the meaning of the grain monopoly. "It means that all surplus grain belongs to the state; . . . that every extra pood [forty pounds] of grain must be taken by the state. How is this to be done? The state must fix prices, every surplus pood of grain must be found and brought in."[19]

At that time the party did not see any other means of harmonizing the interests of the peasants and all small producers in general with the interests of the proletariat and the advance of socialism except with the help of coercion. Moreover, it was even believed that this coercion was ultimately in the interests of the peasants themselves. "And if you, the peasant, make the state a loan and give up your grain," appealed Lenin to the villagers, "the worker will be able to rehabilitate industry. There is no other way of rehabilitating industry in a country that has been ruined by four years of imperialist war and two years of civil war—there is no other way!"[20] The need for the struggle with nepmen* and free grain trade was equally self-evident to the party. If "the petit-bourgeois element" is more dangerous than many old counterrevolutionaries, then, the Bolsheviks believed, there could not be a holier cause than the struggle against the petite bourgeoisie, its power, its influence, and its economic positions.[21] If "small peasant and handicraft economy constantly, inevitably and necessarily engenders this capitalism, he who grants freedom to trade in grain, inevitably permits also free restoration of capitalism."[22]

---

because this group of peasants remain in possession of food products. The middle peasant produces more food than he needs for himself, and since he has surplus grain he becomes the exploiter of the hungry worker. Herein lies the main task and the main contradiction." (Lenin, *Collected Works*, 30:146.)

* A nepman was a person granted permission by the Soviet government to engage in entrepreneurship. A typical nepman owned a medium- or small-scale enterprise or was a trader or an artisan.

To correctly and justly assess the Bolsheviks' actions in this initial stage of the revolution, one should keep in mind that they were deeply convinced of the correctness of the Marxist provision that it would be impossible to eliminate poverty in the Russian countryside if isolated small farms were preserved. Hence, from the very outset they set themselves the task of "socializing agriculture which has hitherto been conducted on a haphazard basis and of transforming it into large state enterprise, whose produce will be equally and justly distributed among all working people under a system of universal and equal labor service."[23]

Note that whenever Lenin turned to the classics for advice on methods of labor organization in the future society, he gave preference to early writings by Marx and Engels. Probably, this is because in the initial period of their theoretical work the founding fathers of Marxism gave top priority to moral, ideological stimuli to work, to class consciousness and the collectivist feeling of the free person, and to socialist emulation. Such a view of the human being appealed to the romanticism characteristic of the initial stage of our revolution. A class-conscious proletarian was for Lenin at that time the "pure human being" that embodied the moral, humane essence of the new system about which all European humanists had dreamt. In keeping with the given approach to the solution of economic problems, the progress of socialism directly depends on the spread of these substantial features characteristic of the front-ranking part of the working class in society and on the growth of society's revolutionary consciousness. Development or progress per se is interpreted as a peculiar emanation of extraordinary social features of the working class from the minority to the majority.

On the one hand, the front-ranking elements of the working class carry with them the rest of the working class by their example and selflessness. They help other workers to overcome stagnation and the routine of ingrained habits. This process, as Lenin thought then, could be greatly promoted by positive examples and advanced labor organization in some autonomous communes.

In Lenin's view, better organization and labor discipline of the working class, its ability to intelligently and quickly resolve economic problems on the new, nonmarket basis would also exert positive influence on the nonproletarian strata. He said, "There are still many unenlightened and ignorant people who are wholly in favor of any kind of freedom of trade, but who cannot fight when they see the discipline and self-sacrifice displayed in securing victory over the exploiters; they are not with us, but they are powerless to come out against us."[24]

Despite all the romanticism, radicalism, and extremes characteristic of the Bolsheviks at this period of stormy onslaught, they did not go beyond the frame of Marx's most general concepts of the first Communist phase. And moreover, as is especially clear today, they did their best and better than their best to model the Soviet republic on Marx's ideal, to completely follow his theory and instructions.

As is known, for doctrinal reasons Lenin, in his debate with George Plekhanov, insisted on the nationalization of land and managed to translate this objective into the agrarian program of the party.*

Hence, it is not accidental that one of the first decrees of the new workers' government proclaimed land a national asset. Note that Stalin also stressed that the practice of land nationalization in Russia was in line with the fundamental concepts of Marxism. In his speech at the conference of Marxist Students of Agrarian Questions, December 27, 1929, he said, "When we nationalized the land, our point of departure was, among other things, the theoretical premises laid down in the third volume of *Capital*, in Marx's well-known book *Theories of Surplus Value*, and in Lenin's works on agrarian questions, which represent an extremely rich treasury of theoretical thought. I am referring to the theory of ground rent in general and the theory of absolute ground rent in particular. It is now clear that the theoretical principles laid down in these works have been brilliantly confirmed by the practical experience of our work of socialist construction in town and country."[25]

Lenin was guided by the same doctrinal reasoning when he opposed anarcho-syndicalism and the attempts to make workers the owners of the enterprises that had been confiscated from the bourgeoisie. His "Notes on the Draft Provision on the Management of Nationalized Enterprises," written with active participation of the Communist Left, said, "Communism requires and presupposes utmost centralization of large production throughout the country . . . it would be overt anarcho-syndicalism rather than communism to deprive the national center of the right to supervise the work of all enterprises of a given industry in all the parts of the country, as the presented draft suggests."[26]

---

* Plekhanov, on the contrary, believed that under Russia's specific conditions Marx's concept of land nationalization would fail to yield the anticipated results. It would favor instead even greater Russian despotic supervision over the peasantry. In his opinion, this was due to the fact that "Russia's agrarian history resembles more the history of India, China, Egypt and other oriental despotisms than that of Western Europe. . . . It so happened in Russia that land was secured by the state together with the farmer, thus promoting Russian despotism. To eliminate despotism, we must destroy its economic basis. Under Russian conditions land nationalization, i.e., state labor organization in agriculture, would be interpreted by the peasants as the revival of corvee" (*The Fourth [Unifying] RSDRP Congress, Official Records* [in Russian] [Moscow, 1959], 59).

Lenin's opposition to market, conditions, and subjects of trade circulation in this initial revolution stage proves better than anything else his adherence to the ABCs of Marxism. We can only add to the above that the draft CPSU(B) program written by Lenin in February 1919 stressed the need "by a number of gradual but undeviating measures to abolish private trading completely and to organize the regular, planned exchange of products between producers' and consumers' communes to form the single economic entity the Soviet Republic must become."[27] As for the peasants' habit of and aspiration to individual work and trade, Lenin suggests it is necessary "to organize the poor and middle peasants so as to be able at every step to combat their gravitation towards the past, their attempts to go back to free trading activities, their constant striving to be 'free' producers."[28]

In my view, Lenin's initial ideas of socialism generally featured strict monism and uncompromising rejection of any concessions on economic development strategy. Later on, in his political will Lenin himself described it as "the very abstract striving for the new, which must be so new as not to contain the tiniest particle of the old."[29]

Those days witnessed hopes for a complete remaking of human nature, humanity's motives for work, and all the structures of production and everyday life, etc. In my opinion, this radicalism in the evaluation of both economic and political programs results from the fact that in that period theoretical doctrines and the conclusions of Marxist political economy overshadowed for Lenin concrete arguments, facts, and realities. That is what actually happened.

For example, Lenin's distinctly negative attitude toward an individual farmer as "semi-worker, semi-profiteer" can be directly traced to one of Karl Marx's works. His major arguments in the debate with the *prodrazvyorstka** opponents were borrowed from the conclusions of *Capital*. Addressing the First All-Russia Congress on Adult Education, May 19, 1919, Lenin said, "I assert that anybody who has read Marx, especially the first chapter of *Capital*, anybody who has read at least Kautsky's popular outline of Marx's theories entitled "The Economic Theories of Karl Marx," must come to the conclusion that in the midst of a proletarian revolution against the bourgeoisie, at a time when landowner and capitalist property is being abolished, when the country that has been ruined by four years of imperialist war is starving, freedom to trade in grain would mean freedom for the capitalists, freedom to restore the rule of capital."[30]

---

* *Prodrazvyorstka* was forced requisition of surplus grain from farmers. Frequently, all grain was actually seized, which provoked bitter opposition on the part of farmers.

Lenin's world outlook in the Civil War period gravitated toward universal historical aims. It was permeated by the urge to speed up the course of history, to accelerate humanity's transition to a new society. Within the frame of this purely politico-economic approach to revolutionary realities the initiated socialist transformations were interpreted exclusively in these universal terms as the beginning of the change from capitalism to communism, the breakthrough in capitalist social relations. All that inevitably entailed a gap between the logic of forming a theoretical image of reality and the real logic of actual development. An individual event or an economic phenomenon was interpreted and evaluated in terms of its place in human history rather than its function and role in the given specific conditions. As a result, the phenomenon was quite often substituted by its abstract substance. Hence, the researcher was no longer interested in actual events and failed to realize what was really happening.

The drawbacks of this logic, the isolation of abstract substance from a specific event, are most obvious in Lenin's distinctly negative attitude toward the grain trade. It would seem that in the context of famine one should draw conclusions exactly opposite to those that were drawn by Lenin in the conditions of the Civil War. Historical experience teaches us that in a starving country peasants should in every possible way be encouraged to produce more grain. In other words, it is imperative to stimulate their wish to work better and produce more. This, as common sense prompts, is advantageous not only economically but also politically. The more peasants are satisfied with the new government, the broader is its social basis and the less bloodthirsty is the Civil War.

But as shown above, at that time Lenin took a reverse view of things. He was guided by the logic of historical movement rather than that of the moment. Therefore, he could not yield the bridgehead won over from capitalism as he believed that any concession or even a compromise would immediately hamper the global offensive already begun on the old system. His reasoning was as follows: Since individual work and free trade historically gave rise to capitalism, the moment we permit free small production, Russia will see the restoration of capitalism.

Such a perception of reality in terms of political economy had another peculiarity. The short-term interests of people currently living were subordinated to those of historical advance and the breakthrough into new dimensions. The present, according to Lenin, was, above all, the field for the anticipated future crop.

The review of Lenin's works of the Civil War period and the analysis of his views on progress and the aims of the October Revolution prove that his character and orthodoxy prevented him from giving up the idea of pure socialism until he tried to realize it and comprehensively tested his original plan of Russia's transition to communism along previously elaborated lines. Hence, in my view, the very victory of the Bolsheviks in October 1917 was pregnant with a programmed attempt to realize the ideal of pure, noncommodity, and nonpeasant socialism. In the initial period of our revolution, Lenin shared with all the other leaders of the party highly radical and, in many respects, utopian views on the feasibility of a collectivist transformation of social life, together with the rate and the depth of this process. He did not realize at that time that interpretation of reality in terms of political economy and its doctrines could not be comprehensive. He failed to see the limits of social life plasticity and all imminent adverse effects of the wish to subordinate the logic of historical development to the Hegelian logic of settling the contradictions.

It is a different thing that the persistence with which we pressed after Lenin's death for the correspondence between Marx's theory and Russian reality was not inevitable. Note that the main leaders of the October Revolution, Lenin and Trotsky, realized within a very short period of time, historically, the utopianism and unfeasibility of their original plans.

Philosophical Meaning of NEP

Characteristically, Lev Trotsky, despite his dedication to left radicalism, was the first to realize back in 1920 that the idea of a complete ousting of commodity circulation and material incentives from social life was unfeasible. As early as February 1920, he submitted to the Politburo a memorandum in which he demanded that *prodrazvyorstka* be replaced by tax in kind and commodity circulation be reinitiated. "The current policies of equal distribution according to the food norms, mutual guarantee in case of grain collection and levelled-off distribution of industrial goods," Trotsky wrote, "are designed to step down agricultural production, to scatter the industrial proletariat and are pregnant with the threat of completely ruining the economic life of the country." He went on to say,

There is a threat of running out of food resources and no perfection of requisitional machinery can help it. It is possible to fight such trends of economic decline by the following methods:

1) requisition of surplus grain should be substituted by certain fixed rated deductions [a sort of progressive tax in kind] determined in such a way that cultivation of a larger plot or better tillage would still be advantageous to the peasant;

2) there should be a greater correspondence between the distribution of industrial goods and grain collected not only by a particular volost [province] or village but also from individual peasants.[31]

Then, at the beginning of 1920, Lenin was still actively opposed to the idea of turning to progressive taxation. He still counted on coercion and hoped for a breakthrough in the economy due to heroic work of the class-conscious part of the proletariat. He still believed in the possibility of a breakthrough of economic difficulties owing to class-consciousness, wonders worked by revolutionary enthusiasm.*

And it is only natural, because only a few months previously Lenin said that the destiny of the socialist revolution in Russia depended on the possibility of extending the practice of Communist *subbotniks*.† He insisted that "every Communist, therefore, and everyone who wants to be true to the principles of communism, should devote all his attention and all his efforts to the explanation of this phenomenon and its practical implementation."[32]

It is revealing, however, that Lenin, who felt very strongly about certain theoretical postulates, felt just as strongly about the need to criticize and replace those postulates once he realized they were erroneous. He was prepared to break away totally from something that he had previously upheld but later found to be wrong.

True, he realized the economic strategy of War Communism was leading the country into an economic and political dead end much later than Trotsky did. It was not until late December 1920 that Lenin understood the need for economic incentives for "shock work"‡. But his analysis of the crisis in War Communism enabled him to reach important theoretical conclusions, something Trotsky had utterly failed to do.

For his part, Trotsky regarded as a tactical measure the substitution of the gradual tax in kind for the *prodrazvyorstka*, or surplus grain appropria-

---

* Trotsky recollected, "In the Autumn of 1919 the number of locomotives out of work reached 60%. It was firmly believed that by the Spring of 1920 it would have run to the tune of 75%. That was the forecast of the leading experts. . . . Engineer Lomonosov who in those months actually managed the transport was demonstrating to the government a diagram of the locomotive epidemic. Pointing to a mathematical point somewhere in 1920, he declared: 'And this is where the death comes.' 'What should be done?' Lenin asked. 'There can be no miracles,' Lomonosov answered. 'Even the Bolsheviks cannot work wonders.' We exchanged glances. We were even more downhearted as there were no experts in transportation among us and we did not know the technique of such gloomy calculations. 'But we shall nevertheless try to work a wonder,' Lenin said coldly through clenched teeth" (Trotsky, *My Life* [in Russian], part 2 [Berlin, 1930], 198).

† A Communist *subbotnik* is an unpaid work day, usually held in time to coincide with a revolutionary holiday.

‡ The name for the very intensive labor performed by volunteers and inspired by lofty Communist ideals.

tion. When the Central Committee refused to back him up, he did not despair but tried to resolve the problem by other means, quite contrary, in fact, to his original design, namely, by applying consistently and rigidly the principles of War Communism and imposing a rigid diktat of the central organs on production and distribution.

Since the transition to market relations had been rejected, I demanded the correct and systematic implementation of 'war' measures, too, in order to achieve real success in the economy. In the system of war communism where all resources are nationalized, at least in principle, and distributed on the orders of the state, I saw no place for the independent role of trade unions. If the industrial sector relied on the state to provide the workers with the necessary products, then the trade union must be included in the system of state administration of industry and distribution of products.[33]

Trotsky did not even try to draw any philosophical conclusions when the economic measures of War Communism had proved untenable. To his last days he held onto the concept of socialist development that had evolved during the period of War Communism, that is, the theory of unmitigated struggle and unmitigated substitution of the old methods of production by new ones. For him it was the socialist proletariat against the propertied peasants in politics, product turnover against consumer goods production in the economy, and spontaneity against consciousness in philosophy. He upheld the theory of an open armed struggle of the proletariat against the bourgeoisie on a world scale. Trotsky ignored everything but the struggle of socially opposed forces, insisted on the absolute incompatibility of the new and the old structures, and rejected everything that was not socialist. Trotsky's *Permanent Revolution*, published in 1930, shows that he was unable to break way from the messianic interpretation of Marxism as a theory of historical revolutionary upheavals that was characteristic of the *Sturm and Drang* period.* He remained of the opinion that Marxism was all about permanent revolution and the eternal struggle to "reorganize" social structures.

Trotsky failed to go beyond the normative and dogmatic approach to socialism and ignored the contradictions that had emerged during the first unsuccessful attempts to make the transition from a capitalist Russia to a Communist Russia all at once, omitting any transitional stages.

What was possible and practicable in the application of theory to real life failed to attract his attention. This may explain why Trotsky did not

---

* *Sturm and Drang* was the period of revolutionary maximalists' domination in the wake of the October 1917 Revolution. It coincided with the epoch of War Communism.

attach enough significance to Lenin's last works and ignored those philosophical and economic ideas that transcended orthodox Marxism. It should be remembered that during the 1920s Trotsky's struggle against the majority in the Politburo was also the struggle against the New Economic Policy.

Unlike Trotsky, Lenin analyzed the crisis of the economic strategy of War Communism on the conceptual plane. He argued that the philosophy of development underlying War Communism (that is, the idea of a direct transition from capitalism to communism and the movement of the revolution "in a straight line") was untenable.[34] Behind the crisis of the economic strategy of War Communism, Lenin perceived another crisis, or rather he realized it was wrong to expect that mercenary interests and private gain would be eliminated in the course of a socialist transformation.

In point of fact, this is the concept of social development that Lenin set forth in his article "A Great Beginning," published in June 1919. As mentioned above, at that time he linked the building of communism and the molding of a new humanity with the need to totally overcome the habit of working for oneself. The article shows that, according to Lenin, "the ability for unpaid work in the interests of society and in the interests of all the working people" was to emerge in conjunction with the ability to give all of oneself to work not for one's own sake or the sake of those who are "close" but for the sake of those who are "distant."[35]

However, his article "On Cooperation," which he dictated in January 1923, shows that at the end of his life Lenin returned to the initial problem of combining private and social interests. What seemed self-evident in 1919, he described in 1923 as a stumbling block for many specialists and an unresolved problem. It is revealing that Lenin was trying to find an answer to the problem that had arisen as a result of the crisis of War Communism, not in the Marxist classics, but in the writings of old cooperators.

It is important to bear in mind that before the October Revolution, and particularly under War Communism, the Bolsheviks took a negative attitude toward Fourierian and Owerian theories of cooperative socialism, which envision a combination of and a flexible connection between individual interests and group or social interests. They also disdained the idea of a balance between the elements of the planned economy and the thrift and enterprise of independent cooperators. The sympathies of the Bolsheviks, and those of Marx and Engels for that matter, were with the opponents of Fourierian doctrines who maintained that social structures should be modeled on factory organization and that production should be based on directive assignments. The article "On Cooperation" began with a reassessment of the dream of the so-called old cooperators and an admission that it was they who were destined to remove the barrier that for a long time concealed the "mystery" of socialism. This can be regarded as clear evidence that Lenin's idea of socialism was beginning to change.

What is important in this case is not so much the change in Lenin's attitude toward cooperation and his admission that the economic principles of cooperation were not incompatible with socialism, as a more profound and detailed analysis of basic notions about the mechanism and nature of socialist development. The important point here is the admission that pure socialism totally independent of the old economic and social mechanism is unattainable and that it is always necessary to look for ways and means to reach an expedient combination of individualistic and collectivist elements.

In a later article, published at the end of 1921, Lenin explained that during the period of War Communist "organization," economic activity was based on the principle of the absolute negation of what had previously been so. Lenin wrote:

We regarded the organisational, economic work . . . from a single angle. We assumed that we could proceed straight to socialism without a preliminary period in which the old economy would be adapted to socialist economy. We assumed that the two systems—state production and distribution and private commodity production and distribution—would compete with each other, and meanwhile we would build up state production and distribution, and step by step win them away from the hostile system.[36]

In our opinion, the excerpt from Lenin's speech delivered at the 7th Moscow Gubernia Conference of RCP (October 1921)* is most important for an understanding of both the philosophical thrust of the initial model of socialism and the philosophical ideas underlying the New Economic Policy.

The difference between them primarily consisted in the interpretation of social contradiction and the possibilities for overcoming it.

The initial model of pure noncommodity socialism that was to be devoid of any traces of the old system relied on the notion that the struggle was absolute and its components were essentially antagonistic. The emergence and development of a new system was conceived of as the gradual destruction and replacement of the defeated elements of the

---

* Moscow Party Conference of the Russian Communist Party.

contradiction by the victorious ones. It was to be a direct armed clash between everything that was new and everything that was old. The leap from capitalism to socialism was to be made by resolutely rejecting the old social structure and everything associated with it. The predominant belief was that without the destruction and total rejection of all the vestiges of the past, the system could not mature. Incidentally, this belief prompted the desire to reduce the wide variety of economic structures to one "pure" socialist type. During the period of War Communism, both foreign policy and economic strategy were formulated according to this belief. The Bolsheviks believed that the world of capitalism was to be transformed into a world of socialism, and the development of the world proletarian revolution was thought of as a chain of "October Revolutions" all over the world.

The initial normative approach to identifying the essential features of socialism had created a situation in which life itself and all existing conditions were interpreted according to this theory. Whenever life came in conflict with theory, which was frequently the case under military communism, the resolution did not necessarily make life better.

At the first stage of the revolution, this kind of rigid subordination of life to theory seemed justified because the interests of the future were believed to have primacy over any current interests. But at a later stage, Lenin realized that such interpretation of the conflict between theory and practice was fallacious. Unrelated as it was to practice and the experience of collectivist transformation of society, the initial model of socialism reflected not so much the interests of the future as the interests of the past.

This view of the transitional period as the struggle of two hostile systems prompted a certain kind of attitude toward the emerging society. At that time socialism was regarded as a temporary stage where the emerging Communist formation with its life-style and mode of production coexisted with the still surviving elements of the capitalist and patriarchal life-styles. In accordance with this line of reasoning, socialism did not have any social quality of its own.

Lenin developed a new concept of socialism as a result of a critical analysis of all the fallacies of the old philosophy of development. For him and the party, the economic and political crisis of the spring of 1921 and the famine opened up a new reality, something that no one had taken into account at the very beginning of the Communist transformations. The real problem for him was to what extent the social fabric could sustain change and survive the bloody struggle between two systems with differing modes of production distribution.

In fact, according to the nineteenth-century worldview that the Russian revolutionaries shared, there was no fear of social self-destruction as a result of the undermining of basic social mechanisms. The initial belief that life was indestructable and would be preserved under any circumstances made it possible to give little thought to the price in human lives that was to be paid in the decisive struggle with the past.

But as the socioeconomic and political crisis in the spring of 1921 showed, there were no guarantees that social structures would be preserved. After a certain critical point had been reached, the reorganization of life and collectivist transformations resulted in human degradation and disruption of production rather than personal development and progress. It turned out that there was a limit beyond which people could no longer accept innovations or live in the state of constant intellectual and moral tension necessary to maintain the struggle with the old world. Speaking at the 10th Congress RCP, Lenin said, "We must recognize the fact that the masses are utterly worn-out and exhausted. . . ."[37]

Lenin had found out that, compared with the outbursts of petit-bourgeois sentiments and the acceptance of petit-bourgeois values by the proletariat, which in the 1918–20 period he perceived as the main threat to the cause of the revolution, there were much more serious threats, such as famine, the loss of desire to work and remain human, and rampant immorality and plunder. The profound economic and social crisis that gripped the country and the threat of millions of deaths as a result of famine, economic dislocation, and epidemics created an "extreme situation" that helped crystallize Lenin's new, more profound, and realistic perception of the objectives and possibilities of the October Revolution. He went beyond the framework of orthodox Marxism and started to search for new solutions.

First came a reassessment of values. It was now clear that life itself must not be sacrificed in the name of an accelerated movement of history toward a collectivist society, free of mercenary interests. Likewise, the fundamental value was not long-awaited equality but human life itself. Reasserted under perestroika, the notions of people's lives as the highest social value are to be found in Lenin's last works. In his speech at the Plenum of the Moscow Soviet on November 20, 1922, Lenin spoke about the burden of destruction caused by the Civil War and recalled that it was because of the war that "we suffered a lot of losses on their account and lost values of all kinds, including the greatest of all values—human lives—on an incredibly large scale."[38]

Essentially, the reassessment of values brought about a change in his view of the very nature of society and transformed the initial paradigm of the analysis of socialist development. During the first stages of the revolution, Lenin sought to speed up the transition of humanity to a qualitatively new stage in order to put an end to the "cursed past" as soon as possible. As mentioned earlier, at that period Lenin's philosophy was largely eschatological, which explains why in many cases he ignored the problems of production while analyzing specific issues of social organization.

But starting from late 1920, with March 1921 marking a watershed in his thinking, Lenin identified the preservation of life and its basic prerequisites as the key value.

The new element in Lenin's approach to the problems of socialism consisted of trying to combine Communist development and the movement to full equality, human dignity, and freedom with the preservation of primary social conditions, that is, people's desire to work, improve production, and make their everyday life better. Now the concept of social order became more meaningful, since the dynamic approach emphasizing change, transformation, and transition of society to a new stage was complemented by a functional approach stressing the primacy of humanity's vital functions and the most essential conditions of the preservation of life.

The new paradigm established the clear-cut and unqualified primacy of the approach that emphasized production and made it necessary that all other interests, including a victorious world revolution, should become subsidiary to the interests of production development, adequate provision of food for the population, and an overall increase in its well-being. During the Civil War, Lenin thought that a drop in living standards was acceptable in the name of an early destruction of the old system. But later he was resolutely opposed to any attempt to isolate social progress from the increase in people's welfare and said that "good harvests are the salvation of the country."*

In his last works, which by a long-established tradition are referred to as Lenin's political bequest, he made it quite clear that the earlier attempts to impose new collectivist modes of production and life-styles were wrong. The emphasis was shifted to the initiative from below, and the masses were to share in the boons of civilization. At the end of his life, Lenin wrote, "This cultural revolution will suffice to make our country a completely socialist country."[39]

---

* Note that in his struggle against the left-wing opposition, Stalin relied on Lenin's idea of socialism and the building of socialism, which linked the progress of the new society with the constant rise in the workers' well-being (see *The Report of Comrade Stalin to the 15th Conference of the All-Russia Communist Party [Bolshevik]* [Moscow and Leningrad, 1927], 458–80).

Moreover, Lenin strongly emphasized the need for peaceful coexistence between the different classes that had accepted the October Revolution and for interaction and cooperation between different social forces. No longer did he pursue the objective of liquidating well-to-do peasants. Lenin came to the idea of a "union of popular forces," later developed by Bukharin.[40] It was to be a union of the working class, which would run factories and plants, and the broad masses of the working peasantry who tilled their own land and were involved in different forms of cooperation.[41]

There are grounds to say, therefore, that at the end of his life Lenin had abandoned his original plan of establishing total state control over the economy and had come to the conclusion that in some cases cooperation would dominate in a new collectivist society. He believed that, in the existing conditions, "for us the mere growth of co-operation . . . is equivalent with the growth of socialism."[42]

The failure of the first attempt to implement the idea of pure noncommodity socialism had cooled the revolutionary passions in the party, and a new and much more carefully considered attitude to the economic legacy of the past began to prevail. It was increasingly realized that "involvement in labour" remained "the most difficult and important problem of socialism."[43] Equally apparent was the necessity to abandon the idea of pure socialism and make compromises and search for ways and means of combining the planned economy with the market economy. It was totally unexpected that Lenin, who used to be an orthodox Marxist, should put forward the thesis that "the right exchange of commodities" between the industrial and agricultural sectors was "the foundation for a really socialist economy."[44] The economic autonomy of enterprises was restored, and industrial production on the whole began to operate "on the principles of financial and economic independence."[45] The principle of personal gain and private interest was once again reasserted.

There seemed no reason to go back to utopia and start new experiments in order to develop pure noncommodity socialism. Lenin had only managed to lay down the rails of cooperative socialism; what remained to be done was to push the wagon of common sense along the track. Seemingly, the crisis that hit the young Soviet republic in 1921 forever discredited the fanciful idea of setting up an economy without markets, totally dominated by state bureaucracy.

In contrast, cooperative socialism looked attractive because it was realistic and could serve the interests of many people. The main thrust of Lenin's idea of cooperation, which he developed in his last works, was in sharp contrast to his previous conviction that people could and should be dragged kicking and screaming toward a bright future.

But contrary to common sense and despite Lenin's unquestioned authority, the top echelon of the party led by Stalin made a deliberate attempt to destroy his brainchild. During 1929 and 1930, the New Economic Policy was dismantled, and, as argued at the beginning of the book, the leadership of the party went back to left-wing dogmatism and the Marxist idea of pure socialism. Essentially, Stalin's victory and the defeat of Leninist teaching on cooperation represent two sides of the same coin. The ultimate question is why Stalin and not Lenin emerged victorious in the dispute about the destinies of socialism in Russia.

NOTES

1. A. Hertzen, *From the Other Shore* (London, 1957), 34.
2. Ibid, 34.
3. F. Engels, *The Dialectics of Nature* (Moscow, 1964), 312.
4. Lenin, *Collected Works*, 26:235.
5. A. R. Williams, *Journey into Revolution* (Chicago, 1969).
6. P. H. Holbach, *Systeme de la Nature ou Les Loix du Monde Physique et du Monde Moral* (Paris).
7. F. Dostoyevsky, *Letters from the Underworld* (London, 1919), 34.
8. J. Stalin, *Political Report of the Central Committee to the Fourteenth Congress of the CPSU(B)* (Moscow, 1950), 102–3.
9. Lenin, *Collected Works*, 5:375–76.
10. Williams, *Journey into Revolution*.
11. *Smena Vekh* (Changing the Landmarks) (Paris, 1929), 66.
12. L. Kritsman, *A Heroic Period of the Great Revolution* (in Russian) (Moscow, 1925), 71.
13. Ibid., 77.
14. Lenin, *Collected Works*, 28:340.
15. Ibid., 28:141, 28:300, 29:203.
16. Ibid., 28:174.
17. Ibid., 30:508.
18. Ibid., 25:328.
19. Ibid., 27:468–69.
20. Ibid., 29:524.
21. Ibid., 27:285, 294.
22. Ibid., 29:190, 294.
23. Ibid., 28:171–72.
24. Ibid., 30:457.
25. Stalin, *Works*, 12:158.
26. Lenin, *Collected Works*, 36:392.
27. Ibid., 29:106.
28. Ibid., 29:79–80.
29. Ibid., 33:497.
30. Ibid., 29:360.
31. Lev Trotsky, *My Life*, 2:162.
32. Lenin, *Collected Works*, 30:288.
33. Trotsky, *My life*, 2:199.
34. Lenin, *Collected Works*, 32:221.

35. V. I. Lenin, *Collected Works* (Moscow: Progress Publishers, 1965), 29:409–34.
36. Ibid., 33:88.
37. Ibid., 32:224.
38. Ibid., 27:254.
39. Ibid., 33:475.
40. Ibid., 44:310.
41. Ibid., 33:484.
42. Ibid., 33:477.
43. Lenin, *Collected Works,* 5th ed., 43:285.
44. Lenin, *Collected Works,* 33:29.
45. Lenin, *Collected Works,* 5th ed., 45:81, 82.

CHAPTER 5

Why Did Lenin Lose to Lenin?

The Initial Tragedy of the October Revolution

To understand why we could not stay on the track of common sense and the New Economic Policy but instead accelerated off the rails and into intolerable left-wing extremism, I think we must go back to the October Revolution and its initial dramatic contradictions.

It is true that, because Russia was not civilized and industrialized enough and lacked urban and municipal culture, the only way it could attain civilized collectivism was by a gradual, mediated, and, therefore, necessarily long and difficult process. This view was prompted by the economic failures of War Communism and the unfulfilled hopes of establishing direct state control over production and distribution in what was a country with a small-scale peasant farm economy. In this situation the key question of the revolution, that is, the question of control, was carried over from the sphere of politics into the sphere of economic development, with economic competition between the large-scale and publicly owned state production sector, on the one hand, and the cooperative and private sector, on the other. The solution to this question and the destiny of the revolution depended on whether or not the Communists were capable of proving the advantages of an economy based on public ownership of the means of production and, principally, the benefits of large-scale agricultural production.

In his political bequest, Lenin put heavy emphasis on this factor of production and argued that the destiny of socialism depended on how successfully it could resolve economic problems. In his article "On Our Revolution," Lenin argued that the October Revolution was necessary not so much to determine the destiny of human civilization as to accelerate Russia's civilized economic development.

According to Lenin, it was necessary to use the revolutionary situation that had evolved in the country as a result of the First World War and the plight of Russia's working people, which had multiplied the forces of the workers and peasants tenfold and "offered us the opportunity to create the fundamental requisites of civilization in a different way from that of the West-European countries."[1] He thought that the socialist revolution in Russian was different not simply because it had its own causes and circumstances and was a "peasant war" and a working-class struggle rolled into one. The important thing was that it had its own specific objectives. It was primarily aimed at resolving the cultural and production problems that in ordinary historical conditions are resolved in the framework of the capitalist economy. The revolution's principal objective was to raise the level of working-class culture/industrial competence, uphold personal dignity, improve general education, and develop the skills of the peasant masses in the use of agronomy and even in commerce. Given this new outlook on our revolution, the implementation of purely Communist objectives—from across-the-board public ownership of the means of production to the development of a classless society—was to be postponed, or more precisely, subordinated to the objectives of the development of civilization and culture.

This new concept of the building of socialism with its emphasis on the natural transition from old structures to new ones excluded in principle the use of violence in the sphere of production. "Nothing is more stupid than the very idea of applying coercion in economic relations with the middle peasant," wrote Lenin.[2] And this only stands to reason, because it is impossible to make people civilized by the use of violence. Any kind of culture, even agronomical culture, can only emerge as a result of free choice motivated by personal interest. This explains why at the end of his life Lenin insisted on the need for the economic independence of the peasants and argued in favor of their creative autonomy. He called for "the greatest possible scope for the development, strengthening and revival of peasant farming."[3]

Lenin's last works show that for him the forms of economic development in Russia became largely a subsidiary question. What really mattered was economic success. First and foremost, this change in his outlook on socialism brought about a change in attitude toward the industrious and civilized peasant. Henceforth, the peasant emerged as "the central figure of economic development."[4]

Given this kind of carefully considered and commonsense approach to a situation in which, according to Lenin, it was necessary to build communism with non-Communist hands, success largely depended on the ability of the party leadership to bridle "Communist emotions" and to rely exclusively on facts that had been checked and double-checked. Lenin knew the prevailing sentiment in the party only too well, and he saw that the membership was prone to adopt the "cavalry attack" tactic that had been its habitual strategy during the heady days of the revolution. That is why he repeatedly emphasized in almost every one of his last articles that it was inadmissible to resort to violence while resolving economic problems. According to Lenin, a social policy bordering on social intolerance and unjustified violence posed a major threat to the young socialist stage, particularly in the agricultural sector and in relation to the individual peasant. He wrote, "Nothing will be achieved in this by doing things in a rush, by assault, by vim and vigor, or in general, by any of the best human qualities."[5]

But as mentioned earlier, since the country was not civilized enough, lacked efficient industries, and badly needed people who were competent in commerce (all of which prompted the Bolsheviks to speed up progress in Russia by the expulsion of the landowners[6]) the implementation of this new and complex program to move the country toward socialism was extremely difficult. Poverty breeds a belief in miracles and feeds revolutionary extremism. Furthermore, the peculiar provenance of Russian poverty must be taken into account. In the majority of cases, this had sprung not so much from any dearth of land as from laziness nurtured by Russian serfdom. No less than half of all the peasants in prerevolutionary Russia, that is, the so-called state peasants, possessed plots of land measuring from sixteen to nineteen *desyatinas*, or twenty-three to twenty-six square hectares. Compared with the other European countries, Russia was a peasant kingdom. For example, land property in Russia was distributed to the much greater advantage of the rural population than in Germany. By 1905, in fifty *hubernias*, or regions, of the European part of Russia, 69 percent of all land belonged to the Cossacks and peasants.[7]

Even before the revolution, in his polemics against the Narodniks' program of land socialization, Lenin stressed that there were no prospects for the redistribution of so-called black land precisely because of the indolent peasants. According to Lenin, if this redistribution was to be carried out in the interests of capitalist development,

the division must be a division among *free farmers*, not among "indolent" peasants, the great majority of whom run their economies by routine and tradition in conformity with patriarchal, not with capitalist conditions. A division according to the old standards, i.e., in conformity with the old forms of landownership based on peasant allotments, will not be the *clearing* of the old landownership, but its *perpetuation*; not clearing the way for capitalism, but rather *encumbering* with a mass of unadepted and unadeptable "indolents" who cannot become free farmers. To be progressive, the division must be based on a new sorting process among the peasant cultivators, which will sift the farmers from the useless lumber.[8]

Frequently, revolutionary maximalists' desire to jump straight into the kingdom of socialism was only the other side of our Russian laziness. This explains the tendency to uniformity, the distribution of other people's wealth, and the harsh treatment of the rich after they were defeated. As a general rule, the uneducated masses favor the simple truths, easy solutions, and unsophisticated methods of achieving their aims.

For the same reasons, Lenin's last works, with their emphasis on the factor of production in the building of socialism, which was to proceed gradually over a long period of time, did not generate enthusiasm among both the people conditioned to Communist sloganeering and Communist bureaucrats. Lenin said time and again that it was necessary to study and work hard, and he did not promise miracles and, what is even more important, did not give any guarantees of success. During the last years of his life, Lenin found it hard to conceal his profound antipathy to the Communist romantics who made up the majority of the membership and dreamed about "pure communism." But starry-eyed revolutionaries, too, were rankled by the undisguised pragmatism and practical concerns contained in Lenin's later writings. One case in point is his article entitled "On the Food Tax," which could hardly awaken enthusiasm because in it Lenin taught how to achieve practical results in the economy and argued that the Communist bureaucrat could and should learn quite a lot from the capitalist.

"Those who achieve the best results in this sphere, even by means of private capitalism, even without cooperation or without directly transforming this capitalism into state capitalism, will do more for the cause of socialist construction in Russia than those who 'ponder over' the purity of communism, draw up regulations, rules and instructions for state capitalism and cooperatives, but do nothing practical to stimulate trade," he wrote.[9]

But Lenin's ideas on cooperation faced many obstacles both intellectual and political in their origin, because cooperation presupposes the full autonomy of the person entering into partnership and guarantees the right to withdraw from it, if that person so wishes. In fact, cooperation represents a purely European idea. Its social base is constituted by the economic and political autonomy of a private person, who is the owner of his or her means of production, and highly developed culture. Cooperation is possible only when society is organized democratically. In

Russia, those prerequisites of cooperation had not yet been sufficiently developed. Only from the abstract "heights" of political economy does cooperation imposed by the state look more mature compared with partnership or group cooperation. In fact, as we have now realized, if cooperation is imposed from the "top" and dominates in the industrial sector, it represents the simplest form of labor organization that can exist even without a sufficiently developed culture and the broad political rights of the individual.

In such conditions, the success of the new drive to move toward a more realistic and human socialism largely depended on how long Lenin was to continue at the helm of the revolution. Now it is perfectly clear that the New Economic Policy, which was a very complex phenomenon, could only be implemented by someone of Lenin's stature. He was the unquestioned leader of Bolshevism, a man who could oppose the maximalists and restrain revolutionary intolerance in the party he had created. He was the only person who was capable of completing the work on a plan of socialism that was acceptable to Russia and had a chance of survival. Only in the economic sphere had the principles of War Communism begun to be gradually abandoned. The policies and political structures that had evolved in the Civil War did not change at the same time, and many things in this sphere needed reassessment.

After the Kronstadt mutiny in the spring of 1921,* this need became very plain at the 10th Congress of the Russian Communist Party when Lenin moved further right than his comrades-in-arms. It is difficult to say how far he would have been prepared to go in that direction if he had lived longer and how close he would have come in his outlook and practical actions to the ideas of West German Social Democrats. In any case, clearly, had Lenin lived longer, his pragmatism, common sense, and ability to take account of the facts would have prevented the restoration of the left-wing attitudes of the Civil War and would have rejected the tactic of cavalry attacks on capitalism and its vestiges.

My profound conviction is that, after the political mechanism of absolute political power had been established in Russia during the Civil War, many things actually depended on how long Lenin could continue at the helm. The fateful, premature death of Lenin has sown a lot of confusion in Russian history and the international working-class movement.

After Lenin's death, the destiny of the country largely depended on who was to control the powerful state system using the equally powerful repression mechanism that had been created. Also, just as important was

---

* This was a mutiny by sailors in March 1921. The sailors were predominantly former farmers who opposed the agrarian policies of the Bolsheviks and the surplus grain tax.

whether Lenin's heir upheld the maximalist or the reformist concept of the renewal of social organization in Russia.

Bear in mind that the all-important resolution *On Measures to Liquidate the Kulak Economies in the Areas of Total Collectivization* of January 30, 1930, which determined the lives of hundreds of thousands of people and the destiny of agriculture in Russia, was adopted by only a few members of the Politburo of the Central Committee of the RCP.* At that time, following the victory over Bukharin's group scored at the April 1929 Plenum of the Central Committee, Stalin acted according to the well-known principle, "If you feel that the law creates an obstacle for you, by slipping it under the tale and concealing it from view you will make your actions much easier." Incidentally, Stalin did not conceal that, since the summer of 1929, the decisions of the 15th Congress of the Party had been abandoned. In fact, he criticized those who unwittingly linked the policy of liquidating the kulaks as a class with previous party decisions. In his article "Concerning the Policy of Eliminating the Kulaks as a Class," he wrote,

Naturally, the policy of eliminating the kulaks as a class could not have fallen from the skies. The way for it was prepared by the entire preceding period of restricting, and hence of ousting, the capitalist elements in the countryside. But this does not mean that it does not differ *radically* from the policy of restricting (and ousting) the capitalist elements in the countryside, that is a *continuation* of the restriction policy. To say what our author says is to deny that there has been a *change* in the development of the countryside since the summer of 1929. To say what he does is to deny that during this period we have executed a *turn* in our Party's policy in the countryside.

What was the point of departure of the Fifteenth Congress in proclaiming an intensification of the policy of restricting (and ousting) the capitalist elements in the countryside? Its point of departure was that, despite this restricting of the kulaks, they, *as a class,* nevertheless were *bound to remain* for the time being. *On those grounds,* the Fifteenth Congress left in force the law on hiring labor in the countryside, and demanded that it should be strictly observed. *On those grounds,* it was again proclaimed that dekulakisation was impermissible. Do those laws and decisions contradict the policy of *restricting* (and ousting) the capitalist elements in the countryside? Certainly not. Do those laws and decisions contradict the policy of eliminating the kulaks as a class? Certainly, they do! Consequently, these laws and decisions must now be set aside in the areas of complete collectivisation, which is spreading by leaps and bounds. Incidentally, they have already been set aside by the very progress of the collective-farm movement in the areas of complete collectivisation.[10]

---

* The decision of the Politburo of the Central Committee of January 30, 1930, on the elimination of the kulaks as a class was adopted unanimously, with Stalin, Molotov, Kirov, Rudzutak, Koganovich, and Ordzhonikidze taking part in the voting, too.

This is the way the destinies of socialism and millions of people were determined. After April 1929, Stalin adopted the simple logic, "I'm my own master." We want total collectivization in the space of a few months, and we will do it. We want to increase the rate of industrial growth two-fold in just one year, and we will do it and make a giant leap forward.* We want to expel all cultured, serious, and prosperous peasants from the countryside, and we will do it, too.†

Lenin repeatedly warned about the threat to the cause of the party and socialism posed by the "unlimited authority" concentrated in the hands of General Secretary Stalin, and it was hardly an exaggeration on his part.[11] Lenin was utterly realistic about the question of power and knew the administrative mechanism of the country, which he himself had established. He knew its strong points and weak points, too. As a philosopher, Lenin realized full well the enormous force of chance (as regards the intellectual qualities and character of a party leader) in a situation in which the state, military, and party apparatuses merged and became all-powerful. He did not see anything mystical in the idea that the personal relationship between two Politburo members, namely Stalin and Trotsky, determined the party's stability and, consequently, the destiny of the first socialist revolution in the world.

Only if one's sense of reality is totally atrophied, can one believe that, in the wake of the October Revolution, Russian history became free from the force of chance and acquired an ideal and fatalistic predestination and logical conformity. In fact, if one remains on the solid ground of facts and common sense and does not deviate from the basics of the philosophy of

---

* In his report to the session of the Central Executive Council on the target figures of production for the following year of 1931, V. N. Molotov, chair of the Council of People's Commissars, said that the growth of industrial output was envisaged at 45 instead of 22 percent as originally planned for the third year of the five-year-plan period. Soon after that, Stalin clarified in one of his speeches that that would mean meeting the main targets of the five-year plan in just three years.

† In the winter of 1929 and 1930, collectivization and the liquidation of the kulaks proceeded in an atmosphere of an unbridled campaign to speed up the dispossession of the kulaks under crude administrative pressure. Up to 10 or 15 percent of the peasants were dispossessed in some areas, although in fact their number did not exceed 3.9 percent in 1927 and 2.5 to 3 percent in 1929. Characteristically, those peasants who used machines (that is, civilized peasants, according to Lenin's definition) were frequently identified as kulaks. On the basis of the resolution of the Council of People's Commissars of the USSR of May 21, 1929, the kulaks were defined as those peasants who had at least *one* of the following characteristics: they systematically used hired labor in agriculture or in handicraft enterprises; owned a mill, a churn, a grain- or millet-crusher, a mower, a wheel-spinner, a grater, a fruit or vegetable drier, or any other machine with a mechanical engine; constantly or seasonally hired out equipment, let floor space for living or enterprise; systematically hired out agricultural machines with a mechanical engine; engaged in commerce, usury, and commercial mediation. See G. I. Shmelyov, "Don't Dare Give Orders," *Oktyabr,* 1988, no. 2:13.

history, one arrives at a totally different conclusion. As the new state apparatus and its repressive mechanism become more centralized and powerful, the force of chance dramatically increases. Even in the old self-regulating economy of commodity production, state power can significantly affect the economic development of society. Engels wrote,

It can run in the same direction, and then development is more rapid; it can oppose the line of development, in which case nowadays it will go to pieces in the long run in every great people; or it can prevent the economic development from proceeding along certain lines and prescribe other lines. This case ultimately reduces itself to one of the two previous ones. But it is obvious that in cases two and three the political power can do great damage to economic development and cause a great squandering of energy and material."[12]

As for state power in the noncommodity administrative economy, its ability to affect the economic development of a country both positively and negatively is far greater. Also, we must take into account that, compared with 1922 when Lenin pointed to the threat posed by Stalin's "unlimited authority," in the summer of 1929 that power was much greater, and not a single member of the Politburo remained who would dare take a stand independent of the general secretary.

It is impossible to understand anything in our socialist history if we do not take into account the fact that the power sanctified by a popular revolution is special in that it is sanctified by the blood of the best and most noble people in the nation and by innumerable sacrifices in the name of freedom and the happiness of people. And the person who usurps this power can remain beyond suspicion for a very long time. It is difficult to believe and, indeed, unthinkable that any mortal would dare use the sacred power of revolution, which had been won in the course of a terrible fratricidal war with millions of victims, to satisfy his pathological cravings or intellectual whims, for example, to exterminate the country's most talented sociologists in order to be able to feel a philosopher genius.

After the summer of 1929, Stalin acquired unlimited power over the lives and well-being of people, and so he easily created the social basis for the implementation of his selfish plans, and, more important, he consummated his own revolution, that is, a radical transformation of agrarian relations. As a politician, Stalin made the optimum decision: He relied totally on the interests and administrative zeal of the average and least qualified but most loyal bureaucrats.

No doubt even Stalin's extensive power had its limits and had to be based on such realities as the sentiments born of the revolution, people's interests, and the need to preserve basic living conditions. Stalin was not free to go beyond the framework of the left-wing social development policy determined by Lenin. He could not openly question Lenin's authority, and in the final analysis, he had to take into account the actual economic results of his policy of the accelerated building of socialism in Russia.

To establish the objective limits of his adventurist economic policy and revolutionary wishful thinking in Russia, where messianic sentiments born of the revolution were widespread and everything labeled with the word *socialism* was sacred, it is necessary not to lose sight of several factors.

First, many economic and ideological methods concealed the truth that the accelerated "implantation" of state control in the national economy was a dead end. Second, arbitrary actions and miscalculations in economic management could be explained away and all blamed on the subversive activity of the hidden enemies of the people and the agents of imperialist intelligence services. Finally, the propaganda machine and servile artists could be relied upon to conceal the actual situation in the economy by creating an illusory socialist reality that one saw in propaganda films.

But the most important "compensatory" factor that offset the negative consequences of our ultrarevolutionary and adventurist economic policy was the long-suffering and undemanding character of the Russian people, who are ever ready to sacrifice all for the sake of their motherland and, what is just as important, the unique natural resources of the country.

Without question the laws of economics are inviolate, and the most revolutionary and "theoretically unassailable" fantasy will collapse like a house of cards when it comes in contact with the "material of life." But we must bear in mind that sometimes those laws are validated over a period of time incomparably longer than the short span of human life. Even if the revolutionary leftism of a leap forward is patently absurd, it takes several generations for the truth to come out and gain acceptance among the majority of people. Particularly revealing is the reassessment of total, uniform, and enforced collectivization that has been protracted over nearly six decades.

The failure of Stalin's accelerated collectivization would have seemed hard to conceal. "The success of collectivization has made many heads reel," wrote Stalin in a famous article, but in its wake came a drop in living standards both in the cities and in the countryside, and a chronic food crisis gripped the nation. It was the natural result of an overall decline in agricultural production brought about by the disruption of age-long methods of organization and stimulation of production in the country-side. The expected growth of grain production did not materialize. By the end of the first five-year-plan period (1939), despite a 20 percent increase in the area under crops, the overall grain production was only 69.9 million tons instead of the expected 105.8 million; that is actually lower than in 1928. The yields of industrial crops such as beetroot, potatoes, cotton, and flax, which determined the success of industrial development, dropped sharply.[13]

But animal breeding was particularly hard hit by the "implantation" of collective farms. In the period from 1929 to early 1934, the number of cattle decreased by 26.6 million, or 45 percent; cows by 10.3 million, or 35 percent; pigs by 12.0 million, or more than twofold; sheep by 64.4 million, or nearly threefold; goats by 6.4 million, or nearly threefold, too; and horses by 17.2 million, or twofold.

Those were the consequences of the leftist and adventurist policy of transferring cattle breeding into public ownership. One of the reasons for the mass slaughter of animals by peasants during the first stage of collectivization was the directive of the Kolkhoz Center of the USSR of December 10, 1929, demanding that all local organizations in the areas of total collectivization should transfer to public ownership 100 percent of draft animals and cows, 80 percent of pigs, and 60 percent of sheep.

Obviously, agriculture was particularly sensitive to the disastrous leftist policy to make a leap forward, because any violation of the laws of land, agrarian and labor economics, and the psychology of human beings provokes a swift backlash in the countryside. Still we have taken more than five decades to admit the utter failure of Stalin's agrarian policy.

These are the dialectics of the objective and subjective factors and necessity and chance in history. In a matter of hours during the April 1929 Plenum of the Central Committee of the VKP(B) (the All-Union Communist Party), Stalin emerged victorious in the ideological battle with Bukharin, Rykov, and Tomsky, and that was the end of the Leninist concept of the building of socialism, the program of cooperation and agrarian science. But we have taken almost six decades to come back to the facts of life and common sense. First, we waited for Stalin's death so that we could call a spade a spade and speak openly about the critical situation in our agriculture, which was not even capable of simple reproduction of labor power. It was Khrushchev who made it public at the September 1953 Plenum of the CPSU Central Committee. But it turned out that criticism alone was not enough to give birth to a new policy while the ideology responsible for the dreadful situation remained unchallenged.

To go back to common sense and the Leninist agrarian policy, we had to wait much longer until the ideology of Stalinism exposed itself as totally untenable. We had to overcome our fixation on giant projects, etatism, pathological craving for uniformity, and automatic rejection of everything old in favor of everything new. We took another three decades, when Russia's mineral wealth was plundered to pay for our fatalistic inability to see the difference between genuine truth and apparent truth, until we began to trust our common sense and our age-old experience.

Thus, at least four factors contributed to the situation that evolved in the late 1920s when our country reentered a period of leftist experiments. First was the untimely death of Lenin, the father of the NEP; second was the powerful state mechanism set up under War Communism; third was the country's fabulous natural wealth and the long-suffering character of the Russian nation, which made it possible to conceal strategic mistakes; and finally was the leftist urge to speed up things, acquired during the great revolution. I think that the latter has had by far the most profound impact on our recent history.

Who Provokes Class Struggle?

In my view, the origins of the maximalism and voluntarism of the 1930s should be sought primarily in the ideological sphere, in the theoretical discussions, and in the way the people of the time *en masse* perceived socialism. We should bear in mind that among Russian Social Democrats the evolution of concepts of a new society and of ways to build it zigzagged tortuously, posing a threat to the new and realistic policies expounded by Lenin. This is not simply conjecture.

We should remember—and this is one of tragedies of our revolution—that Lenin was used to attack Lenin. All those who throughout the 1920s openly criticized the NEP and refused to regard it seriously as a long-term policy (namely, Trotsky, Zinoviev, Preobrazhensky, and, subsequently, Stalin) relied on Lenin's reputation in science to justify their appeals to a more intensified class struggle and a new civil war in Russia.

Lenin's pronouncements on the incompatibility of socialism and the exchange of goods were used to discredit his concepts of self-financing and of combining planning with a market approach.[14] The party line, which in every way encouraged the thrifty and hard-working peasant in 1922–27, was criticized by the Lenin of the Combeds and of the struggle against the bloodsucking kulak. Leaders of all the left-wing oppositions of the 1920s called upon the party to pursue its policies in the country, bearing in mind Lenin's phrase, "The kulaks are the most savage, vulgar and uncouth exploiters."[15]

Moreover, Lenin believed that the remaining small-scale private production sector would be gradually edged out economically—an idea that was opposed to another of his views, namely, that violence was effective when it relied on the power of the working class and corresponded to "loftier principles of a socialist system." To illustrate this point, E. A. Preobrazhensky held that this assumption by Lenin had a general, universal character and was applicable not only during a struggle for power but also at a time of economic development.[16]

Of course, as has been demonstrated above, when War Communism was introduced and when his "Current Tasks for Soviet Power" appeared, Lenin made numerous pronouncements that could be used to justify a new civil war in the country and to discredit the idea of a voluntary and gradual cooperation of the peasantry. This is how Lenin perceived the prospects of the struggle for socialism in April 1920: "The ability to do this is developed by large-scale machine industry, and it has never, in all history, had any other material basis than the productive labor of millions employing large-scale machine industry in accordance with the previously established plan. And here the interests of the proletariat and the peasantry do not coincide. A difficult period of struggle begins—a struggle against the peasantry."[17] This conflict-ridden approach to addressing the peasant issue was chosen by Stalin nearly a decade later.

It is even easier, referring to the Lenin of the time of the Combeds, to justify the policy of total nationalization of agrarian production and to force the peasant to work through legal means. For example, during the period of War Communism, Lenin linked the future of agriculture, which was previously uncoordinated, with "large-scale state enterprise, whose produce would be used equally and justly distributed among all working people under a system of universal and equal labor service."[18]

Since Lenin's perceptions of socialism did change, and this has always been known, it is still possible that Lenin, made wiser by the first experience of a socialist transformation of the structures of society was substituted by Lenin who no longer believed that the road from capitalist Russia to socialist Russia could be traveled in one leap. Moreover, it should not be ignored that, when Lenin appealed for the simplest ways of organizing the new order, called on everyone to perform their work duty, stressed the need for the state to compel people to work, emphasized equitable distribution, and promised the youth that as early as fifteen years later they would live under communism, he was much more comprehensible and was closer to millions of workers and peasants who actively struggled for the new power than when he urged them to build communism with non-Communist hands and to learn to trade.

When hope existed for a shortcut to communism, the formulas of socialism contained in Lenin's works were extremely simple and easy to remember. For example, "the whole of society will have become a single office and single factory, with equality of labor and pay."[19] The underlying reality of the definitions of socialism contained in his political legacy was much harder to grasp. A case in point is Lenin's familiar phrase, "Given social ownership of the means of production, given the class victory of the proletariat over the bourgeoisie, the system of civilized co-operators is the system of socialism."[20]

The rigorous and unambiguous Lenin of the time of War Communism was much more in tune with the feelings of revolutionary workers and, above all, of party members, than the Lenin urging Communists to learn to trade. As is known, the NEP irritated workers and revolutionary intelligentsia the most.

Apparently, this predominant component of the party found adjustment most difficult. Today it is becoming clear that the twenty months of active scholarly life that Lenin had from March 1921 to January 1923 were not enough to instill in the minds of party members a realistic understanding of socialism, the theory of the NEP, and to overcome the leftist radical and utopian perceptions of a future society.

Many party members and, above all, workers still viewed socialism as a total negation of the old regime—money, commodity-money relations, economic independence of the producer, differences in income—a complete and absolute equality. These people fought and made the revolution in the name of that pure socialism that would not retain a single facet of the past.

The image of socialism that took root in the minds of workers emerged in the conditions of hunger and devastation of 1917, when the senseless and harsh life in Russia drove people to despair. That is why Russian workers found socialism attractive, first of all because it offered a prospect of making the transition to feeding people on a collective, Communist basis. This in turn assumed, as Lenin believed at the time (March 1918), "compulsory organisation of the *whole* population in consumer and producer communes."[21] In the minds of the overwhelming majority of party members the concept of "absolute equality," collective consumption, justice, and socialism formed an integral whole. At the beginning of the twentieth century the views of the Russian worker were similar to those of the French worker of the mid-nineteenth century who perceived communism as a network of production and consumer communes that satisfied the most elementary human needs.

Most important, the Lenin they grew accustomed to was simpler than the Lenin preaching a flexible and phased approach. The first Lenin sketched out the future with greater consistency and promised an early disappearance of all social differences. For example, the concept of socialism that Lenin developed in the first months after the October Revolution gave prominence to "organization of competition between various [all] consumer and production communes of the country for steady improvement of organization, discipline, and labor productivity, for transition to superior techniques. . . ." The promise it held was that, thanks to competition in the near future, it would be possible to ensure a decisive change in production "to gradually reduce the work day to six hours" and "to gradually level out all wages and salaries for all professions and categories."[22] Workers liked the very idea of setting up a system of production that would be a radical departure from the previous capitalist production and that would be based solely on moral incentives.

Frankly speaking, I am unable to understand why Soviet authors who undertake to diagnose what causes our long-standing "leftist" disease manifest no interest in the ideological situation that evolved in the party after the Civil War and that determined the conduct and attitudes of the main participants in socialist construction, namely, the most prominent and vigorous representatives of the working class and Communist intelligentsia of the 1920s.

The only difference between the 1930s and the 1920s probably was that between the fourteenth and fifteenth party congresses, when Stalin was engaged in a power struggle with representatives of left-wing deviation in the party leadership (in other words, with Trotsky, Zinoviev, and Kamenev), he himself was opposed to these leftist social attitudes and defended the Leninist concept of a phased development of socialism in the country through various forms of cooperation. At that time he used to say that no superior intelligence was required to revive "the Combed policy of dispossessing the kulaks" or "to rekindle the class struggle in the country" that new deviations led to. He claimed, on the contrary, that "in order to pursue a more complex policy of isolating the kulak through a union with the middle peasant, patience and restraint are necessary."[23]

Zinoviev's assertion that socialism was inherently incompatible with commodity-money relations was primarily made as an attack upon Lenin's theory of socialism as a system of civilized cooperators and upon the economic independence of enterprises and the freedom of the peasant. According to Zinoviev's reasoning, if the enterprises of the workers' state that produce for the market are state capitalist enterprises, then, in line with this logic, cooperation necessarily must be even more burdened with capitalism. Zinoviev claimed that so long as there is free trade and individual distribution and consumption, society is unable to break free of capitalism.[24]

The leader of the Leningrad opposition was most vociferous in attacking both the methods of managing the economy and the forms of control over the private owner's economic activities. In reference to the efforts to involve the private owner (the prosperous peasant) through cooperation in the development of the productive forces of the country, Zinoviev believed that such a production approach to socialist construction ran counter to the class approach and the Marxist idea of class struggle. Criticizing the party line of the time, the leader of the Leningrad opposition declared,

This is not just a debate over terminology, since "an entire school" is now forming around Bukharin that is trying to obfuscate reality and to depart from the class point of view. . . . It was not by chance that this argument flared up, since it is most intimately related to politics, to the fact that this "school" or "little school" wants to present the matter in such a manner that the question "who will beat who?" (capitalism–socialism, or socialism–capitalism?) appears to us to have been resolved, that it is taken off the agenda. This "school" obfuscates class struggle, obfuscates the real relationship between socialist and capitalist elements in our country and attempts to terrorize anyone who points out that it falsifies and distorts the fundamentals of Leninism, so that they turn into defeatists, liquidators and so on.[25]

At the time of the NEP, long before Stalin moved too far left as regards the village in the early 1930s, Zinoviev opposed the policy of a firm and lasting alliance of the working class with the working peasantry, the Leninist policy of deliberately joining the opposites together,* in favor of a policy of class confrontation, the struggle of the working class not only

---

* To be fair, we should recognize that at that time Stalin was as aware of the philosophy underlying Lenin's theory of socialism as a system of civilized cooperators as Bukharin and understood that essentially the problem boiled down to knowing how to unite and combine the opposites. Addressing the delegates to the 15th All-Union Conference of the All-Russian Communist Party (of Bolsheviks) (October 26–November 3, 1926), Stalin posed a question: "What is the principal advantage of the socialist method of industrialization?" He himself provided the answer: "It lies in that it results in a unity of interests in the industrialization from those of the principal working segments of the population, in that it leads *not to a pauperization of masses,* not to a sharpening of internal contradiction, but to their becoming reconciled and resolved; in that it steadily extends the internal market and expands the absorption of that market creating thereby a firm internal basis for proceeding with industrialization." See *15th Conference of the All-Russian Communist Party (of Bolsheviks), Verbatim Report* (in Russian) (Moscow-Leningrad, 1927), 457.

against the kulak but also against the middle peasant. Speaking at the 14th Congress, the leader of the Leningrad opposition stated,

Of course, the middle peasant is no Rothchild, this is not, of course, a classic type of bourgeois; we are fully aware of this. We are also aware that in the long run, when the middle peasant becomes "a civilized cooperation," as Lenin put it, he will not be a bourgeois in any sense of the word. But at present, middle peasants can and should be called petit bourgeois. To ignore that fact means to idealize the middle peasant unpardonably.[26]

The newly created myth of a special peasant leftism of the 1930s that allegedly destroyed the NEP and Lenin's cooperative plan does not correspond to the facts and the history of our party. The truth of the matter is that the 1930s, with their extreme measures, reflected the attitudes and the leftist radical perceptions of socialism that were predominant in the 1920s and that, unfortunately, triumphed. Is it not true that Stalin's well-known thesis, which we have now condemned, claiming that "the elimination of classes is achieved not through a weakening of the class struggle but through its growing stronger," is the logical conclusion drawn from the concept of permanent revolution? Lev Trotsky insisted that the conflict between the working class and the broad masses of individual peasants in a society building socialism was inevitable. In 1922, when Lenin was still alive, Trotsky wrote, in defense of his theory of "permanent revolution," that after seizing power, the proletariat would be locked in an antagonistic conflict not only with the groupings of the bourgeoisie who had supported it in the early phases of its revolutionary struggle but also with the "broad masses of the peasantry who had helped it to come to power."[27]

Generally speaking, one gets the impression that, not only did many of the party's ideologues of the time not accept, but they did not even understand what was original and theoretically new in Lenin's teaching of socialism as a system of civilized cooperators. As can be seen from their work in the mid-twenties, Zinoviev, Trotsky, and Preobrazhensky fully retained their positions on total, integrated, noncommodity state organization of production on a national scale.

It is significant that even such a thoughtful and disciplined thinker as Karl Kautsky did not notice the change of view on socialism in Lenin's last works. In his work "Bolshevism at a Dead End," written in 1930 as a reaction to the beginning of total collectivization in the USSR, he demonstrates a striking lack of understanding of the sociophilosophic and economic essence of the NEP, ignores its achievements, and attempts to portray Lenin as a champion of total nationalization, speculating on the attitudes of a Russian working class keen on equality and confiscation.

The ideological situation that emerged in the party in the 1920s not only failed to contribute to the resolution of the original and dramatic contradictions of our revolution; on the contrary, it made it worse and resulted in a glaring gap between the genuine economic and social needs of the country and the attitudes of those who determined its destiny and ways of development. Few of those who were at the helm of the revolution at the time were concerned with the problems that tormented Lenin in the last months of his life. Significantly, the issues raised in Lenin's article "On Our Revolution"—namely, the problem of strengthening the foundation of Russian social organization, the problem of promoting a general culture of work, and an active attitude toward life and civilized behavior—are totally absent from the works by Trotsky, Zinoviev, Kamenev, and Stalin.

In general, one gets the impression that after Lenin's death the chances for the realization of his concept of a gradual and indirect transition of Russia to socialism dropped sharply, while, in contrast, the prospects of restoring the methods of War Communism and management by decree in the organization of production on a national scale became much more likely.

Of course, there were objective reasons for this. The plan for the transition of Russia to socialism under which all remaining private production would be gradually edged out economically was very complex. Edging out a private owner economically required long-term and meticulous work. To achieve this required demonstrating in practice the advantage of collective forms of economic activities. To join together Lenin's civilizing program and the priorities arising from the strengthening of the foundations of socialism was no easy feat. It was a tough challenge to teach millions of people, including Communist clerks, to trade, to work to make a profit, and at the same time to promote economic management based on planning and decrees. Promoting initiative and the economic independence of the masses while at the same time encouraging socialist centralization was not easy. It was hard, on the one hand, to regard a working peasant as an ally, an equal subject of political and economic life, while, on the other hand, at the same time directing his political development and leading him to socialism.

To simultaneously address these challenges, which appeared mutually exclusive to many—something that amounted to constantly trying to unite opposites—the party leadership constantly had to demonstrate flexibility of thinking, creative attitude to theory, social vision, readiness to take unusual decisions, and, most important, the ability to sacrifice, in the name of the people's good and happiness, its revolutionary ambition and pride in being the first Communist country.

After their victory, the Bolsheviks found themselves in a complicated situation: Although they had engaged in the power struggle, they did not and could not have a detailed plan for all subsequent economic and political measures. In the course of the revolution and later at the time of the Civil War, they, as Lenin put it, were guided by the principle of Napoleon: "First engage in a serious battle and then see what happens."[28] Writing his political legacy in January 1923, Lenin stated, "Well, we did first engage in a serious battle in October 1917, and then saw such details of development [from the standpoint of world history they were certainly details] as the Brest peace, the New Economic Policy, and so forth."[29]

To implement such "details of development" as the NEP, it was necessary to complement them constantly with new elements hitherto absent and to enrich creatively Lenin's theory of socialist construction with new ideas.

However, after Lenin died, the theory and practice of building socialism in Russia, particularly after April 1929, headed in the opposite direction. Lenin's plan of building communism with non-Communist hands not only failed to put on flesh, to develop in detail, but, on the contrary, it became simplified. Many party leaders of the time had neither enough patience, economic vision, and materialism nor the desire to give thought to the future of millions of compatriots in order to find the optimal and least painful way for the people to overcome the difficulties that are inevitable in such a complex undertaking. They were driven only by the desire to bring about as quickly as possible the total socialization of production, the total and final nationalization of all means of production, and to create the first society in the world where not a single facet of the past would be retained as it was under capitalism.

Etatism and the Interests of Bureaucrats

Recently, in some of our publicist articles the view has been expressed that all left-wing oppositions of the 1920s, including the Trotskyist opposition, advocated the preservation of the NEP. This does not correspond to historical truth and the facts. In reality, the situation was quite the opposite. Immediately after the death of Lenin, a frontal attack was launched against the philosophical foundation of the Leninist concept of a gradual transition to socialism. The greatest contribution to the ignoble cause of discrediting ideologically the philosophical and socioeconomic principles of the NEP was made by E. A. Preobrazhensky, a leading theoretician of Trotsky's group.

The etatist concept of socialism, opposed to the NEP and Lenin's concept of a phased and indirect transition of Russia to socialism, took into account not only the revolutionary impatience of the masses but also the aforementioned natural yearning of people for simple and intelligible solutions. Of course, the idea of socialism as one big factory, one big state machine, is more intelligible and comprehensible than Lenin's theory of socialism as a system of civilized cooperators. Just the forms of cooperation alone can be very confusing: agricultural consumer, credit, sales, industrial, etc. The holistic, monolithic socialism based on one form of ownership is quite a different matter.

Preobrazhensky's idea, subsequently translated by Stalin into reality, of a constant and uninterrupted socialization of production accompanied by a wider use of noneconomic methods of socialist accumulation was inherently not compatible with the idea of cooperation nor with the concept of goods-producing socialism. The very nature of cooperation makes it impossible to organize production on a national scale in a way similar to an "all-people's syndicate," presupposing that every economic unit it incorporates follows directives and instructions from the center. A cooperative, as a voluntary union of private owners of certain means of production, assumes economic independence and full self-financing. A cooperative sets its own goals of economic activities. In other words, preserving cooperatives in any form meant a certain degree of economic decentralization in society and numerous independent participants in economic activity entering into economic relations.

In the framework of the perceptions of socialism, shared by Preobrazhensky, that became features of economic life in the 1930s, quite the opposite processes were envisioned. In our view, singling out such an important aspect of 1930s leftist strategy as etatism is important not only to trace its ideological roots but also to determine the most fertile ground for it to flourish. No doubt the etatist interpretation of socialism appealed most to the newly emerging socialist bureaucracy. The nationalization of public production, the scaling down of cooperation, the elimination of the market, and the suspension of the effect of the law of value are, above all, to the advantage of the bureaucrat and the management apparatus.* Such etatist measures expand the scope of the bureaucrat's authority and, consequently, increase the number of vacancies for senior positions, thereby opening up prospects for career development. The idea of scaling down commodity-money relations and of direct exchange of products is

---

* This is a reference to the domination of the party and state agencies and the power of the Communist bureaucracy.

also particularly appealing to the bureaucrat. This strategy of constructing socialism relieves the bureaucrat of an unpleasant controller—the
market—checking the quality of his or her work. Self-financing has
always been frightening to a torpid bureaucrat, unaccustomed to thinking out the economic consequences of the decisions he or she takes, let
alone taking material responsibility for them.

A comparison of the opportunities provided to the apparatus by Lenin's
flexible model of socialism and the ones offered by the etatist concept of
a new society makes immediately clear why we had such difficulty restraining effectively the leftist aspirations for total state control over labor. The
new concept of socialism formulated by Lenin in his last works, a concept
that determined the party's economic strategy in the 1920s and right up to
the April 1929 Plenum, from the very beginning was antibureaucratic in
its thrust and posed a risk to the bureaucrat's well-being and peace of
mind. In fact, one of the principal reasons for the transition from the
administer-and-command methods of management characteristic of War
Communism to economic measures was indeed the need to reduce the
state apparatus that had grown inordinately during the Civil War. As
early as 1920 it already outnumbered the bureaucratic apparatus of tsarist
Russia. By that time, compared with 1917, the number of bureaucrats in
Moscow grew by 46 percent and in Petrograd by 50 percent. Under these
circumstances, reducing nonproductive expenses incurred by the dis-
proportionately swollen state apparatus became top priority.

This challenge could be met only through a significant reduction in the
volume of bureaucratic work and by expanding areas free from direct supervision of the state. Achieving that objective was facilitated by the restoration of self-management rights to peasant communes in the early 1920s.
There was a growing understanding of the importance of reestablishing
horizontal economic ties in the society, that is, cooperation and exchange
emerging at the initiative of producers themselves. For objective reasons,
because of their economic nature, cooperative organizations in industry and
agriculture could in many ways contribute to meeting that objective and,
at least in the context of a given location, help restore the market. At the
same time, the party also regarded cooperation as a direct antibureaucratic
measure to counteract the established incompetence of state bureaucrats.
Indeed, the economic nature of cooperation, its independence and private
commercial elements, barred it from such incompetent supervision. At
the same time, as a rule, cooperative organizations were headed by people enjoying the respect of the shareholders, by people who invested a
considerable amount of their means in cooperative funds and, consequently, were personally interested in running the business rationally.

Thus, from the very beginning the new Leninist concept of socialism came into conflict with the interests of that segment of state apparatus that had to engage in other activities. Against the backdrop of the successful advance of the New Economic Policy, the conflict between the developing production forces in the country and the economic interests of the new bureaucracy was not improving but, on the contrary, was worsening. This was happening because the policy of reducing the apparatus, proclaimed as early the 10th Congress of the All-Russia Communist Party (of Bolsheviks), was not yielding the expected results. Already by 1926 the state apparatus numbered 832,000, while the tsarist bureaucracy had comprised only 432,000. By 1927 it had grown by another 49,000. In some trusts, running the apparatus accounted for 40 percent of the sum paid in wages to the workers. In the early 1920s, the concept of socialism underwent a qualitative change. However, the structure and methods of managing society that had emerged under War Communism remained unchanged. This is where one of the main contradictions of the early 1920s lies. Despite the changes in domestic policy, those same people who had grown used to imposing bans, to issuing orders, writing guidelines, and drawing up projects were still at the top and at the center. Most important, the so-called organizational fetishism was preserved and was multiplying—a conviction that the state apparatus had the right to interfere in all spheres of humanity's social activity, as well as to change it in conformity with the current understanding of socialism. At that early stage, in the mid-twenties, the magic of documents and guiding instructions was becoming more potent, the gap was widening between management activities and reality, the real economic potential, the mental and physical abilities of human beings. More and more often the meaning and significance of management activities were becoming lost in paperwork and reporting procedures. In his last statements, F. E. Dzherzhinsky liked to repeat, "We are suffering from organizational fetishism." For example, when addressing the meeting of ranking officials of the All-Russia Council of National Economy, he stated, "It seems to us that in order to organize something, to construct something, it is sufficient to take a sheet of paper, to sit down in your office and to write: 'Adopt energetic measures,' 'Find the means,' and so on and so forth. This appears to us to be sufficient."[30]

The quicker the pace of the growth of the apparatus, the greater was the danger of the real economic and social challenges becoming methodologized and of being sacrificed to copiously documented organizational programs of various kinds. Under these circumstances, that is to say, beginning in the second half of the 1920s, the question of the future development of the country, of the sources of socialist industrialization, was most intimately linked to the question of the future of the constantly growing bureaucratic apparatus. The alternatives posed themselves in very simple terms: either increase accumulations through the reduction of nonproductive expenses, through reducing the apparatus, or follow Preobrazhensky's prescription—strip the peasants of their possessions.

Reading speeches by Bukharin, Dzherzhinsky, and Ordzhonikidze* gives one an idea of how harshly the dilemma posed itself at that time. For example, in his speech to the July 1927 Plenum of the Central Committee and the Central Control Commission of the All-Russia Communist Party (of Bolsheviks), Dzherzhinsky explicitly proposed the policy of reducing the expenses incurred from running the state apparatus and opposed the policy of dispossessing the village. He emphasized that "we should and can reduce purely administrative expenses of our apparatus."[31] At the same time, he objected categorically to the move, proposed by Trotsky's group, to dispossess the village. Dzherzhinsky emphasized that accumulation resulting from the pauperization of the villages would thwart industrialization. He stated,

The country has to be industrialized, and this will not happen unless we receive increasingly larger amounts of agricultural products. Why? Because we need raw materials from the village, we need bread, we need leather, we need potatoes and wool. We need raw materials from the village. It is impossible to industrialize if one speaks about the welfare of the village with fear.[32]

Finally, we should also bear in mind that the etatist perceptions of socialism were more in line with the technocratic attitudes of the bureaucracy. In a way, they were a direct projection of a perception of the world that was characteristic of the new formation of managers. A passion for large-scale economic reform and directorial command methods of managing the economy grows out of a conviction that the possibilities of organization are unlimited, that it is possible to refashion the social fabric in accordance with the original design, just as a tailor cuts cloth in accordance with a pattern. Faith in the omnipotence of the state forms of organizing labor usually goes hand in hand with faith in the creative force of coercion and bans. Significantly, all the opponents of cooperation rated work duty and political coercion to work higher than methods of

---

* Grigory Konstantinovich Ordzhonikidze (1886–1937), a Bolshevik, led the struggle for Soviet power in the Caucasus and Transcaucasia during the Civil War. Together with Stalin, he pursued the policy of accelerated industrialization during the 1930s. In 1937, he committed suicide because of his opposition to Stalin's policies.

economic incentive in production. At the 10th Congress of the All-Russia Communist Party (of Bolsheviks), Tsuryupa and Frumkin* regarded state-forced labor as "a more perfect" form of organizing labor then cooperation, which, in their view, was "inherently inimical" to socialism.

The nationalization of production appeals to people with this frame of mind first of all because they believe that it makes it possible to exclude the spontaneous, the heterogeneous, and the unpredictible from the economy and to promote the existing order. In their view, progress toward one mode of production must be achieved through a radical reduction of the nonstate options of economic development and explicit bans on those forms of organizing labor that had been enriched by past experience and, above all, by freedom of economic activity.

The philosophy and fundamental principles of the functioning of the cooperative movement are the antithesis of etatism and bureaucratic thinking. Incidently, this conflict emerged as early as the nineteenth century in the polemical exchange between the advocate of the free and voluntary cooperation, Fourier, and the apologist of organized Communist happiness, Saint-Simon. From the very beginning, the first cooperators tried to leave the freedom of choice to the individual and to avoid total control over economic life with no options. They were attracted by the economic independence of a cooperative enterprise because it allowed for the unpredictable, new and unknown developments, and offered hope for a qualitative improvement of the well-being of its members, etc.

Totally state-organized labor along the lines of one big factory, or one post office, was the expression of a desire for complete predictability, for full knowledge of the basic conditions of life and work as well as the trends of their development. The incentive to cooperation, conversely, is maintained by the hope to go beyond what is known and established, to find a new and yet unknown consumer, to expand funds, etc. Significantly, in this context, Fourier described the cooperative system as world anarchism. Yet it is the unpredictable, the faith in the diversity of the world, the hope to reach new, previously unknown and inaccessible frontiers that is the driving force behind the creative pursuit.

That is why the bureaucrats, blindly believing it was possible to totally organize social activity, could in no way become advocates of private agricultural production on the land, of cooperation.

---

* A. P. Tsuryupa (1870–1929) was a Bolshevik and an associate of V. I. Lenin. During the Civil War he was People's Commissar for Food Provisions. M. I. Frumkin (1878–1938), also a Bolshevik, took an active part in the establishment of Soviet power in Siberia.

The mechanism of our state apparatus was not so much the product of ill will as an accurate reflection of the simple machine production predominant at the time. A mechanical perception of reality with its characteristic desire for dominance over all manifestations of life, for subjugating all the foundations of human life to uniform standards, inevitably generated expansionism. The mode of its operation and philosophy drove the state and, above all, the economic apparatus to constantly expand the sphere of its influence. It was urged on by a desire to prove itself through sheer size. In his mind, the state bureaucrat associated the village and the trades primarily with a possibility to demonstrate his organizational knack. He regarded them first of all as unconquered territory, as a convenient bridgehead that could be captured without sacrificing too much but that offered unique possibilities for maneuvers and experimentation. By no accident, the apparatus managing the country grew faster in the 1920s than any of its other sectors. For example, in only three years, from 1925 to 1928, the number of bureaucrats dealing with agrarian issues at the regional and district levels grew by 69.7 percent.[33]

Bear in mind that the mentality of the time of revolutionary storms and upheavals was extensive by nature. That is why it is no accident that territorial conquests related to the acquisition of new social strata were valued higher than material, qualitative victories leading to efficiency, affluence, and the culture of work.

However, even this obvious interest of the constantly growing state apparatus in curtailing the NEP and in abandoning the concept of a gradual voluntary cooperation of peasants is not reason enough to blame it for the leftist excesses of the 1930s.

These attitudes were innocuous in themselves. If they had been crucial for the destinies of the party and the country, then the group of Trotsky and not that of Stalin would have won, since Trotsky's worldview came closest to the technological, organizational, and etatist aspirations of the bureaucrat. Remember that the potential of the state apparatus to exercise direct influence over the decisions being adopted by the party leadership was not all that great. As distinct from the feudal bureaucracy, our socialist state apparatus does not represent something whole. It is not institutionalized, does not have strictly defined rights or political representation. That is why there is always the possibility of playing the interests of different agencies of the apparatus against one another or simply replacing it altogether. As demonstrated by experience, legally and politically, a state bureaucrat in the 1930s was no more protected than a private owner in the village.

In any case, after Lenin's death, the future of our country was not in the hands of technocrats but of politicians, and revolution was their job. They worked Russia into a frenzy and, forever dissatisfied with what was achieved, were impatient to work a Communist miracle.

NOTES

1. Lenin, *Collected Works*, 33:478.
2. Ibid., 29:211.
3. Ibid., 33:28.
4. Lenin, *Collected Works*, 5th ed., 43:382.
5. Lenin, *Collected Works*, 33:488.
6. Ibid., 33:480.
7. P. Maslov, *The Agrarian Question in Russia* (in Russian), 3d ed. (St. Petersburg, 1906), 1:206.
8. Lenin, *Collected Works*, 13:278–79.
9. Ibid., 32:233.
10. 10. Stalin, *Works*, 12:187–88.
11. Lenin, *Collected Works*, 36:594.
12. Marx and Engels, *Selected Works*, 3:491–92.
13. See O. Latsis, "The Problem of the Rates of Development in the Building of Socialism" (in Russian), *Communist*, 1987, no. 18:85.
14. See Lenin, *Collected Works*, 15:138.
15. See Coreport by Zinoviev at the Congress of the All-Russian Communist Party (of Bolsheviks), *14th Congress of the All-Russian Communist Party (of Bolsheviks), Verbatim Report* (in Russian) (Gosudarstvennoya Izdatelstvo [State Publishing House]), 123.
16. See E. A. Preobrazhensky, "One More Time about Socialist Accumulation," *Bulletin of the Communist Academy* 8 (1926):217.
17. Lenin, *Collected Works*, 30:508.
18. Ibid., 28:172.
19. Ibid., 25:479.
20. Ibid., 33:471.
21. Ibid., 27:156–57.
22. Ibid.
23. *14th Congress of the All-Russian Communist Party (of Bolsheviks), Verbatim Report* (in Russian) (Moscow-Leningrad, 1926).
24. Ibid., 102–3, 106.
25. Ibid., 109.
26. Ibid., 121.
27. L. Trotsky, *The Year of 1905* (in Russian), 2nd ed. (Gosizdat, 1922), 4–5.
28. Lenin, *Collected Works*, 33:480.
29. Ibid.
30. F. Dzherzhinsky, *Selected Articles and Statements* (Moscow, 1947), 355.
31. F. Dzherzhinsky, *Selected Articles and Speeches* (Moscow, 1947), 380.
32. Ibid., 376.
33. See J. Bineman and S. Heinman, *The Cadres of the State and Cooperative Apparatus of the USSR* (Moscow, 1930), 104–5, table 6.

CHAPTER 6

The Violence of Falsehood

The Price of a Miracle

One can find another explanation of why Stalin's attempt to do away with the private forms, to destroy the traditional small-scale agriculture and popular life-styles, enjoyed an even broader support in the party than the socialist transformation of the countryside that had begun in the summer and autumn of 1918. Apparently, NEP, with its well-fed cities and Russia's usual abundance in the marketplace, with its measured pace of life and its atmosphere of political tranquility, failed to live up to the expectations of those who had partaken of the joys of making history. Too much of the new socialist reality was reminiscent of the past; this resemblance was especially strong in everyday life.

Seemingly, the plentiful food and quiet labor of the peasant who had received land failed to justify the shocking experiences and unimaginable sacrifices suffered during the Civil War. As to the benefits of equality, many became accustomed to them as easily and quickly as to the absence of the hateful tsar.

Surprisingly, however, not only the victors continued dreaming of the "nontrivial" but also those who were defeated and lived abroad. Even the *Novaya Vekhi* liberals, who seemed to be pleased with the results of NEP, its flexibility and wisdom, continued to desire something even more significant and impressive.* Therefore, to achieve something of major importance through a common effort, they demanded that the liberal intelligentsia reconcile itself to the Bolsheviks, that those who failed to accept the revolution should make peace with those who had accom-

---

* This is a reference to the authors of a collection of articles about the Russian intelligentsia entitled *Vekhi* (Landmarks). Among its contributors were prominent Russian thinkers representing the liberal sectors of the intelligentsia, including N. A. Berdyayev, S. N. Bulgakov, P. B. Struve, etc.

plished it. "Without the Bolsheviks," wrote the émigré Yu. Klyuchnikov, "the revolution would be a mere coup, a riot, a pogrom, or anarchy with no glimpse or hopes for the future."[1]

In the view of this adherent of *Smena Vekh*,* the Russian nation was faced with a tragic dilemma after the revolution: Either it must achieve even greater headway to the future and thereby assert its greatness or accept the guilt for appalling crimes.

Is it possible to imagine how bitter this great nation will become if the immeasurable sacrifices it has suffered during these trying times do not lead to magnificent and all-justifying results? Will it have sufficient moral strength in the future to bear the burden of self-condemnation or the condemnation by other nations? Will it be able to survive with the clear understanding of being a criminal, a scoundrel, an idiot who, while not being drunk or possessed, has destroyed everything and in return . . . nothing! Absolutely nothing!!!

So queried Yu. Klyuchnikov in 1921. And his own answer was,

No, let everyone know that presently there is only one alternative left to us: either all Russians taken together are criminals, or we are promoting a noble cause. We are criminals if we are simply ravishing and killing our much suffering Motherland so that we may return to the old and get a kopeck's worth of the new. We are great, if our sufferings end with the triumph of the genius of the revolution.[2]

If that yearning for greatness, for a miracle and the expectation of a "breakthrough into the future" was the yearning of a liberal intellectual, someone who was far removed from the revolution, can one imagine how driven those people were who had literally shed their blood to create that which had no prior existence—greatness, a kingdom of the future, the unique society? Imagine how simple it was to seduce those people by asking them to make just one more leap and a few more, final sacrifices so that never again would they be called upon to sacrifice anything.

As a matter of fact, Anatoli Rybakov portrays Stalin in his novel *The Children of Arbat* as thinking in exactly the same way when he decided to launch a new series of repressions: It's not worth worrying about sacrifices, for all are doomed to death and will be forgotten, only the great will be remembered—"only those are remembered who sent people to death."[3]

---

* A collection of articles, *Smena Vekh* (Changing the landmarks) was compiled by a group of Russian emigre writers who called for cooperation with Soviet Russia. As a political and public movement, *smenovekhovstvo* (the spirit of *Changing the Landmarks*) of the Russian liberal intelligentsia marked an end to the struggle against Soviet power and its de facto recognition on the part of some Russian intellectuals. The ideologists of this movement, primarily N. V. Ustrelov, hoped that Soviet power would change its identity in the conditions of the NEP.

It is startling to note that all our original thinkers had premonitions, long before the revolution, that we Russians would not resist the temptation to astound the world. Eighty years before our first attempt to make the great leap and to vault directly from capitalist Russia to Communist Russia, P. Ya. Chaadayev wrote in his first "Philosophical Letter":

In a certain way we are an exceptional people. We are one of the nations that don't seem to be part of the humanity and exist solely for the purpose of giving some sort of important lesson to the rest of the world. Of course, the lesson we are called upon to teach will not be in vain, but who can say when will we find ourselves among humanity and how many misfortunes shall we suffer before our predestined task is accomplished.[4]

Chaadayev did not remain with Nikolai Gogol's thought that it is foolish "to be thinking of the future while ignoring the present." He pushed it still further and showed the extreme danger, both for the present and the realistically foreseeable future, in attempting to diminish the value of the present. If our "present" life is worth nothing except a "heartfelt sympathy," wrote P. Ya. Chaadayev,

if the present life of Russia is not worth . . . being loved and mere compassion suffices, then, consequently, the people's life may be interrupted without any shocking effect; consequently, one fine morning the people can reject their former life-styles and begin living a new life; consequently, it'll only take some type of strong will in order to shove aside the entirety of the people's past and graft upon the past some kind of artificial present for them; and, finally, what sort of a wretched people is it that so easily tosses aside its heritage for no reason at all.[5]

When a future lesson rises to a level where it is idolized, the present indeed seems highly doubtful and unstable. When the approach to both the past and present is clouded with doubts, there is no firm ground upon which one can determine any reliable criteria to assess the quality of socialist work. One remains unable to distinguish between the necessary transformations that are ripe and mature and those that are poorly timed, hasty, or simply detrimental; there is no ground for realism. The idea that has been instilled in the minds of our philosophers for decades—to the effect that the criteria of what is of Communist nature and what is not are contained in communism itself and that one should not believe in what was and what is but only in what will be—may have resulted in mysticism, for nothing else is possible. How is it possible in a real, material world to rely on something that might or, possibly, might not happen?

A concept of the future that is abstract, unspecific, and disassociated from the real life of Russia and the character of real Russian people leads to an equally vague concept of what is good and what is evil, what will benefit the country's population and society and what is harmful for them.

The criterion of morality as being that which serves the cause of consolidating communism is justified if and only if our knowledge of the future is reliable and is of a positive and constructive nature. But of what use as a tool for guidance is this criterion if communism is associated with dreams of the impossible, for instance, with the withering away and disappearance of national languages, state borders, sovereignty, money, classes, etc.? How many stupid things could have been done by the proponents of forced collectivization, given their faith in the forthcoming universal brotherhood and their willingness to teach even the chickens in the villages to lead a collective life, before it became obvious that their romantic visions of a radiant future were merely a utopian dream? The initial vagueness and indistinctness of the concept of the future that so charmed and inspired people during the first five-year plans inevitably led to people's nondifferentiated (i.e., organic) attitude toward their environment, toward their present life. The mystical image of the future immediately shattered into the tasks that were unrealistic from the very outset, given a sound understanding of the past and present and given the ability to see the world (and especially humanity) as it is.

For this reason, as long as the vast majority of the people retain a mystical, utopian conception of the future, they are in principle unable to work in a meaningful and fully thought-out manner and are unable to create a differentiated (i.e., viable) reality.

This helps us better understand Stalin's mechanistic approach, or as the philosopher E. Batalov described it, the inability to see the plastic nature of the life of society and its capacity for resisting all kinds of turbulence. A devaluation of the present enhances the technocratic illusions of our time and the popular view that life is merely the "soil"—and people, the "material"—and that given the will and appropriate organizational pressure everything can be changed, remade, and reshaped.

When there is lack of clarity concerning good and evil in this life, then the criterion to judge about this is the "lesson" itself, the possibility of something that has never before existed, for example, a "nontrivial" national economy unconnected with the law of value. Through a mystification of the goals, one is inevitably led to attaching an absolute value to the process itself of transforming life and battling against the past and the present. In this case, the greatest evidence of progress is found in the fact of a minor change, a dissimilarity in that which has been newly constructed as opposed to that which existed in the past.

Following this logic, the advocates of the theory of a specific socialist integrity attempted to prove to us only four years ago that even the most unprofitable state farm is ten times better due to its social merits than the most efficient private farm.

A person who is convinced that the most important events in history will take place in the future and that our present life and work are of no value in comparison to the uniqueness and fabulousness of "genuine history" cannot adequately evaluate either the past or the present. Involuntarily that person becomes an enemy of culture.

The tendency to destroy is the inevitable price paid for a romantic (i.e., unrealistic) attitude toward the future, the price of the right to live, even if only for a moment, in a visionary's world where life is having a feast.

Mikhail Bakunin's belief that revolution is creation did not disappear but just the opposite. As Russian society was becoming more and more radical, this view became ever more popular. The levity with which our compatriots resorted to violence, to destruction, is simply amazing.

In a situation where even the professors of the Imperial University were prepared to agree that a revolutionary need not think about sacrifices, that "unfortunately, history knows neither a price which is too high nor one which is too low,"[6] it was fully understandable that Trotsky's theory of a permanent revolution and leftist radicalism appeared. The author of the quote, Professor N. V. Ustrelov, considered violence and its historical role in exactly the same terms as the second-most important leader of the socialist revolution in Russia. "Any great historical event," the leading ideologist of *Smena Vekh* wrote, "involves destruction. Generally speaking, the humanity's culture is viable only because it is being constantly destroyed and recreated, by consuming itself in fire and then rising renewed from the ashes like a phoenix and by consuming its offspring like Saturn."[7]

I see no difference between this statement by the liberal Ustrelov and the affirmation by the left radical Trotsky that only revolutions create personalities.

Considering the growing popularity of Ustrelov's works today (some publicists quote his views on the purpose and nature of our revolution, considering them to be absolutely correct), I would like to remark that both he and Trotsky were wrong. A multitude of European nations have currently reached the summits of spiritual progress and economic prosperity without having destroyed the material and spiritual culture inherited from their ancestors and avoiding outrages upon that which is sacred to them. The history of France, with Bartholomew's night and the repressions and horrors of the Jacobinic dictatorship, to which

Ustrelov referred, cannot lay down the law for every nation or serve as an example to follow. The civilization of ancient Athens, which Marx regarded as the summit of the fully developed human spirit, knew of no class revolutions or professional revolutionaries; its rise was the result of commerce, of the labors of free farmers, and of democracy, which permitted creative freedom, various philosophical schools, and a multiplicity of viewpoints.

Revolution in and of itself creates nothing. A personality is the creation of productive work, culture, the arts, reflection, and a developed religious feeling. Revolution is able to enhance the sense of personality and human dignity and to remove that which inhibits the personality's creative self-expression. This is a great deal, of course. But still revolution in and of itself creates nothing. And I am referring now to a revolution whose purpose is to pick the fruit already ripened on the soil of the old society, take it and give it a breath of fresh air. Things become much more complex in the case of revolutions whose fundamental aim is simply to change the world and create something that never before existed (for instance, a "nontrivial," "non-petit-bourgeois" economy). One cannot be overly cautious of these revolutions, for one is never completely certain regarding the possibility of creating something that has never before existed, such as large grain factories in a patriarchal Russian village. Therefore, one has to be constantly on the alert, retain one's common sense, a sense of proportion, and a sense of responsibility for the lives of people, as well as to be morally prepared to retreat, change the route, or to courageously and without delay abandon one's most alluring and beloved dream if this dream becomes a destructive force rather than one of creation.

All this is possible if the revolutionaries do not become unrealistic, are always guided by humanistic values, and share the desire of the people desperately wanting happiness. The problem, however, is that the left radicals' belief in revolutions as the sole creative force of personalities from the beginning deprives them of any chance to see things as they are. This view of history turns everything upside down and results in a reversed system of values, or rather a world of antivalues.

It removes the attention from the individual and focuses it on the revolutionary process and the seizure of power; it substitutes a possible method of achieving an aim for the aim itself. This ultimately leads to a situation in which the transformation of society and the very process of the change of the established life-style, of the productive sphere, and of family relations are held to be the main social goal. Trotsky's theory of permanent revolution and his all-consuming desire to agitate are the consequences of his fundamental position that only revolutions create personalities and promote progress.

Once a revolutionary has contracted the infantile disorder of leftism, he cannot stop, for if whipping up the old world is the ultimate goal, the meaning of life, then importance lies not in the result but rather in the process of changing things, of rejecting all that was in the past.

I am firmly convinced that all the main deformities currently associated with "Stalinism" stem from this apocalyptic view of history so typical of our radical intellectuals, from this desire to question humanity's so-called absolute values. As long as we are chained to this old and deeply ingrained passion for trampling underfoot that which currently exists and lies before us and as long as we consider the abstract goal to be more valuable than living people, we shall not be able to overcome what party history manuals call "Trotskyism." We shall not overcome the events that actually took place under the motto of "battles for socialism."

As a rule, it is precisely the intelligentsia, which serves as the bearer of critical conscience, of the spirit of doubt and common sense, that enables a nation to refrain from senseless sacrifices and extremes even in the most critical, explosive periods of its history. Among our intelligentsia, however, were very few people who, like Erasmus Roterodamus, sought a compromise solution for even the most complex situations. The majority of them believed the opposite, that only extreme and extraordinary measures could lead to something of true significance.

Perhaps, the dangerous element of our radical thinking did not consist so much in the cavalier attitude toward violence and destruction but rather in the convictions that the strength of the future edifice depended on the thoroughness of the initial destruction and that nothing of importance can be built without major sacrifices. Sometimes one gets the impression that many Soviets hold dear not that which has innate value as significant in itself but rather that which has cost them much suffering. This outlook is a tremendous hindrance to a realistic assessment of the history of socialist development. Many people sincerely wonder whether it is possible at all to be critical about collectivization, which was implemented with such a great sacrifice. This vision of where the road to the Great Society lies makes it difficult to see basic differences between a Russian professional revolutionary and a Russian poet.

Bukharin, who said at the 7th Party Congress that "in case of necessity we can and must sacrifice tens of thousands of workers," was at that moment no more bloodthirsty than, for example, the poet Alexander Blok.

At the same time, in early 1918, Alexander Blok wrote passionate praises of the destruction caused by the revolution, its scope and aspirations, and invited all to "arrange things, life so that everything will be new." He agreed to nothing less or "more moderate" than this because what is "more moderate" is "more lowly," a "riot," a "coup," but not a "revolution." The latter, he wrote, is

like a thunderous whirlwind, like a blizzard always carrying in itself the new and unexpected; it not only deceives many; its vortex can easily cripple a worthy man; it often washes the unworthies ashore unharmed; but these are details that neither change the general direction of the current nor the current's ominous and deafening roar. Regardless of everything, this roar is always the trumpet of the Great.[8]

Not surprisingly, therefore, this country was destined to be particularly stubborn in its attempts to achieve the ideals of pure socialism and to repeat over and over the leftist experiments of the period of War Communism. Bukharin, who taught realism and compassion for the poor Russian peasant, simply had to lose the power struggle with Stalin, who called for an attack upon the stars, for the impossible, and who taught that fear of great sacrifices was unwarranted. Everyone wanted so badly to break through to the new, the unexplored, and they were prepared to sacrifice anything, even one's life, to quickly achieve the pure socialist society and the development of the true human personality.

It must be noted that Marx was the first to see the danger of this mystical approach to the Communist future and history's universal values. He was sharply critical of the American socialist Krighe, who preached that "communism is the religion of love for humanity" and that a Communist should exterminate "selfish egoism" from his soul.[9]

"Krighe's good intentions" helped Marx to see clearly the danger of the Communist movement being engulfed by and adapted to Christianity's moves and philosophy. He therefore decided to disassociate himself from the Christian "tendencies" of asceticism and "man's self-defilement" that had been propagated by Herman Krighe in an attempt to peddle all the abominations of Christianity under a tavernlike signboard of communism.

Unfortunately, and this should certainly be emphasized, our Russian working-class movement has equally failed to escape this tendency towards Christianizing Marxism. There were, of course, objective reasons for this, such as the spiritual heritage of Nechayev and Bakunin's "revolutionary's catechism," the psychology of the underground struggle, and, finally, the low educational and intellectual level of the people who took the path of revolution.

The Christianization tendency revealed itself not only in the utopian interpretation of Marxism but also in this utopia becoming a symbol of faith and its political utilization.

Nobody cared about such minor details as the spirit of Marx's intellectual quest or his doubts as a researcher. Only the end result, the final conclusions and clear-cut Marxist formulas cast in bronze, were in demand. Trotsky wrote, "We needed Marxism not only to do away with populism which only brushed against us, but above all to launch an uncompromising struggle against capitalism on its own territory."[10]

The fact that Marx throughout his life continuously progressed as a scientist, having overcome the influence of Hegel's cosmopolitanism and fatalism, was ignored.

Marx's thought concerning the future associative society underwent a genuine revolution between the period when he wrote that communism was an enigma aware of being an enigma and when he later, in a letter to the editor of *Patriotic Notes*, argued against attempts to view his theory as a doctrine of the universal destiny of humanity.

What about those who regarded themselves as Marx's followers, especially those who were rank-and-file members of the revolutionary battles? Have they been able to carry out the same revolution in favor of a scientific, nonfatalistic conception of history? It is well known, for example, that a number of the leaders of the October Revolution, who lacked a university education, never read Marx in the original; they were simply unable to read it. Even Trotsky, a nonclassical secondary school graduate from Odessa, who considered himself to be an educated person and boasted of his self-confidence, was convinced that the slave-owning system had been replaced by the more progressive feudal relations as early as the fifth century and that at that time the German barbarians were at a higher stage of development.

We need hardly demonstrate that the Communists, workers, and peasants who first participated in the armed uprising and later in the Civil War needed to accept the idea of communism as something messianic and fatalistic, like the Christian paradise or the kingdom of God on earth.

These people obviously needed a mystified Marxism clothed in religious, messianic garb; they wanted it to be a doctrine of the "Great." The more majestic and further removed the aim of the revolution was, the more confident these revolutionaries were, and their field of action and opportunity to demonstrate their talents and satisfy their ambitions enlarged.

This type of revolutionary needed not Marx the scientist, the researcher, but rather Marx the prophet, Marx the soothsayer, a Marx who had peered into the secrets of human destiny. From the wealth of

Marxist ideas, our revolutionary messianism highlighted only those that could be put in the terms of our native, apocalyptic tongue. We perceived Marxism to be a doctrine of history's revolutionary drama and associated it with a sea of blood, which must be crossed in order to progress. We welcomed it as a doctrine of the inevitable destiny of the world and the surety of a global proletarian revolution.

Could the people who dreamed of a new global holocaust have perceived Marxism any differently—people like the poet of the revolution and scholar A. Gostev, who awaited a new messiah, "the messenger of miracles and catastrophies"? They awaited history's triumphant hour when "terrible night shadows will darken the day, and the temples and museums will crumble, and mountains will move apart, and hurricanes will sway the land, and oceans will attack the shores, and the sun might rise in the north."[11]

This approach to Marxism and communism has obviously enhanced the traditional messianic character of our intellectuals' consciousness and our typical custom of subordinating the present to the future, public interests to those of an evil individual, the spiritual to the material, etc. The goals struggled for grew in their importance and became increasingly more distant from the fleeting moment of our present life. We aspired not only to overthrow the hateful tsarist government and liberate the Russian people but to liberate all working people and build a worldwide kingdom of workers and farmers. The life and concerns of a single individual viewed from the summits of these goals appeared so infinitesimally unimportant that they seemed inconsequential and could be neglected.

As a result, the life and interests of living people were sacrificed from the outset in favor of the future, a dream. Under these circumstances all that remained for an individual was to have his or her "personality dissolved in the collective spirit of the Party." From the very beginning, this interpretation of the class approach justified all manner of cruelty toward an individual person, especially someone of nonproletarian origin. Trotsky's political thinking is particularly characteristic of this interpretation of the class approach. Trying to justify his behavior at the Brest-Litovsk peace negotiations,* he wrote that the loss of the Baltic area and the Ukraine, as well as the inevitable death of soldiers during a new offensive to be launched by the Germans, would not be too great a price for the class-awakening of the German proletariat and the opportunity to bring closer the conflagration of world revolution. "I demanded at that time," Trotsky writes in his memoirs, "that there be no haste in conclud-

---

* In January–February 1918, L. Trotsky led the Soviet delegation at the peace talks with the Germans in Brest-Litovsk.

ing a peace treaty and that even at the price of loosing our territory we should give the German proletariat time to grasp the situation and to have its say."[12]

It is not simply an expression of Trotsky's individual personality but the result of the matrices of social thinking that determined the actions of the most radical-minded elements of the revolution, of which Trotsky is the most eloquent spokesperson. These people were certain that the progress of history, caused by the class struggle, could justify anything and that the class struggle, therefore, as V. Stanishevsky, a party journalist, wrote, "knows neither the so-called laws of warfare nor the laws of humanity, it spares neither the old nor the young, neither women nor children."[13]

It is here, in the gap (created by our archrevolutionary, superspiritual conscience) between morality and the economy, between a dream of a new human and the real living human, that many of our good beginnings perished. The culprits in all this are the insane extremes of our intelligentsia who wanted to remove in one fell swoop all the eternal contradictions of human existence. Nikolai Gogol wrote that "the cause of all our troubles is that we do not look at the present but we look into the future. The whole trouble with us," continued the author of the "Selected Passages from the Correspondence with Friends,"[14] "is that as soon as we have taken a good look at the present and noticed that certain things in it are pitiful and sad, while others are simply nasty or are not being done in the way we would like them to be done, we wave our hand at all this and begin looking towards the future."

Philosopher E. Batalov, a contemporary investigator of the pecularities of the Russian revolutionary conscience, believes that this euphoric and utopian approach to the future—the loss of a solid grounding, the sense of an almost complete freedom from economic laws and the power of the past, an unlimited freedom to remake society and an overestimation of both one's own potentials and the plasticity of the social fabric—appears during the process of a victorious revolution.

This proposition is probably correct as a general rule. However, many of our revolutionaries were, even here, exceptions. Long before the victory, even not knowing when they would achieve it, many of our revolutionaries felt free from the past and the present and both overestimated their own capabilities and the plasticity of social life. The deification of the future and the tendency to moral extremism and the moral approach composed a religion for our revolutionary, atheistic intelligentsia.

Even "Vekhi" contained a detailed explanation of the Russian revolutionary extremism. S. Bulgakov wrote, "A certain otherworldliness, eschatological dreaming of the City of God and the forthcoming kingdom of truth . . . as well as the desire to save humanity from suffering if not from sin, are known to comprise the immutable and distinctive feature of the Russian intelligentsia."[15]

Lenin also spoke with irony of the striking "boldness" of the Russian intellectual in theoretical argumentation and the implementation of "some great universal agrarian revolution."[16]

F. I. Chaliapin also gave a particularly incisive description of this weakness in our revolutionary conscience, which he as an émigré discerned from outside the country:

I cannot be blind and biased to such a degree as to fail to notice that deep at the heart of the Bolshevik movement there was a desire to rebuild life on principles which Lenin and some of his followers believed to be more just. The trouble was that our Russian builders could not stoop to design an ordinary human structure in accordance with a reasonable human plan; instead, they were determined to construct a "tower to the skies"–a Tower of Babel! They couldn't be satisfied with the regular, good and healthy pace of a man going to and from work. They had to rush to the future with seven-league strides. . . . "The earth shall rise on new foundations. . . ." "We'll renounce the old world. . . ." So they had to immediately sweep the old world so thoroughly that not a root, not a speck of dust was left. And the main thing is that our clever Russian heads amazingly know all the answers. They know how to transform a hunchbacked shoemaker into an Apollo Belvedere, how to teach a hare to strike a match and they know what that hare needs to be happy. . . . [17]

F. I. Chaliapin failed to notice, however, Lenin's attempt to bring the builders of the Tower of Babel back to earth. It is no wonder he overlooked this, however, as many party leaders failed to notice it also.

In all fairness we should recall that even Stalin briefly supported Bukharin's attempt to show that socialism without enough food for the farmer and the worker was not socialism but a chimera. The author and director of the most terrible human-made famine in the history of Russia criticized Trotsky at the 15th Bolshevik Party Conference for separating the tasks of building socialism from those of raising the living standard of the peasantry. "A comparison of comrade Trotsky's position," Stalin said at the congress, "with Lenin's statement that 'a good harvest could save the country' shows clearly how mistaken the claims of comrade Trotsky are."[18]

To our misfortune, however, the builders of the Tower of Babel never returned to this sinful earth. The traditions of the Russian revolutionary radicalism proved to be stronger. With Stalin's assistance, Trotsky's idea—that we needed not merely a good harvest but one that "could become a factor of accelerated economic development towards socialism"—became deeply ingrained in our consciousness. Until recently they were commonly found on the pages of our party press, fighting against "certain comrades who are attempting to use their work on subsidiary farms for their personal enrichment."

On the whole, this servile attitude to the future was fully and consistently upheld.

As we read today Alexander Prokhanov's pronouncements—that we needn't try to catch up with the West in the ability to make apparatuses, conduct public opinion polls, and organize production management; that we shouldn't worry about the fact that "our Soviet hospitals offer inferior treatment in comparison to Western hospitals"; that Soviet computers are not as fast and Soviet cornfields are not as rich as those in the West; because we are destined to pursue some other, nontrivial objective—we can see in all this absurdity the same old defect, which has become a part of our national conscience, a pride beyond measure, and a satanic arrogance. We wish not merely to catch up to other nations and have what they have but to accomplish something that nobody else is capable of or would dare to attempt.

This conscience is easily manipulated. People who are blinded by their ambitious idea to amaze the world and teach all of humanity the proper way to live—that is, to work and live in accordance with a plan—who never doubt their step and are convinced that, as Nikolai Gogol wrote about them long ago, "the whole world is lying and only they alone speak the truth," are unable to even notice that they have already set one foot over the precipice. One can indeed do anything with them, even cause them to bring about their own destruction.

So the European dream of a pure humanity and a pure socialism had no better soil in which to take root than our passion to amaze the world and be first in line on the road to eternal salvation.

A Hatred for the Routine, A Hatred for Life

There is enough ground to affirm that the Bolshevik mettle, revolutionary extremism, and readiness to sacrifice one's own life in the name of ideals were in a certain sense typical of our intelligentsia as a whole.* Otherwise it would be, to say the least, difficult to explain why our Right has always lost to the Left and why we never stopped our Communist

---

* "Judging by general frame of mind of the Russian intelligentsia and its taste for a special kind of tactic, which was described in 'Vekhi,' and not by the concrete socio-political programme, the majority of the Russian intelligentsia," Yu. V. Klyuchnikov wrote, "were quite definitely Bolshevik" (*Smena Vekh* [Prague, 1921], 22).

experiments of the Civil War period but continued driving Russia further toward the "heights" of noncommodity socialism.

Of course, a striving for novelty is characteristic of all nations. A truly scientific philosophy of history cannot evolve unless people's ineradicable passion for the unknown—the desire to see the time when, in historian Ustrelov's words, "the world would be ruled by fantasts" and the "people of real life" thrown aside and crushed—would be immersed in a world of specters. Sooner or later comes a day when history seems to have tired of common sense, of realistic policies, of the monotonous, sober-minded, and measured pace of progressive movement, and history itself begins to fantasize and create a legend.

One must keep in mind that this bitter feast of history occurs in different ways in various nations. The strength of the hand raised against the mundane, against what has become hateful, depends not only on the acuteness of the political and economic antagonisms but also on the psychology of those whose hand it is, on the degree to which they have become integrated into the old world, into its "minor affairs."

In Europe, people's natural striving for what is new, unusual, and unexplored has always been constrained by the equally natural fear of loosing that which has already been attained. Our hopes for improvement are not always fulfilled. The old with all its deficiencies is, however, real.

Apparently for this reason, that is, this restraining mechanism, the Western European nations, which had the objective and subjective prerequisites to implement Marx's socialism at the turn of the last century, failed to undertake any serious attempt directed toward this end. At the same time, in Russia, however, where those objective prerequisites for a transformation to a pure, complete socialism had only begun to mature, several consecutive attempts were made to reach this unknown.

Seemingly, the exact same objective requirements for the further development of social relations or for doing away with what has become hateful acquire different meanings in different cultures.

In Russia, our attraction to that which was available and our restraint from embracing a romantic vision were not as powerful as those of other nations, which had been trained in the art of realism and sober-mindedness by capitalism. Apparently, the phenomenon Lenin described as "Asiatic" included not only social inefficiency, a lack of knowledge, and widespread illiteracy but also the absence of a motivation to suppress extremism. This "Asiatic" or "Tartar" phenomenon also includes an adoration for the natural forces and destruction and the readiness to force one's way forward at all costs.

Lenin said that Russia stood on the border between the countries of the civilized world and the Orient, the non-European countries. On the one hand, we were prepared to accept the West's most radical ideas and, on the other hand, due to our intermediate location we lacked the conditions for their objective appraisal.

This resulted in, as A. I. Hertzen foresaw in the 1840s, an "optical illusion." The Russian intellectual is interested only in the end result of Western science and rarely in that which preceded, contradicted, and disagreed with it. In the West, however, "modern science" and the popular conservatism that opposes it through its "stubborn singularity" constitute two eternally competing halves of a unified whole. There the "results" of interest to the Russian student "never exist separately, in the same way a man's head thinks just so long as his neck keeps it fixed to his body, otherwise it's an empty vessel."[19]

The optical illusion is that, although we do see the Western new, progressive idea, our vision of it is not broad enough to take in the entire integrated picture. This defect in our intellectual perception of Western social ideas became especially obvious when the conditions for their implementation began to appear in Russia. Philosopher Sergei Bulgakov again reminded our intellectuals that the achievements of Western social thought required more cautious study and that the tree of European civilization had, not only fruit and branches, but also roots that provided it with nourishment and that ensured a natural balancing of the idea. Therefore, continued S. Bulgakov, even negative (revolutionary) doctrines circulating in their native land among other powerful spiritual currents that oppose them have a completely different psychological and historical significance in comparison to when those same doctrines appear in a cultural desert, claiming to be the entire truth, and become the basis of Russian education and civilization.

To this one could also add that the radical and revolutionary doctrines born in the West are balanced not only by other tendencies but internally also. Incorporated within them is the foundation Bulgakov described as the roots of Western civilization, that is, positive thinking and a pragmatic approach to life. This intrinsic balance was also characteristic of Rousseauism, but it was particularly obvious in Marxism.

Yes, Marxism was the most radical, revolutionary doctrine in the history of European thought. No one before Marx and Engels had ever thought of the possibility of drastically changing the entire course of history, the possibility of proceeding from prehistory to a completely different, genuine history. The young Marx dreamed, literally, of a miracle; he linked communism to a fundamentally new approach to life, a new conception of space and time, a complete and final resolution of all the contradictions of human existence, a "genuine resolution of the conflict between man and nature and between man and man – the true resolution of the strife between existence and essence . . . between the individual and the species." To him, communism is the "riddle of history solved, and it knows itself to be this solution".[20]

It seems that the history of humankind has never known such extreme demands of the future, in which the future is treated as being a laboratory clean and pure. Even Jesus Christ couldn't promise such purity as the resolution of contradictions in the hereafter. This first impression of Marxism is, however, deceptive. For once one penetrates the core of Marxist philosophy and carefully considers the substance of what it associates with that pure future, one sees many links to both the present and past, to that which we still customarily describe as "bourgeois culture" or the attributes of a "trivial" economy and "petit-bourgeois" life-style. What will this future society look like? There will be efficient and rational production, an exchange of substances with nature at the lowest cost, living conditions "worthy of human nature," a protection of individual autonomy, and all the benefits of the urban "petit-bourgeois," burgher civilization. Ultimately, this means normal human happiness. Yes, happiness, and happiness for the vast majority of society at that, including the petite bourgeoisie who seem so hateful to our present critics of Stalinism. "And if it should perhaps appear to some of you," Engels said in January 1845, "that the raising of the hitherto abased classes will not be possible without an abasement of your own condition, then you ought to bear in mind that what is involved is to create for all people such a condition that everyone can freely develop his human nature and live in a human relationship with his neighbors, and has no need to fear any violent shattering of his condition. . . ."[21] In the works of Marxist classics, the ideal is very earthly and the future has a firm linkage with the present. They have always been quite straightforward and direct about it. To them, communism was not an ideal but a movement that ends the intolerable situation of the proletariat and all working people.

Here the construction of socialism is tightly bound to tangible improvements in the material conditions of people's life. This was prompted by common sense. The conditions for and limits placed on the application of what we currently call the class approach or class viewpoint were set on the basis of a realistic humanism.

The revolution protects its own interests and the conditions for individual development. The matter in question, however, should be concerned with currently living people, the protection of genuine social benefits, and the prerequisites of social health.

Therefore, a European radical or Communist, who thinks in realistic and positive terms and applies the logic and values of his or her culture, does not see danger in the inevitable imperfections in the plan of the future born of the festival of history. He has no need for a future without efficiency, prosperity, and individual autonomy. He will immediately reject it as a farce. In this case, his decided preference would be for an imperfect but existing present rather than for a beautiful, impossible, and unachievable future.

Russia, as noted above, lacked sufficiently effective counterbalances to leftist radicalism and the dream of living in a fantasy world where the human will and thought would have no limitations and where the most unrealistic aspirations for a better life would probably come true. What the Slavophiles believed to be our national heritage was, in fact, our misfortune. The antibourgeois, nonconstructive outlook of our intelligentsia did us a great disservice. In contrast to intellectuals abroad, the Russian intelligentsia failed to root itself in the soil of real life, to master the basics of economic management, and to rise en masse to the heights of professionalism. It was, therefore, unprepared, from the very beginning, to play the role of creator of an economy more efficient than capitalism.

Of course, the romanticism, dreaminess, and maximalism of Russia's revolutionary intelligentsia did find their niche during the turning points of our history. Without these dreamers, Lenin said, the October Revolution would have been impossible. Our tragedy was that the majority of people who were spiritually prepared for accomplishing the miracle of the revolution lacked an adequate understanding of its creative, economic objectives; they lacked the skills of creative thinking. They were unaccustomed to considering the economic consequences of the transformations they launched. They failed to consider the industrial, creative side of the matter; frequently, they showed little regard for the concerns of the common, nonrevolutionary, rank-and-file workers and farmers, for the concerns of the mere mortals.

Lenin saw the danger of the dream of socialism becoming divorced from the daily concerns of the working people. In 1901, his book *What "the Friends of the People" Are* sharply criticized attempts to mystify social ideals. "The loftiest ideas are not worth a brass farthing so long as you fail to merge them indissolubly with the interests of those who participate in the economic struggle, to merge them with those 'narrow' and pettty everyday problems of the given class, like that of a 'fair reward for labor,' which the grandiloquent Narodnik regards with such sublime disdain."[22]

Yet the desire to link the ideal to "minor," "petty," everyday problems was not consistent among the Russian Social Democrats and especially among the Bolsheviks. Many of them, just like the populists, were ill with the same disorder of a haughty neglect for the daily concerns of the masses. Even during the famine of 1919, many revolutionaries were more concerned with getting all the people to work and eat together than with supplying bread, cows, sheep, and chickens to those people.

Many people were attracted to socialism by the beauty and uniqueness of its "form." Only now, during perestroika, the old-time tradition of contrasting the objective of achieving sufficiency to that of building communism is being discarded. This former tradition stemmed from our much-boasted national aversion to everything "petit bourgeois" and our "anticonsumerism."

I believe that were it not for the Russian intellectuals' traditional disdainful attitude toward mundane life, toward what is haughtily described as the "trivia of everyday life," Stalin would have been unable to convince the party that it was necessary to cut short the New Economic Policy and that it was possible to build socialism on an empty stomach and without even minor conveniences.

What Engels regarded as an unquestionable value (guarantees of individual welfare), many of his Russian followers viewed as an attribute of the despicable petit-bourgeois way of life. Perhaps the tragedy of the Russian revolutionaries was that they could find for themselves no clear, tangible values in the life they observed outside the country.

The Russian revolutionaries intensely despised the Western bourgeois, philistine society with its wealth and comforts of everyday life. But our own patriarchal way of life with its measured pace and oppressive atmosphere irritated them as well. This is the reason it was so difficult for them to link the dream of the unusual, nontrivial future to something positive, durable, and real.

Professional revolutionaries, working illegally, were particularly sensitive to this cleavage with reality, with the world of trifling issues and its daily petty duties and concerns. People who had known imprisonment, exile, and solitary confinement found it hard to resume living a common life with its routine, values, and morals. They looked at this world with different eyes, and it seemed to them that they knew secrets of life closed to others. But that which a member of an underground revolutionary organization considered to be normal (take, for example, Stalin's views on the proper life for a Communist) was, in fact, something strange, an abnormality.

The Russian words *meshchanin* and *obyvatel* (philistine) reflect this contempt for the commonness of everyday life. (In contrast, the Polish word *obivatel* means a "citizen," a "pillar of society." The German *bürger* also means a "citizen".) With us both *obyvatel* and *byurger* are people who oppose progress and the spiritual development of life. All our present sufferings stem from our disdainful attitude toward people's everyday needs and concerns.

The deification of the future inevitably led to a skeptical attitude toward the present, toward current problems.

The conviction that one cannot be a true revolutionary without despising the trivial nature of daily life and all that is stable and repetitious in humanity's existence became established in Russia in the last century, when the ideas of Bakunin and Tkachev dominated the minds of the intelligentsia. A good example is "The Revolutionary Catechism" by Bakunin and Tkachev and their advocacy of self-denial: "The revolutionary is a dedicated man. He has neither personal interests, nor affairs, nor feelings, nor attachments, nor property, nor even a name. Every part of him is absorbed by one sole interest, one sole thought, one sole passion: the revolution. . . . Strict with himself, he must be the same with others. All feelings of affection, all the softening feelings of kinship, friendship, love and gratitude must be stifled in him by a unique and cold passion for the revolutionary cause. . . . Pursuing this goal coldly and without respite, he must himself be ready to perish and to destroy with his own hands all that which obstructs the achievement of this goal."[23]

This pledge to hate the routine, habitual aspects of life can be found in the works of many Russian Social Democrats. Trotsky's thoughts are again interesting in this context. One gets the distinct impression when reading his works, especially his autobiography, that throughout his rich and eventful life as an active revolutionary he was interested not so much in obtaining social and economic results of one kind or another as in changing and disrupting everything that existed. He seems to be interested in imparting a constant and universal character to the revolution and in accomplishing something unprecedented. His theory of permanent revolution was based precisely on this inner conviction: that an established equilibrium, regardless of people's attitude toward it and its utility, is intrinsically evil, and therefore there can be no more noble task than to spare no effort in exploding the normal order of things.

Long before Stalin did, Trotsky pronounced an anathema against equilibrium as the most unworthy state of human existence. Society, he insisted, must "continuously shed its skin"; "Each phase of transformation is a direct result of another. . . . Revolutions in the fields of economy, technology, knowledge, family, everyday life and morality unfold through a complex interaction with one another and prevent society from reaching a state of equilibrium."[24] He was not merely looking to transform poverty into sufficiency; his revolutionary ardor was also aimed at more material things. Judging by Trotsky's memoirs, it was the "strapping Siberian women who brought roasted chickens, sucking-pigs, milk in bottles and mountains of baked bread to sell at the railway station" that reinforced his belief in the necessity of destroying the old world to its very foundations and of devoting his life to revolutionary activity.[25]

Our writers of the so-called patriotic orientation share with Trotsky much of this deadly hatred for "consumerism" and for what they call "quiet philistine happiness." Trotsky was also convinced of no greater evil in history than that of receiving "material benefits" from one's labor, and therefore his preferences were for a barracks-style leveling of pay and the solidarity of half-starved workers. He also believed that revolutionary morality usually declined when people were no longer starving, and therefore death from malnourishment during the period of War Communism was, in his view, far superior in moral terms to the life led by millions of well-fed workers and farmers during the NEP.

Authors who would have us believe that the decline of the Russian people began thirty years ago when, owing to Khrushchev's concessions, the farmers stopped starving and defiled themselves by yielding to such "gross elements of existence" as prefabricated, five-storied apartment houses and modest incomes, should know the origin of the ideas they are now repeating.

Our contemporary writer Yuri Bondarev has also revolted against the quiet and normal flow of life. He decided for some unknown reason that our Soviet person is threatened by "life in paradise groves and in the thoughtless blessing of satiety, satisfaction and pleasure" and recently began ennobling our former life by praising the "obstacles, descents, pits and ascents" we've had to surmount.[26] I wonder if other nations have writers who would consider history's pits (the author "apparently" meant the tragic events of the 1930s) as being more worthy than material sufficiency, but we have such writers. Our tragedy has always been contained in the fact that our "engineers of human souls" (and I have in mind not only writers) are great moralists who simply love to expose ills like "self-interest," "material benefit," etc. Unfortunately, all these critics of philistines are not accustomed to thinking prudently about life and the world. They wish to know nothing about the factors that support life, production, and their own existence. They simply refuse to accept the fact that, just like them, all other people want to derive some material benefits from their work and have the right, just like them, to "touch" in their one and only life such "gross elements of existence" as an apartment, a private country cottage, or a car. Why are these "gross elements of existence" not an obstacle to the moral purity of writers though they are considered, by the writers, to taint the morality of mere mortals?* Who has proven that starvation and the eternal "pity" of our existence enrich the soul more than the comforts of our modern, civilized life? The famine we experienced in this country during the early 1930s and late 1940s proves the contrary. Hungry people become brutal and wild. Some of them break down, kill their like, and eat them. Indeed, the world is much more complicated and contradictory than the way it looks in the pictures drawn by the new guardians of Russia's moral purity. How much more of our land, rural population, talent, metal, cotton, and coal must be destroyed and wasted before we understand the harmful and antihuman nature of a system of production in which a laborer is refused the right to his or her share of the "material benefits." Nothing is more terrible than our Russian unwillingness to respect common sense.

During the recent 19th Party Conference I talked with two students from Kaluga. They asked me for help in finding philosophers and sociologists who could assist them in convening a national rally in support of restoring communes of young producers and consumers. Naively, I asked them about how things were in their commune. It turned out that they hadn't yet established a commune of their own.

These young people explained to me that, if one wants to accomplish something, one must first set up an efficient organization and develop a clear-cut program of action. They insisted that in this case the program should provide for the voluntary, gradual communalization of the life and work of the youth and also provide for the steps to be taken against consumerism.

I then made an even greater mistake. I shared my thoughts about individual autonomy with them. It seems that autonomy presupposes the individual's right to develop his or her own version of personal happiness, and it also presupposes a right to build one's own everyday life on Communist principles. Further, people should be entitled to live as they themselves see fit and enjoy their own "philistine" happiness. The young people never expected to hear anything like this from the author of *The Idea of Socialism* (Moscow, 1976). The radiant blue eyes that had met me moments earlier became hardened. The young people had no further

---

* "In the last thirty years," Yuri Bondarev writes, "moral notions such as honor, conscience and respectability have undergone a sort of revision and humiliation as a result of gross elements of existence, and they have been tarnished by hypocrisy, flattery and indifference, while self-interest and material benefit have moved up to positions of moral predominance" (Y. Bondarev, "Pain and Hope," *Literaturnaya Gazeta*, June 22, 1988).

questions for me. Before we parted they said, "Real happiness is the fight against consumerism and *meshchanstvo* [philistinism]."

Messiahship, or the deification of a great idea or ideal, is not merely a weakness, a romantic passion, but rather it is a cardinal sin before humanity, before one's own people. The hatred for life's routines, however noble its motives, has always meant a hatred for life itself. For without this so-called routine, this constant concern for our daily bread, shelter, our children's happiness, and without this contact with the "gross elements of existence"—there is no life.

The so-called hatred for philistinism, which is typical of our intelligentsia, did not ennoble but, rather, emasculated our reason and our will to seek the truth. Of course, in certain specific cases this hatred enabled us to overcome "bad circumstances" and preserve ourselves. In most cases, however, it enhanced the illusion of the possibility of building a life without routine, without the petty everyday problems, without the tedious duties. And it strengthened the fantasy of managing our economy without appeals to humanity's innate egoism by excluding "material benefit" and "self-interest" from our life once and for all.

Incidentally, our leftist opposition has always lived off this illusion. Some of our present-day writers inveigh against the economic reforms for allegedly corrupting the person in the street by promises of prosperity and economic stability and corrupting the farmer, by independence. In the same way, Trotsky and G. Zinoviev railed against the New Economic Policy of the 1920s for being "an expression of the philistine attraction to order and peace." Indeed, there is nothing new in this world.

By attacking philistinism, the utilitarian spirit of the bourgeois way of life and its consumerism, we indirectly justified our inefficiency in industry, trade, and everyday life. That is, we justified our inability to provide enough goods for the people and ensure their well-being. The struggle against the so-called primitivism and mercenary spirit of bourgeois thinking helped us to justify our traditional inability to keep account for, analyze, and foresee things.

The opponents of the present economic reform are most afraid lest, God forbid, our Russian people start accounting for things and have enough food, consumer goods, normal living conditions, and, in this sense, resemble Westerners. They are deeply convinced that our traditional poverty and unskillfulness in all fields related to manufacturing high-quality consumer goods are of a greater moral and spiritual value than the comfortable life of a Western burgher. Moreover, they attempt to prove that the experiences of famines, undernourishment, repressions, and traditional shortages are less dangerous for the moral health of the nation than cost accounting, lease and family contract, incentives, enterprise, and earned good income. The patriotism of the present saviors of the Russian people, their purpose, their aspirations are simply incomprehensible to me. To what camp does a Russian writer belong if he is indignant over the fact that the Russian peasant has finally begun to be free from the guardianship of the overseers of collective and state farms and to take back the economic independence of which he or she had been deprived? How should we label a Russian man of letters who expresses his outrage over the fact that the Russian worker has regained his right to speak out and freely judge who can and who cannot satisfactorily manage production.

Before the revolution, a writer opposed to democracy and freedom would have been called a *krepostnik*, an "advocate of serfdom." Today he could be called a defender of Stalin's model of barrack socialism. For example, A. Slootsky's report, "Perestroika and Socio-Political Journalism," at the plenary meeting of the board of the Russian Federation's union of writers exemplifies, in my view, precisely this line of thought that justifies Stalin's enslavement of the workers and peasants. Possibly, the author didn't understand what he was doing. I am absolutely convinced, however, that the report's political substance is opposed to humanity's freedom and is permeated with a mistrust of the worker, the farmer, the intellectual. It justifies the prohibitory trend, the former harsh methods of administration by injunction, Stalinism, and the economic absurdities that resulted from it. In fact, he questions our people's ability to even approach the heights of democracy and freedom.*

Leftist Dogmatism or an Ideology of the Absurd?

The British political scientist Jeff Glaismer, who came to Moscow to gather material for a book he intended to publish about the debates connected with perestroika, once told me frankly that he couldn't understand some of our philosophers and writers who were actively opposed to economic reform and Gorbachev's agrarian policies. He approached

---

* "Will not the reliance on independently operating factories run by the all-consuming desire to profit at all costs leave the nation without inexpensive medicines and consumer goods because of group interests which are due to substantiate departmentalism? Aren't we, by dividing the property of strong collective farms and confusing a form of ownership with a method of work, turning the lease-contract business into one which resembles the former maize campaign? Aren't we undermining the State's power by eroding its monopoly of foreign trade and breaking up its hard currency resources? Aren't we at times taking steps toward anarchy and a dictatorship of pure utility by holding alternative elections?" (*Literaturnaya Rossiya* [December 23, 1988], no. 51).

me with an excited look on his face soon after an interview he had with one of the active opponents of the "ideology of economism."

"These people are very peculiar," he said. "They can't see what is right in front of them. At the same time things that have never existed, neither in the East nor in the West, and of which they themselves have only a vague idea, seem to them to be extremely important and correct. There must be a secret here, some strange logic that turns everything upside down."

The British guest seemed depressed and even frightened during our conversation.

"Your entire press, all your publications concerning your history, indicate that the only reason the Soviet economy [which was created by Stalin and free from the 'ideology of economism'] stayed afloat until the mid-1980s was the Soviet people's unpretentiousness and the vastness of your national wealth. Notwithstanding, your 'patriots' continue to defend Stalinist methods and his command system as the sole means of saving Russia. How can one defend a policy that causes hunger, poverty, and shortages? It is common knowledge—Western authors wrote about this long ago—that Stalin's collectivization deprived the farmer of land and economic independence and thereby undermined the productive capabilities of the Russian village.

"Today your own people write that the Russian villages in the non-black-soil zone are losing farmers and gradually disappearing. Your 'patriots' insist, however, that the danger lies in the farmer's independence, economic initiative, and trade—all of which Stalin had eradicated and which are now being reestablished. They say that the commercial system being introduced by Gorbachev will transform your farm lands into a desert. Why should the application of economic methods and criteria ruin your country while it has fostered efficiency and well-being everywhere else?"

"What are the motives of the defenders of Stalin's economy?" the British guest asked me. "What's the reason for their hatred of economic criteria and methods? Why are they looking for other, noneconomic methods? They seem to have no idea of how this peculiar economy, which will ignore economic rationality and the laws of commerce, is going to operate. Why are they defending something they are unable to even describe? What sort of people are they? How can an intelligent, well-educated person rely on something that can't be tested and for which there are no reasonable arguments while at the same time casting away what has proven to be effective both abroad and in your own experience?"

I tried, as best as I could, to calm him down. I told him that the logic of the absurd we had witnessed doesn't determine our present life in this society and very few people, at least among the intelligentsia, still believe in the miracle of a noncommodity economy. However, I failed to answer a number of questions our British guest asked me. We have never given any serious thought to the motives of our Communist romantics who currently oppose the ideology of economism and the country's economic progress. Nor have we considered the reasons for their obsession with finding some type of more efficient, nonmaterialistic criteria for the economy. What sort of an ideology is it in general? Is it an echo of that same European romance with pure socialism and the creation of a genuine human being, or is it something quite new?

A discussion of this topic was begun by *Pravda's* editorial of April 5, 1988, which attracted a great deal of attention. For some reason, however, the discussion soon came to an end. Nobody wanted to continue it and convince people of the methodological flimsiness of Nina Andreyeva's anti-perestroika manifesto, explain its false patriotism and misanthropic nature.*

A serious, academic discussion concerning the origins of modern leftist dogmatism and rhetoric has actually never begun. We seem to shy away from criticizing leftist radicals if they are our own. This is the reason we still have blank spots in the history of leftist extremism during the period of War Communism. We have never seriously considered the motives that guided our Russian radicals to constantly hustle a dream, doom people to suffer along the road to an unknown future, and instruct people of all ages to mistrust both the experience of their forefathers and also what they saw with their own eyes.

This is strange, even abnormal. No other socialist country has suffered so much as a result of these dreams of specific, noneconomic criteria and Communist rates of development.

It is difficult to say whether we spent more time and effort on exercising our leftist leaps or on healing the wounds they caused. Look at our seventy-year history from this angle. Isn't it amazing how devilishly we have persisted in preventing people from leading a normal life and causing them to suffer?

It seems that after an impressive and far-reaching revolution such as the one of October 1917 no other nation would seek further "profound" transformations. It seemed that Lenin's brilliant compromise between our

---

* Nina Andreyeva, a faculty member at a Leningrad college, sent a letter to the editorial board of *Sovetskaya Rossiya*, which the newspaper published in its issue of March 13, 1988, under the title "I Cannot Abandon My Principles." The letter was an open revolt of leftist dogmatics against the philosophy and practice of perestroika.

revolutionary ambitions and Russia's modest economic potential was in earnest and would last for many years. So much blood had been shed, and so many things had been destroyed and lost forever. Life was only beginning to return to normal. The farmers, workers, and intellectuals had only begun to enjoy the fruits of the revolution, sufficiency, human dignity, free creative labor, the right to till one's own land. But only one year after Lenin's death another leader of our revolution, L. D. Trotsky, demanded revenge. He wanted to astound the world with fantastic development rates through a rapid revolution in our industry. "The average annual rate of our industrial growth before the war," Trotsky wrote, "was 6 or 7 percent, which was quite high. But this figure seems quite insignificant when compared with the present rate of industrial development which is 40 to 50 percent per annum." It would seem that even the most impatient revolutionary should be satisfied with the 48 percent rate of Soviet industrial development between 1924 and 1925. But Trotsky hurried the country and our industry in particular. "The question of development rates," he wrote, "is a question which concerns socialism's place under the sun of history." He was not satisfied with the motto of taking "at least one step toward socialism every year" put forward by the State Planning Committee. "This phrase, if interpreted literally, might lead to wrong conclusions. Words to the effect that by making 'at least one step' every year we shall successfully progress towards socialism may be interpreted in the sense that the question of rates is, in fact, irrelevant: if the overall movement is directed towards socialism, we shall allegedly reach our goal anyway." "But," Trotsky concludes, "this conclusion would be fundamentally wrong."[27] In 1926, he claimed it was necessary to swiftly industrialize agriculture and introduce collective farming methods.

Another example is September 1953. Seemingly, life had again punished us for our desire to astound the world and live by unique standards. A Plenary Meeting of the CPSU Central Committee acknowledged the fact that Stalin's agrarian policy had been a complete failure. The policy of administration by command and political coercion directed against the farmer paralyzed the productive capabilities of the village. The party performed a leap in the direction of realism and rejected the practices of the surplus-appropriation system and the methods of forcefully keeping the peasants on the farms. The benefits of this realistic policy were obvious. During the second half of the 1950s, our agriculture achieved unprecedented successes. But the desire to astound the world and reach the bright future as quickly as possible triumphed again. Beginning in the late 1950s, we resumed our "accelerated" development toward our "ideal," a "Communist purity" of farming that excluded the use of the "trivial" household plots by collective farmers, and along with this it also excluded the "trivial" milk, meat, and, as became evident by 1963, bread in many cities and towns.

The failures of the 1965 economic reform are still fresh in our memory, for they happened during a period of our social awareness. However, no sooner than three years after the March and September (1985) Plenary Meetings of the CPSU Central Committee, "new people" appeared on our society's political scene. They started a campaign against market socialism, economic criteria, and methods, and against Libermans, Birmans, and Shiks.* These people advocated the idea that the summits of prosperity could be reached only on the basis of a spontaneous "self-development of the general Communist principles," by continuously bringing the collective farm and cooperative form of ownership nearer to the communal ownership, and through an integration of collectivist principles and Communist ethics with the entire fabric of our production.

The consequences of this fifteen-year-long campaign to strengthen the "general Communist principles of socialism" were thoroughly discussed at the Plenary Meetings of the CPSU Central Committee held in January and June 1987. The Communist purity of socialism was maintained by supporting the heavy drinking habits of the working class and by robbing our children and grandchildren, that is, through wasting our natural resources and cheating good workers. Instead of the expected growth of collectivism and consciousness, there was a leaplike growth in corruption and malfeasance, which was entirely without precedent in the history of Russia.

Finally, the era of perestroika has arrived or, as we call it, a revolution for realism and common sense. Perestroika has focused on the interests and concerns of not imaginary but real living people, on rationality, economic and social efficiency. Seemingly, under these conditions there is no place for leftist doctrinaire attitudes, new attacks against common sense, or the advocacy of all sorts of social mysticism. This sense of security from the danger of leftist adventurism was, however, deceptive.

For the umpteenth time in the not-so-long history of socialism in this country, a large-scale and vehement campaign was mounted against all our present values, against democracy, the criteria of rationality, the principle of autonomy, respect for human dignity, faith in people, humanity's moral values, kindness, charity, and all other things so essential in the world today. Under the pretext of fighting against "triviality," "petit-bourgeois trends," "pseudo-intellectualism," and "biased criticism," our

---

* Liberman and Birman are Soviet economists. Otto Shiks, a Czechoslovak economist, was active during the Prague spring of 1968.

"unbending" radicals are again trying to dominate the political scene, seeking to regain the right they lost to order people around and dispose of both the fruits of other people's labor and their lives as their dreamy and nontrivial conscience sees fit.

I am deeply convinced there would be more ideological guarantees for the triumph of perestroika if in March to April 1988 (when Nina Andreyeva's anti-perestroika manifesto was the focus of public attention) we hadn't limited ourselves by criticizing only Stalin's crimes. We could have gone further and started a substantial analysis of the damage the Communist fantasies of leftists like Stalin did to our country, to its land and natural environment, to genetics, and to people's morals. That would have fully exposed the antihuman nature of those leftist hustlers and high priests of "Communist primogeniture" and would have shown the danger of relying on the unknown with no regard for the experience of our ancestors and the achievements of other people. However, we failed to do that, and as a result, we are facing the developments that so greatly frightened our foreign guest.

Now, the opponents of perestroika do not openly defend Stalin; they are more cunning. They attack perestroika as being opposed to the leftist ideals of communism and accuse us mortals, who support and defend the radical economic reform, the current agrarian policy, and the concept of a law-governed state, of betraying communism and working-class interests. This is how things stand today.

Nina Andreyeva is again lecturing the party on the policies it should pursue. This time, however, she is doing this in the world press as an internationally known author and champion of the ideals of the working class and communism. Such is the price of underrating the very serious nature of leftist extremism. The absurd hero has wrapped herself in the bulletproof jacket of "party program." This hero is calling upon the party not to indulge in perestroika, for, as Nina Andreyeva claims, the CPSU is not a party of perestroika but a Communist party. She reproaches the 19th Party Conference for being silent about "the country's Communist perspective" and for concentrating instead on democracy, glasnost, and the food problem. Simply put, she accuses the perestroika militants of violating the "fundamental interests of the working class."

It is obviously stupid to counterpose the tasks of perestroika against those of the establishment of communism, and the policy of raising the Soviet living standard against the vital interests of the working class, as Nina Andreyeva did in her interview. It is purely immoral to slur those people who desire a better life for the Soviet people, better food for our children, a reduced infant mortality rate, fewer lines (for mothers to stand in), less drinking by fathers and more caring for their children, and finally that our unmilked cows stop wailing for the whole world to hear. What kind of communism (the communism of Nina Andreyeva and, unfortunately, a great many of her adherents) conflicts with democracy and openness, with an increase in the worker's freedom and initiative, and with people's well-being and happiness? What Communist criteria are in conflict with the criteria of economic rationality, social efficiency, kindness, charity, and respect for human dignity? Will the concept of communism have any meaning if we, the Soviet Union, the mother of the socialist revolution, fail to become a civilized, democratic state with at least minimal rationality, living standards that are, at least, comparable to those of other industrialized countries, and technically equipped production? Do the true, vital interests of the working class consist in the maintenance of our present level of agriculture, which was destroyed by the Communist visionaries? Are we to continue frightening humanity by our amazing inefficiency, long lines, and inability to work well and rationally?

There are many reasons for revealing the misanthropic nature of this form of "communism" and its "Communist perspective," which is defended by people who speak Nina Andreyeva's language and are again attempting to mislead our people. Every statement they make is simply rubbish, intended to deceive, frighten, and mislead uneducated people, and aimed to arouse doubts about the present reforms in our country.

The purpose of this book is not to show all the fallacies in Nina Andreyeva's position or analyze all aspects of her basic views, which are, in my opinion, misanthropic. One can only label as misanthropic her attempts to justify, by references to class struggle, the campaign to dispossess the kulaks. This is, in effect, a justification of the first-degree murder by Stalin of hundreds of thousands of innocent peasant children and infants, not to mention his murder of the adult population, their parents, in the snow-covered woodland of Siberia.

What interests me now is analyzing, on the one hand, the nature and the motives of the deliberate advocacy of obviously false ideas and violence and, on the other, our infantile, passive attitude toward those people who defend these ideals and their dreams of revenge. It is indeed beyond belief. A number of our people are still afraid of many things, and yet, no one is frightened to publicly, in the presence of many people, propagate foolish or even vile ideas while fully knowing that these ideas are foolish and vile. For example, they fearlessly affirm that a situation in which many millions of victims were repressed is less terrible than one in which millions of people lose faith in Stalin's ideals.

Poor learners from our own mistakes, we still underrate the danger of the seemingly innocent discourse on the possibility of incentives more effective than increased economic independence or higher wages or of some other criteria of progress or well-being that differ from those humanity has always used.

We lack immunity or a fully developed protective reaction against the absurdities that actually threaten the very basis of life, the lives of millions of people, both those currently alive and those yet to be born. It is not accidental, after all, that the proponents of the "general course" toward total famine feel so free and independent while lecturing both us and our guests from abroad on the nature of humanity. But it is indeed a dangerous situation if people think the way they do here, if they are willing to sacrifice lives both present and future, happiness and well-being, for the sole purpose of preserving what they term "the country's Communist perspective." A sane person is hardly rational who insists more truth is found in some quotation from the classics than in practical experience, than in the hundreds and thousands of facts that disprove that quotation.

One could surely enumerate many objective reasons that have led to the loss of the immunity to absurdity.

Unfortunately, many have the unquestioning admiration of a provisional youth who has been admitted into the temple of knowledge and has discarded the common sense of a simple person before reaching the point of scientific doubt.

For half a century we were able to cogitate about the laws of the development of socialism and its transformation into communism and about the dialectics of the general Communist principles' self-development, while failing to make the effort to study the society in which we lived.

Our philosophy courses at higher educational establishments offer little for the intellectual and spiritual development of young people; they do, however, infect a person with a virus of mistrust in the validity of an individual phenomenon, a fact, thereby deforming a person's consciousness. The so-called substantive approach makes it unnecessary to think in terms of proofs—for those who must show or demand them.

The reasons for our strange logic, which astounds foreigners, are perhaps to be found in our spiritual past. For a long time the life we, as a society, lived was illusory and unreal. Not surprisingly therefore, many of us have never learned to distinguish between imaginary and real values, between a world of ideas, of symbols, and the world of material objects. As future historians study the last quarter of this century, they will undoubtedly be amazed by the mass resistance to obvious truths of life, by our amazing ability to disregard that which is most important and most directly affects our future. They will be surprised to find that several generations of people outwardly professing materialism and scientific knowledge and actively fighting against idealism have never given thought to the events happening around them because they believed that importance lay not in the obvious but in that which was hidden from sight but implied. I think that the most fanatical mystics were less at variance with the most elementary principles of objective economics than are we who consider ourselves materialists.

It is true, however, that by the end of the 1930s it became necessary to support the faith in the coming of a Communist society in the near future with something tangible in order to allow people to really see some evidence of the forthcoming miracle. Stalin felt this necessity and set out to create tangible proofs to support these hopes. As a rule, though, this was accomplished through propaganda. The time came for setting all kinds of "records," on the surface and underground, in the north and in the south. Then, "records" began to be set in the transformation of nature and the climate through the use of Lysenko's genetics. "The Kuban Cossacs" movie-picture world of "record crops" helped keep people in two parallel worlds. People became so accustomed to this that, in the early 1960s, when Khrushchev said that "the current generation of Soviet people shall live under communism!"* many believed him. Possibly, he himself believed it, or he simply felt it necessary to sustain people's hopes; otherwise they would be unable to continue waiting for the promised miracle.

To be quite frank, however, our unwillingness to resist absurdities is a result not only of our old habits. More often than not, our passive attitude to publications, such as Nina Andreyeva's anti-perestroika manifesto, is caused by an elementary fear. Many are simply frightened to argue with these people; they are afraid of demagoguery based on revolutionary rhetoric. Unpreparedness for serious philosophical debates enhances this fear, thereby strengthening the position of the Communist phrasemongers who for decades terrorized our society by the specter of "revisionism," "deviation from principles," etc.

The opponents of an economy based on commodity production are not afraid to advocate hunger and call upon the country to perpetuate

---

* The transition to communism meant free basic consumer goods for all. When Khruschev said that "the current generation of Soviet people shall live under communism," he meant that, within the lifetime of the current generation of Soviet people, the Soviet economy based on the principle of communism will be developed enough to provide free basic consumer goods.

poverty and wretchedness. Every single case in history of attempts to base an economy on morality resulted in a shortage of daily bread. Yet, we are afraid to expose those people as advocates of misfortune and disaster.

One of the astonishing things about this situation is that these rather simple methods of intimidating our intelligentsia and all those who are sincerely concerned about the country's present and future are not new to any of us. The old and "all-conquering" strategy is still in effect. This strategy requires no analysis, work, or investigation. All that is necessary is to accuse a person of having lost his or her "Communist orientation"— that is, resort to the time-tested method of *donos* (secret denunciation)— and success is assured.

We know full well, for instance, the price our country and people paid for the "Communist orientation" of L. I. Brezhnev and M. A. Suslov. It resulted in the termination of the 1965 economic reform and all attempts to create a rational economy, and it undermined both the application of the Schyokino progressive methods of economic management and the team contract system. Among its consequences were the country's economic crisis, an increase in the scientific-technological gap between the USSR and the developed capitalist countries, exhaustion of the soil, and loss of farmers, and in some areas, loss of whole villages.*

We know the price to be paid for neglecting real issues in the name of fictitious ideals. Is it possible for a sensible politician, responsible for the life and prosperity of the country, to be guided in an economic policy, not by the principles of economic rationality and efficiency, not by the people's interest, but rather by a "Communist orientation"? Is it not evident, for instance, that the mid-nineteenth-century ideal of an affluent society with unlimited consumption is an absolutely utopian dream in light of the imminent ecological, energy, and food crises?

Why, then, are we afraid to tell our Communist demagogues to stop propagandizing and let people work and think for themselves? One can't continue to blackmail the party and society forever, for it's also a crime in the long run. Why are we afraid to tell those people that they are merely parasites on the population's political illiteracy and the fear that remains in people's souls since the time of Stalin, and that the ideal they desire to enforce upon society is not, essentially, an ideal?

---

* L. I. Brezhnev (1906–1982) was general secretary of the Communist Party of the Soviet Union from 1964 to 1982.

The Schyokino methods were a form of labor efficiency stimulation by redistribution among workers of part of the money saved by eliminating redundant jobs at an enterprise.

Noncommodity production, a farmer who is no longer farming, property that has ceased to be property for it belongs to no one, a personality divorced from its age—who and when considered this to be an ideal, a good?

The ideal of humanism, including the realistic humanism of Marx and Engels, has always been a contented citizen free from all forms of alienation. The ideal has always consisted of the dignity of a free human being, the autonomy—above all, the spiritual autonomy—of a person, an individual's right to an opinion, to err, and to enjoy the cultural achievements of the past and present. This is exactly that which is gradually returning to us in the course of perestroika. Stalinism is impossible in a society based on these humanitarian values.

We should learn to distinguish between revolutionarism—a necessary method of justified resistance to violence, cruelty, and exploitation—and ostentatious revolutionarism, which is caused by ambitions, a passion for innovations, or a simple desire to revenge oneself for humiliating circumstances.

Archrevolutionarism, or leftist dogmatism, for which revolution is an aim in itself, brings, in effect, more violence and injustice. The policy of national self-annihilation, such as was caused by Stalin's leftist experiments and the Pol Pot regime in Kampuchea, which was brought about by the leftist radicalism of students, could only undermine the basis of life. Stalin's domestic social policy contained not a single creative element.

The Egoism of Dreamers

Is there a way to tell an honest revolutionary, a Communist, who is prepared to sacrifice his or her own life for justice and the happiness of the suffering and oppressed, from archrevolutionaries who bring violence and death? There can be only one answer to this question, and the world has known it for centuries: Judge them by their deeds.

Lenin had attempted to develop criteria by which one could distinguish an ostentatious revolutionary, a leftist radical from a true revolutionary. As he was thinking about the reasons for the "terrible revolutionarism" and "haste" of all kinds of visionaries, he concluded that the reasons should be sought for in the existence of a gap between theory and practice. The motives that bring adventure seekers to the revolution are shallow, not serious, and this, of course, is immediately evident in their theoretical carelessness. These revolutionaries simply cannot devote themselves to the quest for truth because they are not interested in knowledge as an innate good but rather in knowledge that enables them to engage in disrupting the world, their favorite pastime.

I believe society does not seek self-destruction. Society is weak and defenseless, but it hardly encourages people to destroy the condition of their own existence. This can only be done by unskilled and inaccurate theorists.

And, then, has everyone sought truth in Marxism and revolution, has everyone been honest in choosing their road in life? Judging by what we now know about the life and activities of the leaders of the October Revolution, we can't answer this question in the affirmative. To some, Marxism was only a convenient means of achieving their ambitious goals. I personally am inclined to agree with Z. Fainburg, a Soviet sociologist, who said that "the revolution was varied, complex and contradictory due to its composition, its personages; most of the people who were drawn to the revolution were either those with noble ideals and high moral values and from different social background, or hopeless people who had no hopes under the old social system but who wanted to rise above their fate."[28]

Fainburg is right. What career could Joseph Dhugashvili, a shoemaker's son and a seminarian, hope to establish upon graduation from a theological seminary? At best, he could have hoped to become a priest of a small town (to be commissioned to a larger parish he needed a patron, and it was hard to fine one).

The career of a professional revolutionary was more attractive to him. Even though risky, it focused public attention on the personal qualities of a leader, freed him from the inferiority complex caused by his ailing arm, and opened opportunities for wielding enormous power.

No doubt Trotsky, the most aspiring of all the ambitious Russian revolutionaries, was guided by similar motives. In fact, he made no secret of this. The egocentric nature of his revolutionary activity stands out vividly in his confession *My Life:* He agreed to nothing less than the role of a leader of the world proletarian revolution. Furthermore, because of his Jewish origin, his chances of finding, in the Russian state, a place adequate to his talent and ambition were even slimmer than those of Stalin.

But, I repeat, what led these kinds of people to become professional revolutionaries was not their origins or humiliated status but innate adventurism and an ambition to rise in the world. Lavrenti Beria's* life is even more typical in this respect. That people with beastly hearts often associate themselves with the noblest of ideals is not surprising, nor is

---

* L. P. Beria, chief of the NKVD (the People's Commissariat for Internal Affairs) from 1939 to 1953, was a close friend and associate of V. I. Stalin.

the fact that they exploit the ideals of collectivism to satisfy their utter, unbridled egoism. Even in the hardships of prison and exile they seek an opportunity to assert themselves, get out of the rut, and reach beyond the limits of a trivial and insignificant life.

There is no need to prove how much these people needed to mystify Marxism, give it some religious, messianic coloring, and turn it into a teaching about the "Great." The more majestic and distant was the aim of the revolution, the more confident they became, the more things they found to do in this world, and the more opportunities came their way to satisfy their ambitions.

This type of revolutionary needed a Marx the Prophet, a Marx the Soothsayer. Out of the wealth of Marxist ideas, they picked out only the teaching about the revolutionary upheavals of history when progress forges ahead through a sea of blood, a teaching about the ineluctable fortunes of the world and ineluctable proletarian revolution worldwide.

How else could Marxism be understood by people who dreamed of a new global disaster, who, like the revolutionary poet and scholar A. Gostev, were waiting for a new messiah, "a harbinger of wonders and disasters," and who longed for that heyday of history when "the ghastly shadows of night pass through broad daylight, temples and museums come crashing down, mountains spread apart, hurricanes rush by, the oceans rise over the masses of land, and the sun comes up in the north."[29]

"Inapt theorizing" over seventy postrevolutionary years has produced many programs for a leap to be induced by force and coercion. Fortunately, many of them failed to gain support and never got off the ground. But they were all divorced from the existing situation, from how people lived and what they were expecting of the party.

We are now arguing a great deal about possible alternatives to nation-building, starting with the crucial year 1929. Many doubt if another choice, except for the one made by Stalin, was possible at all. I am not quite sure if there is a way to prove, in retrospect, the possibility of what never happened. Nor is there much difficulty proving that Stalin's strategy of ripping off the countryside to build up industry at the peasants' expense was devoid of any scientific, social, and economic substantiation. Simply read Stalin's speeches, "On the Rightist Deviation in the CPSU(B)" or "On Matters of Agrarian Policy in the USSR," made at a conference of Marxist agrarian scientists on December 27, 1929, to become convinced that Stalin's general course was not based on any calculations. Nor was it backed by serious studies of the potentialities of the forms of labor organization that had been established by that time. More than enough arguments were given in the two speeches to support the new course, but they were all of a purely normative nature and based on conjecture. Stalin's main argument was as follows: There cannot be what there must not be or what is not stipulated in the political economy of socialism; there must be what is stipulated. Thus, he insisted that, in comparison with family farms, large grain factories would ensure expanded reproduction, thereby setting the stage for more rapid industrialization. But none of his arguments was backed by fact. No economic proof was given to show that family farm production had outlived itself. (How, in this case, could one explain the striking success of NEP in farming?) There was no proof—and there could not be any—that, when transplanted into the countryside, the factory type of labor organization based on command would bring about a breakthrough in grain production. Many serious doubts to this effect were expressed at the time. Such doubts were raised in the writings of A. V. Chayanov. Stalin rejected Chayanov's arguments using a method of his own: "There is a person, there is a problem; no person, no problem."

E. A. Preobrazhensky, the father of the project to industrialize the nation at the peasants' expense, in the party was reputed to be a better-educated Marxist than Stalin and a more capable and conscientious researcher. Yet even in his writings you will not find any desire to provide substantiation for his leftist plans and programs to effect a forced march toward unisectoral socialist production. He, too, in fact, never tried to prove anything, for he pinned all his hopes on "things that must be" and on theoretical projections of a socialist future. Without any doubts or scruples, he referred to these theoretical projections as he sentenced the Russian peasantry to bear the brunt of the industrialization they never opted for. And what at least needed to be done before saddling the peasantry with all the hardships of industrialization was to study the reserves for accumulation in the industrial sector, devise ways to raise the workers' productivity of labor and their interest in using raw materials with more economy, and consider possible reductions in the already bloated management structure.

But Preobrazhensky made no bones about those minor details. He believed that, when laws and fundamental decisions were at issue, there was no need to go into particulars.

Little wonder, Lenin used to call leftist doctrinairism an infantile disorder. It is like a spoiled child's whim, "That's the way I want it," which defeats the dictates of reason and common sense. From the very beginning, a leftist doctrinaire is put out by the dictates and truths with which a mortal gets on through life.

And not just that. If Preobrazhensky, not to mention Stalin, had been a little sympathetic toward the peasants they were sentencing to poverty, they would have weighed the pros and cons a hundred times before they blustered out their laws dooming millions of people to suffering. But a leftist doctrinaire takes no heed of human needs or happiness. These "theorists" never feel any responsibility before the people. To paraphrase Pushkin, "there are millions of two-legged creatures and only one tool for them"—mortal human flesh, with the help of which the "laws" of history forge ahead.

A leftist extremist consciously incites revolutionary intolerance and conflict in society and instigates violence in economic relations. He urges the people to show "historical obedience." Not surprisingly, in all phases of our revolution—in the years of the Civil War, in the 1920s, 1930s, and even nowadays in the conditions of perestroika—appeals for establishing a nontrivial economy and nontrivial criteria and methods have coexisted with appeals for asceticism and restraint that, supposedly, take us closer to the ideals of communism. One gets the impression that our leftist doctrinaires and dogmatists subconsciously realize that their special methods cannot ensure well-being.

Note that, as the time when Lenin began to ponder over the intellectual and moral sources of the left-wing disorder recedes further into the past, the disorder itself has become ever more dangerous and its symptoms have grown ever more diverse.

As experience in the field of economic methods and criteria accrued, inapt theorizing and contempt for facts and the dictates of reason became increasingly aggressive.

Decade after decade the so-called substantive approach has battled the "phenomenon," destroying it more and more.

This is understandable, for nothing can be more frightening for a leftist dogmatist longing for a nontrivial economy than our existing reality. The reality itself (especially the state of the market and the agrarian sector) unmasks him and lays bare his groundless hopes.

The left-wing radicalism of the Civil War period, craving to reform all life on new, Communist principles, can be explained away by lack of experience. But how can one justify the leftist opposition and that extremist, Stalin, who were aware of the effects of surplus-produce appropriation and yet continued to insist it be implemented as the universal, Communist way of organizing production and consumption? How can one justify the leftist doctrinaires of the 1970s and the first half of the 1980s who, despite shortfalls in meat and milk supplies, continued to castigate non-Communist methods of food production, ordering farmers' private orchards to be cut down and their cattle slaughtered. What the Soviet people needed, they insisted, was not simply well-being but the kind of well-being created through nontrivial, Communist methods that increasingly revealed the general Communist nature of socialism.

I don't think it was by chance that Nina Andreyeva's anti-perestroika manifesto, and later her interview with the Yugoslav weekly *Vestnik*, were devoid of a grain of materialism or even a hint at an attempt to analyze our economic experience and the present socioeconomic situations in all socialist countries. She puts herself forward as a champion of people's interests but for some reason ignores the things that make up the lives of millions of Soviet people, overshadowing their daily existence and happiness. She doesn't seem to care that "general laxity," indifference to work, and sloth have become our national scourge, that with every passing year ever fewer skilled specialists and workers have remained in our society, that our goods have been of ever-deteriorating quality, or that the Soviet Union's prestige as a manufacturer has been falling.

One can say that this sort of thinking is a relapse into egalitarian, utopian socialism, which by its nature is preoccupied with redistributing somebody else's wealth and is totally unaware of how to get down to the job of organizing production. Egalitarian socialism, which has now come to grips with perestroika, cannot offer society any positive program for development.

In this case, individuals who claim to be defending the interests of the working class and all of Soviet society are consciously misleading people away from the main danger, the erosion of the foundations of production. It is a kind of utopianism that results from outright cynicism, not from inapt theorizing.

How else can one explain the dogmatists' attempts to justify Stalin's crimes by references to the laws of class struggle? Obviously, as Yu. Koryakin* has said, only a cynic, who pities nobody but himself, will try to justify the killing of the innocent.

The tragedy of communism was and is rooted in the fact that all too often diehard egoists with beastly hearts incapable of any empathy have posed as defenders of Communist ideals. Never has a more abhorrent kind of egoism existed than that which grew in the field of struggle against individualism professing to defend the collectivist, socialist principles of life. Just think of the social and philosophical meaning of Stalinism. Has there ever been another time in history when so many human lives were sacrificed for the ambitions and craze for power of one criminal individual? Hardly so.

---

* Yuriy Karyakin is a prominent Soviet publicist and people's deputy of the USSR.

Left-wing dogmatists, those revolutionary radicals of various shades and intellectual powers, have never been collectivist-minded. As such, they have never been Communists, that is, people caring for the common weal. Each of them has been selfish for his or her own reasons but never out of a wish to help others or make lives better. No doubt about that.

One cannot consider himself or herself a Communist and a champion of human happiness while ruthlessly destroying the mainstays of life and urging millions of people to make meaningless sacrifices. Only the naive *Vekhi* philosophers, who appear to be out of this world just like all true believers in God, could think that revolutionary zealotry and left-wing extremism came from pious respect for the people, from a blind wish to sacrifice life and limb for workers and peasants. A revolutionary loving the people and caring for their future cannot step over the truth or facts. A Communist, just like anyone else, can make mistakes and believe in the illusions of his or her time. Like anyone else, Communists are powerless to foretell the future or foresee all the consequences of their decisions and actions; they are unable to resist the devilish temptation to make goodness immortal. But they have no right to ignore the knowledge already gained for their covert passion.

Leftists are unwilling to stand on the firm soil of reality for the simple reason that they find it boring. They are not interested in delving in details, facts, in the economy. "A madman, he searches for a tempest," trying to keep public and political life on the brink of an explosion when people like him or her are very much needed.

Revolutionary dogmatism, revolutionary radicalism is based on the most dangerous kind of egoism known in human history, which bears out the beast in a human being. This is intellectual, jesuitical egoism, "an ambition to impose one's views on the world," impose one's ideas about human values. As the noted Soviet historian S. Averintsev has observed, "Any utopianism means that a certain type of values, which empirically are not universal values, are made binding on all."[30] Egoism shows itself in a striving to keep revolution and public life in a condition that suits the leftist dogmatist and accords with his or her character. This enables them to conceal their weaknesses while parading their merits. In this case, egoism and self-centered interests are not necessarily aimed at gaining more of the benefits and comforts of life, despite the fact that following the revolution all preachers of a shared, Communist life ensconced themselves at private *dachas* (summer houses in the countryside) in Serebryanny Bor. Even such a mighty stimulus as the opportunity of grabbing attention or hard-won power is not basic to a radical's intentions. Leftists are motivated first of all by a desire to recarve people's lives to their own yardstick and impose their own values and their ideas about goodness and evil and the laws of history. Leftists make a religion of persuading others that they have accurately defined the laws and values of life and that their criteria of life are the authentic, universal ones.

Perhaps Trotsky strove for permanent revolution just because he could not live any more without rallies and assemblies or could not visualize his political future without being able to boss people around and decide their lives. Who knows? Anyway, to understand the reasons for his revolutionary intolerance is not so easy as it might seem at first glance.

Unfortunately, Stalin's mystery died with him, and we will never know what he really thought of himself, the party, the world, or the kind of socialism he was building. Apparently, this is a loss, too, as even the vilest and ugliest soul is still a human soul. It would be a very useful thing to know what this sort of man feels when he passes death verdicts on individuals, classes, and even whole nations. Indeed, the omnipotence of revolution that fell into Stalin's hands for no particular merit of his own corrupted him absolutely. But this was also his protest against the entire world, entire humanity, and everything that had been built up over millennia. What was it that angered him and made him revolt against his nature? After all, every angry boy rising to omnipotence will not dare to commit evil on a global scale. Perhaps, that was a mediocrity's revolt to avenge itself for being a nonentity.

Left-wing radicals think it exceptionally important to sustain the "awesome revolutionary zeal" of the masses and their flat rejection of all things old. That is why in all phases of our progress along the socialist road, left-wing radicals have always been opposed to any national accord or any reconciliation with whatever they denied the right to exist. What irritates them most of all, quite naturally, is the daily running of the economy and serious talk on how best to organize production. They are put out by these things as they remind these radicals of their vain efforts to "get rid of the past" and of the "ideology of economism." They remind them about the existence of eternal and insuperable economic laws and about things immune to their revolutionary willfulness. So in their capacity as leaders, ideologists, or theorists, they try to do everything possible and impossible for people to stay at high frontiers of revolutionary, messianic abstraction and historical obedience and never set foot on the soil of concrete economic facts, comparisons, and practical interests. The latter things annoy them as they constantly expose their Communist utopias, dogmatic illusions, and propaganda of success and prove them inadequately fit for competent leadership and conscious, serious work. Hence, their desire to impose a moral and purely emotional approach to the economy and keep public awareness at the level of simple, moral indignation about some people being rich and others poor and about so much injustice in the world. As a rule, their reasoning never goes beyond the limits of general, abstract comparisons between socialism and capitalism. They are unaware of facts, blind to things that exist, and unable to face the truth. Still more important, they do not have the slightest idea about the specific problems attending a transition from the old society to the new.

It appeared at one time that there was no way of extricating left-wing dogma from its social seedbed, the intolerance and embitterment of the oppressed and the humiliated. But now left-wing dogmatism obviously can do without broad social support and exist as a sect of gloomy and aggressive individuals, who very often prove to be bad learners or overall failures. What holds them together is their common fear of new conditions of production and life and their satanic yearning to bring the social environment into line with their ill temper. They try to prove that rejection of well-being, of a normal life and of normal human contact, along with denunciation and malice, is indeed the rule of life. They try to prove that they have lived in probity, while all the others have lived in "petit-bourgeois" sin.

Today, in conditions of perestroika when many of the left-wing Communist myths have collapsed, the champions of "Communist purity" who used to terrorize our social thought clearly include many sickly people afflicted by congenital jesuitry and prepared to torture others for the simple reason that their own internal disarray has tortured them all their lives. Stalin might have been this kind of self-torturing Jesuit. Little wonder, he is revered by the same type of people. In this case we are faced with a highly complicated and insufficiently explored mechanism whereby an ideologist, a politician, or simply an activist arrives at an equilibrium within himself by distorting the world around him.

Usually, gloomy and reserved people opt for the rhetorical model of socialism based on command, prohibition, and "state sacrifice." In an effort to avoid thinking of their own failures and warped mentality, these sorts of theorists try to prove to themselves and others that they are the way all people are and that their own selves are typical of human nature. Just take a close look at the lives and mentalities of our present left-wing Notescals. What groups them together is the absence of any strong links with the world at large, with the substance of human life.

As a rule, our opponents of economic incentives and people's material comforts, who so much hate "personal benefit," so-called material acquisition, and "the narrow circle of a cozy home," have lost all hope of enjoying life as all normal people do. More often than not, their malice is like a narcotic drug that helps them forget about the present and become engrossed in the "mortal struggle" of the two worlds and the two ideologies. Hence, their nostalgia for the time when "millions were on the crest," having abandoned their daily work and cares. Our leftists today are simply bored with their lives, bored with their routine work, bored with raising children and improving themselves. To them, life that makes its measured progress from childhood to old age, with all the human joys and cares, is like routine, like trudging along in a rut—a choice an outstanding personality cannot take. They feel uncomfortable in this time and want to compress it and break it up. Like the Notescals of the 1920s, they call it all getting nowhere, sliding back into capitalism, and betraying the cause of the revolution. They dream of great transformations taking us much closer to communism. They dream of commanding new battles and creating a new and unprecedented history in which they will leave "their own traces."

NOTES

1. *Smena Vekh* (Changing the Landmarks) (Prague, 1929), 32.
2. Yu. V. Klyuchnikov, *Smena Vekh* (Prague, 1921), 36.
3. A. Rybakov, *The Children of Arbat* (Moscow: Khudozhesvennaya Literatura, 1988).
4. P. Ya. Chaadayev, *Articles and Letters* (Moscow: Mysl Publishers, 1987).
5. P. Ya. Chaadayev, "A Letter from Ardatov to Paris," in *Articles and Letters* (Moscow: Mysl Publishers, 1987).
6. P. Ya. Chaadayev, *Articles and Letters*, 38–39.
7. N. V. Ustrelov, *Smena Vekh* (Prague, 1921), 94.
8. A. Blok, *Intelligentsia and Revolution* (Moscow: Khudozhesvennaya Literatura, 1972), 5:399.
9. Marx and Engels, *Collected Works* (Moscow: Progress Publishers, 1988), 4:14; 23:545.
10. Trotsky, *My Life*, 1:153.
11. V. Frige, "Poetry of the Iron Race"(in Russian), *Vestnik zhizni*, 1918, no. 2:29–30.
12. Trotsky, *My Life* 2:192.
13. V. Stanishevsky, "The Paris Commune in History and Literature," *Vestnik zhizni*, 1919, no. 3:49.
14. N. V. Gogol, *Collected Works* (in Russian) (Moscow: Khudozhestvennaya Literatura, 1978), 6:285.
15. "Vekhi: Collected articles on the Russian intelligentsia" (Moscow, 1909), 41.
16. V. I. Lenin, *Selected Works* (Moscow: Progress Publishers, 1966), 700.
17. F. I. Shaliapin, *The Mask and the Soul* (Moscow: Moscow Worker Publishers, 1989), 241.
18. *15th Conference of the All-Union Communist Party (Bolshevik), Steno Report* (in Russian) (Moscow-Leningrad: no publisher, 1927), 459
19. A. I. Hertzen, *Collected Works* (Moscow: Fiction Publishers, 1955), 2:11.
20. Marx and Engels, *Collected Works*, 3:296–97.
21. K. Marx and F. Engels, *Collected Works* (Moscow: Progress Publishers, 1975), 4:263.
22. V. I. Lenin, *Collected Works* (Moscow: Foreign Languages Publishing House, 1963), 1:391.
23. K. Marx and F. Engels, *Collected Works* (Moscow: Progress Publishers, 1988), 23:545.

24. Lev Trotsky, *The Permanent Revolution* (Berlin: Granat, 1931), 13.
25. Lev Trotsky, *My Life*, 137.
26. Y. Bondarev, "Pain and Hope," *Literaturnaya Gazeta*, June 22, 1988.
27. L. Trotsky, "Towards Socialism or Capitalism? (An analysis of the Soviet economy and its development trends)" (Gosudarstvennoye Izdatelstvo, 1926), 26–27.
28. An unpublished manuscript of a book about Stalin.
29. Quoted from V. Frige, "The Poetry of Iron Dew," in *A Harbinger of Life*, 1918, no. 2:29–30.
30. S. Averintsev, *Yunost*, 1988, no. 5:10.

CHAPTER 7

Humanity Cannot
Betray Its Nature

Crisis of the Idea of Total Control over Production

Certainly, leftist dogmatists still hold strong positions in our society. They deftly play on the egalitarian sentiments of the needy who are unprepared for systematic and highly skilled work and on the values and ideals of Communist romanticism. Yet, I am convinced, the long, seventy-year period of recurring leftist leaps is now a thing of the past. It is difficult to imagine someone taking another risk at reining Russia back into a kingdom of pure, noneconomic socialism.

The four perestroika years have uprooted the myths that used to nurture leftist dogmatism, especially the myth about completely socialized production and about the farmer turned an industrial worker.

Our fundamental advantage over the Communists, Marxists of the 1920s and 1930s, is that we have at last realized the natural and insurmountable limits to centralization and, in our case, to state control over production. For instance, our present positive attitude toward cooperation as a necessary and productive form of socialization of the means of production is based on the firm conviction that total state control over production is a wrong, and harmful, way of running the economy and ensuring economic growth. Now we know that total state control over production can be an effective and essential instrument, and in this sense a progressive step, only in the grueling conditions of war and the repulsion of foreign intervention.

In effect, complete centralization of economic decisions, complete and effective centralized control over lower economic structures, and, consequently, directly socialized work as conceived by Marx are impossible in principle. This is of crucial importance to a new understanding of the role of cooperation in socialist society.

This primary follows from the law on the transition of quantity into quality. The economic experience of socialism has shown that planning, centralization, and coordination of production operations on a scale typical of a large industrial factory cannot be reproduced on a national scale, especially in such a big nation as ours. The number of economic facilities cannot expand endlessly. Overstepping the reasonable limit of centralization in the field of economic decision making is bound to result in a steep decrease in the effectiveness, competence, and reliability of state control over the economy.

The logic is simple. The higher the centralization level of economic decision making, the further, in time and space, the subject of management from its object and the less knowledge about existing relationships and the content of economic processes being regulated. Supercentralization typical of existing socialism has resulted in a situation where economic decisions originate three or four (or even more) levels higher than the level at which information necessary for these decisions is actually available.

In the center of a socialist nation it is difficult to assess the specific daily requirements of people living in various other regions. Within a "rigid" production program planned in advance and handed down from above (and any plan is always burdened with the past), there is no way to react to changing market conditions and fluid demand. With the program being designed for several years and sometimes even decades, an even greater problem is that of reacting to scientific and technological progress and using its achievements in production.

Being far away from the target of decision making, all management bodies experience a chronic shortage of competence, and decision making turns into an exceptionally slow process. In these conditions, incompetence is not so much the result of the managers' personal qualities as the inevitable consequence of the existing mechanism of decision making.

The very nature of social and economic life has placed insuperable obstacles to the omnipotence of the center. Even when only a small percentage of the economic performance levels are planned on top, this work is too much for the planning bodies. The central bodies of the state just cannot control all the 500 billion economic links existing in society.

For this reason, as has become clear now, it is impossible in principle to ensure the economy against any spontaneity, that is, activities and actions that were not planned at the center. Considering modern production, the scientific and technological revolution, and the present mobility of producer and consumer needs, there is no way in principle to implement the concept of directly socialized work as absolute centralized control over production, a concept that up to now has been included by inertia in our manuals on political economy. Without a degree of spontaneity (i.e., the right to economic initiative not planned by state bodies), the development of production and the preservation of human civilization are altogether impossible.

Note that from the experience of War Communism Lenin realized the difficulty of ensuring state organization of production on a national scale by analogy with a large factory. Speaking at the 10th Congress of the RCP(B), Lenin said, "Theoretically speaking, state monopoly is not necessarily the best system from the standpoint of the interests of socialism. A system of taxation and free exchange can be employed as a transitional measure in a peasant country possessing an industry—if this industry is running—and if there is a certain quantity of goods available."[1] Yet, in this case, as the quotation indicates, Lenin linked the limit of state control over production primarily with Russia's specific conditions. He described total state control as "foolish and suicidal" because it was "economically impossible" given the existence of millions of small-time producers.[2]

The present understanding of the role of cooperation and small-time private production in socialist society stems from another kind of criticism of illusions about state monopoly over production. As he criticized "a blind faith in the omnipotence of management" at a Plenary Meeting of the CPSU Central Committee in June 1986, Mikhail Gorbachev said that in the present conditions it was inadmissible—and practically impossible—to solve all questions at the center.[3]

Now what is of *crucial importance in the present stage of socialist development?* An objective obstacle to total state control over production and the omnipotence of plans and directives is human nature and the mentality of men and women as intellectual beings. As the development experience of our country has shown—and so has the experience of all other socialist countries that have adopted our supercentralized, command system of economic management—state control over national production is bound to result in a disastrous collapse of economic initiative at the grass-roots level, in the growth of apathy and indifference in society, and in reduced responsibility for the results of one's work and the state of the economy at all levels. So far none of the socialist nations has succeeded in stimulating good work and encouraging professional excellence in the state sector. Full employment, a spin-off of state control over production, suddenly made workers less interested in the results of their work. In the words of the Polish sociologist Jan Szczepanski, it has led people to realize that "in this social system one can make a living without working or by pretending to work. It is a fact that employment is not synonymous with 'work' in the precise meaning of the word."[4]

The very idea of direct and complete subordination of people's work to the instructions of a centralized plan is fraught with a trend toward curtailing people's economic activity. In conditions when all aspects of economic life, including each production operation, are programmed by a system of approved standards (quality, costs, etc.), any producer's initiative is out of the question. He or she becomes a pure operator divorced from all creative and socially important functions, such as an artisan's or a farmer's independence in work, planning, supervision, and use of the products created. Total state control over production, which is stipulated by the mechanical concept of directly socialized work, dramatically reduces the field for creativity, democratic involvement and, in general, for the intellectual development of a personality. It is now perfectly obvious that under state-controlled socialism based on command it is impossible to achieve the main social objectives of socialism, that is, pave the way for people's creative work and effective self-expression. The ideology of total control over the producer is incompatible with the ideology of all-around and harmonious development of a personality.

Certainly, in the conditions of simple machine production of the nineteenth century when the concept of directly socialized work was formulated, all the negative consequences of a centrally controlled economy were not so evident. Furthermore, Engels viewed the ascendancy of the machine over the worker and the worker losing his or her freedom and creativity at work as a norm and inevitable payment for economic and technical progress.[5]

Then, in the last thirty years of the nineteenth century, one could not discern all the aspects of the profound antagonism between the nature and the main social requirements of human beings and their role as a cog, a part of socially needed work to which the industrial system had relegated humanity. For the same reason, many of the now obvious advantages of individual and family work in farming and the advantages of agrarian work over industrial work were underestimated. But now that creativity becomes an acute necessity, what with the growth of educational standards and with the unprecedented mobility of human needs, total control over production turns into a flagrant anachronism.

One of the worst negative consequences is that ordinary workers, who make up a vast majority of the population, have lost all sense of responsibility for the state of production and the economy as a whole. When even a factory manager cannot decide anything, when there is no choice to make, no sense of responsibility can appear. As a result, mistrust in the value of initiative spreads at all levels, from top to bottom. At the same time lumpen sentiments, sponging, and illusions about all-powerful state bodies that supposedly can either raise or lower living standards at will, grow, and they grow especially among the less-skilled workers.*

Hence, people underestimate their own initiative, effort, work, and personal dignity.

Clearly now, supercentralization ultimately destroys whatever remains of the self-established economic democracy. Thereby, it deprives people of the opportunity to work effectively and deprives society of the opportunity to function normally. Without people's initiative, without initiative as such, no horizontal ties whatever can form in society. Therefore, state-controlled socialism deprives itself of extremely necessary, horizontal ties in production that make for economic stability in general. An economy based on indirect ties, that is, an economy in which all ties between individual enterprises pass through the top of the pyramid, is an immobile one, and its effectiveness entirely depends on the state of the upper structure. The absence of natural horizontal ties causes as much harm to the social climate.

Politicians and economists in the European socialist nations are agreed that the unwarranted centralization of property and production, coupled with the fallacious policy of total state control over industrial production, was the chief reason for the drop in social production growth rates at the turn of the 1980s, the inadequate improvement in the standards of living in their countries, the growth of bureaucracy in economic management, and the deteriorating moral standards. The same factors are viewed as the cause of the chronic shortfalls in essential supplies and the ever-widening lag in the technological race with the industrialized capitalist nations. Most of basic industry in these socialist countries is operating at a loss and is subsidized.

Supercentralization has caused the swelling of the state apparatus and the growth of nonproductive costs. At the same time the overwhelming majority of workers have grown ever more apathetic and indifferent to work as they have lost the right to supervise production and decide how

---

* "Out of the ideological concepts of the past decades we have inherited a view of the state which belongs to monarchic mentality rather than socialist mentality. It is a view whereby the state is a kind of boss, or rather a leader standing at the top of the state machinery, a boss who can rain the people with favors once he is begged to do so" (O. Latsis, *Izvestia*, April 15, 1987).

the products they create are to be used. Even more important, an economy under total state control, like no other economy in human history, has proven susceptible to arbitrary decisions and economic adventurism.

State control of the nationalized means of production based on command has failed to restore the sense of ownership that the workers forfeited under capitalism. State-controlled socialism has never solved the problem of ownership of public property. It has not found a party involved in economic affairs that would not only own property but bear economic and political responsibility before society for the economic decisions it adopts. Ownership of property still remains anonymous. In the obtaining conditions, enterprises turn into an appendix of the state's administrative bodies at various levels. State control over production results in a situation where administrative bodies supervise all economic activities by enterprises. This easily leads to bureaucracy, blind commanding, and violations of objective economic laws. Instead of earlier forms of alienation from the means of production, new ones have appeared, of a different social and psychological nature. Whereas previously the means of production were viewed as *"somebody else's," "the boss's,"* now they are viewed as *"nobody's,"* as *"abandoned property."* Being *"nobody's,"* ever more socialist property has been stolen in all countries of the socialist community. The economies of all socialist countries have suffered from theft. At the same time, the gap between the interests of the workers and managements has widened. In an administrative system, the manager is accountable only to the state's economic bodies and is exempt from any economic and political responsibility before the employees. For this reason factory managers in all socialist nations have had to act on instructions from superior administrative bodies irrespective of how economically valid and expedient these instructions may be. Their well-being under this system did not depend on the economic performance of the enterprise and their salaries were not affected even if the enterprise had suffered serious damage from an instruction handed from above.

All these factors, especially the absence of levers to monitor management's actions, led the workers to see the means of production as belonging to nobody, at least not to them. Naturally, they lacked any motivation for productive work, initiative, and creativity.

Another factor contributing to inertia and passivity, rooted in the idea of directly socialized work, was and remains the monopoly of individual enterprises to produce some specific items. To date, this monopoly has generated commodity scarcities in all the socialist nations without exception. The scarcities, in turn, have made the manufacturers uninterested in improving product quality. As a result, the quality of products has deteriorated, and they have become less and less competitive in the world market.

The directive system of management, as has now become clear, fails to provide any stimuli for economic self-growth and for scientific and technological progress. State monopoly and total nationalization, far from opening up the floodgates to scientific and technological progress, in which Kautsky and Hilferding* sacredly believed, in effect block it in most cases, as experience has shown.

In the opinion of F. Burlatsky, a noted Soviet political scientist, the reason lies in the structure of economic management, which is susceptible to arbitrary decisions from the center or is devoid of a mechanism to resist economic voluntarism. He writes,

Technological and technical stagnation is the punishment for this. Inside the system itself there were no stimuli encouraging continuous technological renewal, the introduction of new machinery, or ongoing progress. Built on an "order-execution" principle, this economy had difficulty coping with the economic plans drawn up on top. It had neither the reserves, nor the material resources, nor even the motivation to ensure ongoing technological modernization and achieve higher productivity of labor.

What novelties of science and technology should be implemented? And how to do this? As a rule, a plan handed down from above fails to envisage technological renewal: this renewal is bound to interfere with the attainment of current objectives as it involves the restructuring of technology and management. In this case the only solution is to look over the fence to other countries that are more scientifically and technologically developed. For decades the chief stimuli for technological progress have come from abroad.[6]

We must admit, however, that the idea of total state control over production has suffered the worst defeat in the agrarian sector. In agriculture, the state model of organization of production particularly reveals its mechanistic and inhumane nature. Our experience of state-controlled organization of production, which is a little less than sixty years old, has graphically shown that this is no way to keep the farmer attached to the land. It has failed to ensure steady growth of farm output and to resolve the food problem that resulted from the excesses of collectivization. For many a decade, our country, which accounts for much of the world's plowland, including black soil (150 million hectares), has had to buy half the grain it needs from other countries.[7] Over the last four five-year-

---

* Karl Kautsky (1854–1938) was one of the leaders and founders of the German Social Democratic movement and the 2d International.

Rudolf Hilferding (1877–1941) was a prominent economist and one of the founders of the 2d International.

plan periods, sizable capital investments into the agrarian sector have failed to produce any tangible growth of farm output, which has remained lower than population growth rates all these years. For dozens of years, milk yields per cow have remained frozen at 2,000 kilograms a year. Such is the situation in the Smolensk, Bryansk, Ivanovo, Volgograd, Saratov, Orenburg, and some other regions.

State control over farm work as applied in the USSR, far from strengthening the agrarian sector of socialism as Trotsky and Stalin hoped it would, has in effect eroded it. Large-scale, state-controlled farm production has destroyed all personal motivation for good work, the ultimate result being the erosion of the Russian peasantry. Many factors contributed to this, including the famines of the early 1930s and the latter half of the 1940s, which carried off millions of lives, and the forcible uprooting of the better-off and more knowledgeable peasants and their families. This caused considerable "losses" of the best gene pools of the peoples of Russia, especially the Russians and the Ukrainians.

And yet, the worst damage to agriculture was caused by the state-controlled, bureaucratic organization of farm production that deprived farmers of independence in their work and destroyed family land-use patterns that had evolved over the centuries. Once deprived of their independence, that is, the right to creative endeavor and responsibility and the right to their own produce, the farmers lost interest in their work. Several generations of rural people have now grown up without any idea of how to care for the land. In effect, they need nothing at all—land or cattle or even the houses in which they were born. No love of land is possible without the right to work it independently. In the words of the writer Vasili Belov, country people can be creators only if they are free to do as they please, that is, only when they are not bossed around or taught how to do the plowing and what to sow or given another unwanted instruction. Still more important, "freedom is not at all freedom from the land. . . . Freedom of action without the land and the home is empty, bogus freedom."[8]

Following the coercion and the recurring surplus appropriation of the 1930s, mass exodus from the countryside has continued for over fifty years, exodus from the forced, unfree work. Hence, the depopulation of the countryside, especially the non-black-soil region, and the abandoned villages and fields.

Clearly now, the idea of organizing farm work on a national scale on the same footing as the state-owned railways was an out-and-out pipedream. It contradicted the nature of agricultural work and was totally divorced from the concrete conditions of farm production. On the whole, the attempts of state-controlled socialism to mechanistically implant the production methods of basic industry in agriculture proved to be an oversight and a blunder.

The blunder was due to the fact that the specific nature of farm work, which is substantially different from factory work, was underestimated. Unlike the industrial worker, the farmer deals with living nature, which dictates the rhythm of human work and greater human involvement in this work. Detailed specialization from operation to operation typical of industry is unnatural for stock breeding and crop growing. Base pay rates cannot be applied in agriculture, for until the harvest has been taken in, the quality of any particular operation cannot be judged. The process of life, being whole and indivisible, requires the wholeness of farm work. The nature of farm work involves personal responsibility for the entire production process up to harvesting, with one farmer having to do many different operations, and with one group doing its work independently of another. The wholeness of farm work requires greater self-control than the work of an industrial worker. Farm work is done on a large territory, hence it is more difficult to monitor with the help of another person, a superintendent, or a quality inspector. Likewise, monitoring the amount, quality, and technology of farm work is difficult.

Consequently, farm work, being more whole than the work of an industrial worker, requires more conditions for self-control and self-organization. By its nature, it is incompatible with "external care," pettifogging regulation, and rigid centralized control. The farmer alone must decide the work to be done on any particular day. And this requires economic independence, which clears the way for a more rational strategy of economic development.

The Soviet agrarian scientist V. Bashmachnikov has amply shown in his articles that when Stalin substituted his collectivization for Lenin's theory of cooperation, he, in effect, substituted metaphysics for dialectics. Essentially, all the philosophers and political economists who, from the 1930s to the mid-1980s, insisted on direct socialization of farm production on the factory model were entrapped in metaphysical set schemes. They all, writes V. Bashmachnikov, failed to grasp the socioeconomic content of a transition from small-time farm production to large-scale collective production. They spread some of the economic laws and principles to the agrarian sector without considering its specific conditions. They never learned the dialectic relationship between socialist and nonsocialist forms of organization of production. "Only ours" or "not ours at all" was how they understood the problem. This approach resulted in great losses in agriculture and prevented the experience the countryside had accumulated over the centuries from being used.[9]

We must say that our earlier unwillingness to consider the specific nature of farm work and get at the root of the problem stemmed in a very large measure from our erstwhile theoretical boorishness and our barbaric attitude toward the social knowledge gained. And we must know that it was Kautsky who had done a lot to update the Marxist agrarian program—a fact acknowledged by Lenin. Kautsky was one of the first Marxists to say that agriculture heavily depended on what we now call the human factor and that it presupposed

intelligence, independence and interest in the process of work without which successful application of modern technology and science in agriculture is even less possible than in industry. For, contrary to the factory with its unchanging and ever equal conditions always requiring the same manipulations, agriculture deals with nature and its quickly changing conditions to which we only have to adjust machines and modern farming methods.[10]

The present comeback of cooperatives and pluralistic views about the socialist economy is closely linked with recognition of the specific and complex nature of farm work. The more evidence we obtained proving it impossible to build a total economy with total centralization and concentration, the more often we turned our gaze to such natural and simple forms of collectivity as voluntary cooperation. This was the case in the early 1920s when we moved from the policy of War Communism to the New Economic Policy. Symptomatically, the reason why cooperation was rehabilitated in the early 1920s was, again, the crisis of the idea of total state monopoly, the crisis of the military methods of organizing production based on mobilization.

But, unlike the 1920s, today we have much greater insight into the reasons for the cooperative organization of socialism and for the preservation of individual and group forms of property on a large scale. At least now we have irrefutable proof to the effect that the economic and social potentialities of small-time forms of farm work, especially family work, remain untapped. This is a great stride from the way the problem was understood in the Marxist literature of the last thirty years of the 1800s. It is a breakthrough in the agrarian concept of Marxism, and this should be as clear as daylight.

It has now been recognized that cooperation, which links the interests of the family with those of all of society—cooperation in various forms and, more important, voluntary cooperation—must prevail in the countryside. Our agricultural experience, far from refuting, has proved correct the proposal of V. Chayanov (a prominent Russian agrarian specialist who fell prey to Stalin's repressions in 1937) to the effect that the cooperative form of expanded and socialized production must grow from small-time, family production; it must build on it, not destroy it.

In all these cases the chief argument in support of cooperation is that it provides more independence at work and better suits the mentality of a normal, healthy individual. The "rehabilitation" of the human factor and the basic social needs and motivation for work, occurring in the present stage of socialist development, has brought about a new and more realistic approach to the role of cooperation within the framework of a Communist formation. The thing is that much more can be done to realize the social ideal of Marxism under voluntary cooperation than under state-controlled organization of production.

Not surprisingly, in the present conditions of perestroika, more enterprising, creative, and better-skilled individuals prefer to work in cooperatives. Today we acknowledge the need to preserve and promote cooperation by referring to a new kind of "mentality" and new cultural and intellectual values. Whereas in the past, cooperation was associated with an inadequate level of civilization and with inert and patriarchal mentality, now it is linked with people wanting to be more independent in their work (thanks to their increased cultural standards resulting from our educational policy) and with their desire to come into their own in production, bear material responsibility for it, and influence its organization. As educational standards in socialist society have grown and more people have been trained for highly skilled and creative work, the practice and ideology of total state control of public life have increasingly been rejected and more interest has been shown in less formal organization of collective work. Recent press stories about cooperative ventures indicate that people prefer smaller enterprises, as these ensure more independence at work, more sense of "authorship," and better conditions to apply their skills. As a rule, top professionals seeking more opportunities for creative self-realization are setting up cooperatives. They seem to tell the truth when they say they are more interested in achieving independence in their work and showing initiative and expertise than in earning high wages.

These publications also suggest a new area of research into the reasons why cooperation has retained its stability and why society still needs it. The latest Communist party documents have emphasized the necessity of paying greater heed to the psychological aspects of production. Obviously, it is time to study the socialist-tested forms of organization of work and production management in the context of the mentality of economic creativity and the main social needs of humanity as a genus.

Yet, from a philosophical standpoint, nothing is unexpected in our present reappraisal of the social merits of cooperation. The earlier political economy of socialism simply failed to verify its tenets against such social realities as human mentality, the sociopsychological constitution of human beings, and their main generic needs. The conceptual crisis of socialism as one big factory only proved the fundamental principles of humanism to be correct. It has reaffirmed the creative nature of humanity. Under no circumstances will the individual agree to be a cog of the industrial system but will always strive for work granting him or her more independence and more opportunities for creative endeavor and self-realization. Individuals will not opt for complete determination and pre-set conditions of work, or even for equal remuneration. They can hardly bear to be a cog even if convinced that this is something justified and useful. Individuals strive to retain the right to their own initiative, competition, and certain autonomy. That is why, consciously or instinctively, humans resist despotic patterns of work that leave no room for initiative. An unskilled worker serving conveyer-belt production is forced to put up with the loss of work autonomy. Under certain, extreme conditions the whole of society may put up with it, as well as with egalitarian distribution. But the system of total state regulation, even if society may have to accept it for some time out of historical necessity, still remains an unnatural thing.

Once there is no way in principle to build all production management vertically, from the center, it is desirable to keep the various self-regulatory economic entities capable of creating the horizontal ties society needs. Inter alia, a cooperative as a self-sustained organization can quickly react to a deficit of horizontal economic ties.

The ideologists of the cooperative movement in Russia in the early 1900s realized that "the advantages that large-scale production and updated technology yield in agriculture are not so great as the advantages that they produce in industry. Small and technically weak farms can put up great resistance to their larger competitors, which is totally impossible in industry." For this reason, said A. Chayanov, "whenever cooperation becomes sufficiently firm and strong in our socialist state, it will be entrusted with more and more areas of economic work in the countryside that was previously done by the state apparatus consisting of specialists and employees appointed by the centre."[11]

Rehabilitation of the Land and the Farmer

All in all, one can say that the present reassessment of values is primarily due to the humanization of our social thinking and the overcoming of a series of atavisms that we now call vulgar, simplified interpretations of class consciousness. The rehabilitation of cooperation is closely linked with the rehabilitation of the farmer and with recognition of many social advantages of farm work over industrial work. Recognition of the farmers' right to voluntary cooperation amounts to recognition of their social and political autonomy, that is, their right to decide their economic strategy independently. This is bound to undermine a great many stereotypes evolving Marxism over the past century in evaluating the social qualities of the farmers and the role of their culture in the progress of human civilization.

In this context, the current reassessment of the crucial role that the farmers and the agrarian sector play in society is particularly important. To my mind, the decisions of the 19th Communist Party Conference signaled a breakthrough. For the first time in CPSU history, a party forum called for facing life as it is and understanding that in such a country as ours general well-being depended first of all on the prosperity of the countryside and that, as long as our fields produced scanty harvests and the countryside remained desolate, we would never become a healthy society or win prestige in the world.

It is now clear as never before that many of our present problems result from a perfunctory attitude to the agrarian sector, from the old enmity of city toward country fueled by dogmatic Marxism, and from the fact that we disfranchised the peasants and entrusted the working class with organizing farm work.

Persistent comparisons between the industrial working class as being progressive by its nature and what dogmatic Marxists viewed as the ingrained conservatism of the propertied peasantry made it possible to portray the forcible collectivization as a great, blessed undertaking freeing the peasant from the scourge of private property.

For this reason there was no way to revert to common sense, the history-tested forms of farm work, and the centuries-old experience without social and humanitarian rehabilitation of the farmers as one of the pillars of human culture and civilization. As soon as the point came home to us, we realized there was no political or social or, even less, economic need to turn the peasant into a worker, that is, destroy the specific socialization of the peasants that took centuries to evolve. Obviously now, the thesis on the social, economic, and political reforming of the peasantry as formulated in the early 1800s by Fourier, Saint-Simon, and Owen, and later by Marx, was a great delusion of modern social science bearing out its superficial attitude to the agrarian problem and, in general, to the preservation of life.

We have now realized that, in addition to the problem of obliterating the distinctions between the workers and the farmers that dominated the minds of the pioneers of the new society, other problems exist, for example, protecting the environment, the family, life, human motivation for good work, effective and rational organization of work, and society's ability for innovation, and curbing beastly instincts in humanity.

Take a look at the social communities of different classes from the standpoint of all the problems of the world and life that have presented themselves to us and you will become convinced that the previous distribution of rights and duties between them was an unjust one.

Indeed, Marx was proved perfectly correct to say that the peasantry could not play an independent role in a socialist revolution.

But the peasantry's inability to be a leading force in revolution did not at all mean that it needed working-class patronage in all matters: how to organize production or how to organize their lives. People like Davydov, a character in M. A. Sholokhov's novel *Virgin Soil Upturned*, could teach the peasant how to deal with the kulak, how to start cultural education, and how to cope with illiteracy, but they could not and had no right to teach the peasant how to work his or her fields or grow crops.

I think that humanism, or more precisely the depth and wisdom of the social mentality of perestroika, has particularly manifested itself in our present attitude toward the farmers and their social qualities. We have come to see many merits of this central figure of agricultural production. V. Bashmachnikov, who was mentioned earlier, lists these social qualities as follows: the relatively broad universal nature of a farmer's knowledge and work skills; on the one hand, caution and prudence in using the land and other natural resources (i.e., a certain conservatism, combined with gumption and an ability to readjust production to changing conditions in a flexible and creative manner), and on the other hand, thrift, frugality, and a measure of stinginess in anticipation of hard times (i.e., harvest failure), combined with a readiness to help out the neighbor; individualism as expressed in a striving to have "his own" business and "her own" production facilities, combined with a readiness for team, communal cooperation. V. Bashmachnikov writes,

The specific nature of agriculture requires that the farmer show great responsibility, care, persistence and readiness to peg away at his work under any circumstances, in disregarding time and strain. For this reason the farmer is so often called a "toiler." Farm work is a "toil" not so much because of physical conditions as because of permanent creative strain.[12]

We must admit now that our previous, so-called class approach to the peasantry, which dominated our political consciousness for decades, was a one-sided one. In the past we Marxists viewed the peasant only from one angle (i.e., how interested he or she was in abolishing private property and socializing the means of production). And since, unlike the working class and the progressive-minded intellectuals, peasants had the least interest in socializing work on a national scale, they used to be regarded as the lowest class on the ladder of political virtues. This interpretation of the "class approach" ignored the problem of preservation and reproduction of life and also the peasantry's decisive role in securing these vital conditions for human civilization, including the vital conditions for ensuring a future socialist approach on the part of the working class. More important, that parochial approach underestimated the moral, cultural, and civilizing significance of peasant socialization, especially the peasant's rationalism and attachment to land.

We have suffered from our old, utopian view of the world in which there was no room either for the peasant as an owner of the means of production or peasant culture or love of land.

Clearly now, Stalin's postulate about the unavoidably "petit-bourgeois" nature of the peasantry under any conditions was indeed the main obstacle to developing a rational domestic policy. It was the root cause of the famines that carried off millions of lives and of the eternal food shortages that have marred the lives of several generations of Soviet people.

But, of course, the roots of this political discrimination against the peasantry go deeper, just like the roots of socialism. They are based on the earlier habit, which goes back to nineteenth-century Marxism, of hooking progress to a simplification of social and economic structures and to a growth of likeness and uniformity and on the belief that history is headed for an ultimately ideal state, a kingdom of world brotherhood of all working people.

The negative attitude toward the peasant and any small-time producer in general was generated by the faith in pure, noncommodity socialism, a society in which large-scale socialized production would oust all other forms of work organization, especially small-time production, in which all distinctions between the peasant and the worker, the wheelbarrow pusher and the architect would die out, and in which new moral stimuli would defeat a peasant's traditional interest in work.

Stalin's doctrines were indeed based on consistent logic strictly conforming to the philosophy of pure socialism. In his mind, just as in the minds of many other representatives of the old guard, the concept of the market merged with that of capitalism. Therefore, anything burdened with the market and free trade, especially the free peasant as a property owner, was viewed as a capitalist vice and as the last, most widespread, and, consequently, most dangerous obstacle on the road to a kingdom of pure socialism.

Hence the pervasive feature of Stalin's writings—and those by Trotsky, Zinoviev, Kamenev, and Plekhanov—of using Christian, church motifs to describe a propertied peasant as a devil, a tempter trying to mislead the "pure," "clean" working class and plunge history and society back into the scourge of private property.

Note well: None of those party leaders, none of the party's recognized theorists—Preobrazhensky, Goltsman, Kritsman, Larin, or Pyatakov—would talk of the Russian peasant just as a man who had his family, his children, and his special interests. In the latter half of the 1920s, when Bukharin and Dzerzhinsky tried to explain to them that most of the so-called kulaks were poor people wearing shabby clothes and eating scanty meals and that there was nothing more in their lives than strenuous, backbreaking work, the theorists of pure noncommodity socialism accused them of being populist-minded and unable to rise to a scientific, politico-economic view of the world.

The peasant, like the artisan, was invariably viewed as a social force, a carrier of some social impetus, objectively hindering the progress of history and the salvation of the human race.

Hence the attitude toward classes associated with the market as antichrists and renegades standing in the way of the true faith. Hence the conviction that any humanity that fails to accord with this law of historical progress toward a class-free society is not true humanity but transient humanity, that is, something untrue.

Just as the crusaders did not observe the conventions of standard morality when they dealt with pagans, the believers in the early triumph of a universal kingdom of pure noncommodity socialism felt no restraint when they dealt with the propertied peasantry, that is, the overwhelming majority of Russia's population.

Now we understand there are no perfectly virtuous or utterly inferior classes. Those who pray for the working class as if it were an icon more often than not prove insincere people, politicos. By the way, the working class has always felt this insincerity and realized the true reasons for servility to itself.

The beliefs that many of the present publicists continue to preach are clearly out of date. On the one hand, they are appealing for economic reform and the development of money-commodity relations. But on the other, they are trying morally and ideologically to discredit commodity producers, the classes that created human civilization. The socialist romantics of the nineteenth century were at least integral and consistent persons. They believed in the extinction of commodity production and, therefore, sincerely hated the petty commodity producer.

We, however, have never set our world outlooks in order. On the one hand, we justly condemn Stalin for destroying the productive forces of the countryside and ruining the nation's gene pool, and on the other, we are putting Stalinist labels on the farmers and trying to make them wholly responsible for the economic adventurism of the 1930s, for the repressions, for the abhorrent victims of arbitrary rule, and for our own troubles.

It is impossible, at least in one essay, to draw on both mutually exclusive world outlooks.

The first attempts to see the world as it is and embrace all the fundamental problems of reproduction of life in their unity. It was formed through an analysis of the reasons for our economic failures. Consequently, it sets particular store by the social prerequisites of effective work, expertise, and motivation for work.

Under this approach to public life, which condemns violence against the countryside, peasant socialization is understood as an inseparable part of human culture and a major achievement of human civilization.

The other paradigm, which views the peasantry as the cause of the leftist leaps, reflects the earlier one-sided and simplified attitude both to social life and to human history. In this case the production approach to life is replaced by egalitarianism and normative sociology. All social phenomena are judged only according to their ability to serve the designs of history and promote rapid progress toward a class-free and noncommodity society. Social and political appraisals within this conceptual framework are based on very simple logic. Whatever helps to speed up the destruction of private property is considered a good thing, and anything hindering the early advent of a kingdom of universal equality is frowned upon. In this case, the worst treatment is meted out to the peasant and the artisan, for they constitute the last obstacle to the final abolition of private, individual work and are particularly attached to private property. This is a normative approach since neither the Marxist classics nor we have ever collected exhaustive factual evidence about the possibility of starting large-scale farm production on a nonprivate, collective basis and, therefore, of achieving noncommodity socialism.

I think all the present attempts to blame the Russian peasant for the tragedies and leftist excesses of our socialist history constitute a relapse into the earlier normative, sociologically vulgar attitude toward history. Purposefully or not, all this vague talk of the peasantry as a land mine that the working-class, socialist revolution may hit at any moment justifies Stalin's violence against the Russian farmers. Ideologically, it stays within the limits of Stalin's speech at a Plenary Meeting in April 1929 when he argued for the need to incite class struggle in the village. For if the proprietary or patriarchal village had indeed been the chief enemy of progress and socialism, Stalin had done a great thing by destroying family farm work, by destroying the peasants' *we*.

Let us be realists. Could Ignashka Sapronov, the character of Vasili Belov's novel *Kanuny*, or the social type of the village he represented, influence the party captains' decisions? Hardly so. The share of village people in the party in the 1920s was negligible. The Central Committee's Political Report to the 14th Congress stated,

As for the share of village people in our Party, things appear rather unseemly. By the 13th Congress, the rural population aged from 18 to 60 years totalled 54 million and by the 14th Congress, over 54 million. By the 13th Congress, there were 136,000 communists in the village, i.e., 0.26% of the adult rural population, and by the 14th Congress we have 202,000 peasants in the Party, i.e., 0.37%[13]

The peasant Communists' left-wing sentiments did not play any significant role in those years, not only because the peasants were a minority in the party (under one-quarter of all members), but because they enjoyed less say as Communists from among the peasants. They were first and foremost the carriers of party policy in the country. Compared with worker members of the party and especially with employee members, they wielded less influence on the political struggle, which focused on the cities. Keep in mind that everything in Russia had depended on what was going on in Petersburg and Moscow. After November 1917, when the *muzhik*, rifle in hand, voted for the Decree on Peace and for the Social Revolutionaries' "black reallotment" supported by the Bolsheviks,* he had no more possibility of *directly* influencing the political and economic decisions adopted by the socialist state.

Anyway, even if the egalitarian sentiments of the extremist-minded poor peasantry had been politically expressed, they would have resulted in nothing else than another campaign to strip the well-off peasants of their belongings. The egalitarian sentiments that did exist among the

---

* A *muzhik* is a Russian peasant, and the Decree on Peace was one of the first laws by the Soviet government proclaiming peace with other nations.

poorer groups of the peasantry did not as such produce a desire for collective farming.

To my mind, a farmer can never devise the idea of total socialization of all the means of production or total state control over the economy. All these ideas, which were basic to the left-wing sentiments of the 1930s, reflect a perfectly different kind of social experience: first of all, urban mentality.

Industrial workers can grasp the idea of state control over national production and its unification and standardization. At least, this idea has some bearing on the conditions of their lives and work. The idea of integral, one-dimensional production appeals even more to party ideologists, intellectuals who are accustomed to dealing with abstract and induced notions. Expansionism and the infinity of free discursive thinking are closely linked with each other. For this reason intellectuals, politicians who daily travel in a world of ideas and notions, can believe much more quickly in overstepping the limits of the has-been, the limits of the existing reality, than the peasant Ignashka Sapronov. Peasants can mutiny and play it off the cuff, but they cannot project a new mode of production fundamentally different from the one to which they are accustomed. In these matters, they are sooner reactionaries than revolutionaries. They are linked with life's matter, nature, more closely than intellectuals or industrial workers, and for this reason peasants are more sober-minded and more suspicious of all manner of innovations, such as Stalin's large grain factories.

We have now realized, or rather been led to realize by suffering, that our earlier barbaric attitude to the stronger representatives of peasant socialization caused as much damage to the mainstays of our social life as the mass destruction of what had remained of the traditional Russian intelligentsia. To my mind, the noted Soviet historian V. Dashichev is correct in drawing a parallel between the social nature of Stalin's reprisals against the intelligentsia, including the party and the military intelligentsia, and the forcible collectivization of the peasantry.*

---

* "Stalin was always hostile and suspicious toward the intelligentsia. He sabotaged Lenin's advice to enlist the efforts of bourgeois specialists for the building of socialism. He had ordered thousands of them to be shot in the Civil War years. Later he started mass-scale destruction of Soviet specialists. He is to blame for destroying 'the thin stratum of revolutionaries,' most of them intellectuals, who had led the October Revolution to victory . . . . After announcing his motto, 'The Cadres Decide Everything,' in the 1930s, he in effect masterminded their ruthless extermination. We can still feel the disastrous effects of that. Stalin's reprisals appear particularly gruesome against the background of the huge losses our people had suffered after 1919. Just consider these figures: in the First World War Russia lost one million and a half dead or missing; the Civil War carried off eight million lives, and in the Second World War we lost over twenty million people. And on top of that loss of life, millions fell prey to Stalin's repressions! . . . And the peasants?" (V. Dashichev, *Izvestia*, April 12, 1988).

Restoring a well-wishing and humanitarian approach to the peasantry as a class, as a necessary form of life, is important not only for saving our economy. This is even more important for saving our souls and the moral health of society. I am deeply convinced in the justice of Vasili Belov's thought that "not to love the peasantry means not to love oneself. . . . Not to understand it or to humiliate it is like cutting off one's nose to spite one's face."[14]

Moral protest against a crime does not cut off a person from his or her national history. It cuts off evil from goodness and exposes all pretense at goodness. At least, as I see it, the sense of guilt our society has increasingly felt before the farmers as a reminder of their past hardships and of Stalin's crimes against them holds much more truth than scientific studies about the universal responsibility of the peasants' *we*. A normal person who has not lost a simple moral instinct feels that all our urban, "scientific" attitude toward the farmer contains something unhealthy that fails to accord with the elementary ideas about justice and sometimes with elementary common sense.

What line of reasoning should one use to become convinced that the oldest and most stable class of human civilization, the farmers, has failed over the millennia to work out any genuine idea of a better life and things to hope for? What sort of people are they, if we are to believe our present urban pedants, who cannot begin to understand the meaning of life, the meaning of why and what for?

Why did the townsfolk come to think they knew better than the peasants how the latter should organize their work and what was better for them? By the way, many Russian intellectuals and revolutionaries were tormented by that question, being unable to accept immediately, at face value, the Marxist idea about the erosion of the peasantry. "By what right should workers impose on the peasants any form of government or organization? Where did they get that claim of theirs, as ridiculous as it is impudent, and as unjust as it is harmful, to impose their political and social ideal on ten million peasants who do not want it?" These questions were formulated for the first time by Mikhail Bakunin.[15]

I, for one, am not sure at all that we have provided any comprehensible or exhaustive substantiation for the right of the city (i.e., the working class and the intelligentsia) to decide the future of the countryside. If we had ever given serious thought to the problem as formulated by Mikhail Bakunin, we would have discovered that our routine and hackneyed philosophizing about the social, moral, and cultural superiority of the intellectual or the hired worker over the propertied farmer was morally blemished. It is based on the conviction that a better educated and more civilized social stratum is entitled to impose its ideas on those who have not grown to the urban level of knowledge. But this premise about an imaginary or genuine supremacy of intellectuality, education, or worker civilization over peasant civilization, as first discovered by Bakunin, can serve to justify any violence. Addressing the French socialists who insisted on a right to judge the destinies of the parcelle peasants, Bakunin said,

> But do you know that by using such a principle one can legitimize any conquest and sanctify any oppression? Moving from nation to nation, just like from one class to another, this fateful principle, which is nothing more than a principle of authority, explains and justifies all invasions and all conquests. Didn't the Germans use it to justify their attempts against the freedom and independence of the Slavic peoples and to legitimize their forcible and cruel Germanization?[16]

Today, at least, considering how the building of a new life has proceeded in other countries and remembering such a fall of humanity as nazism, we must be cautious about any attempt to accuse people—let alone a whole laboring class that has shored up society for thousands of years—of being socially or civilizingly inferior. We must be cautious about any attempt to draw a line between those who bear the imprint of the urban *I* and those who bear the imprint of the farmers' *we*. We should not forget the tragedy of Kampuchea. It was caused by the same professed principle whereby one part of society is believed to enjoy civilized, "socialist" superiority over another. This time, however, under the influence of new intellectual trends in the West, Kampuchea's socialist intelligentsia exchanged the plus sign for the minus sign and turned the entire might of revolutionary authority against the city, against bookish, or what they considered, bourgeois civilization.

The socialist townsfolk, not to mention the socialist intellectuals, must hold down their pride and recognize the fact that attempts to teach the farmers how they should work and live have failed to produce any other result except for a crisis of our agriculture. One should not overestimate the prophetic depth of urban judgment about the meaning of life and of history, and even less the meaning of farm work. Many directives handed down from city to country have proven confusing, once again convincing the villagers that they can pin little hope on the city, let alone socialist intellectuals. Even what appeared the best elaborated urban idea, that of turning agricultural work into a kind of industrial work (i.e., organizing it by analogy with factory production), largely resulted in damage to the mainstays of the agrarian sector. Yet in other socialist countries that took heed of the experience of village civilization and of the farmers' opinions and efforts to be as independent in their work as possible, the country-side embarked on a meaningful life and began to gain strength.

All told, I would identify with those who are calling for more respect to be shown to rural civilization, seeing not only its weak points but natural advantages. And, even more important, it is time to give up the morally and economically fallacious idea that the country is indebted to the city and that it exists for the sole purpose of meeting the needs of the city, industry, the army, what not.

I cannot begin to understand how our humanitarian ideals and our talk of equality, brotherhood, and justice can measure up against our practical, daily attitude toward the country and the farmer. Is it an unimaginable situation in a socialist society that one laboring class remains ever indebted, while the other laboring classes have no moral or social duties before them?

It turns out that this is possible. Until now, many socialist intellectuals, specialists in the field of philosophy and sociology, have been complaining that collective farmers are not conscientious enough and that instead of applying themselves in the common field, they save some energy for the family plot, for growing potatoes, cucumbers, and onions.

I, for one, am convinced that this socialist lordliness and biased attitude of townsfolk toward farmer holds back the development of the free ego and democratic liberties in our country much more than what remains of the peasants' *we*. Until we recognize the farmers as an equitable and free social class, until we recognize that they have the right to decide their future themselves and that they have a right to protect and uphold their own interests, we will not be a free society. Until we get over the old attitude toward the farmer as a means of socialist accumulation, an attitude going back to E. Preobrazhensky, we will not gain the desired moral health.

We need to admit that our earlier views on the peasantry, as formulated at the April 1929 Plenary Meeting of the party's Central Committee, contained much injustice contradicting elementary notions of legality and morality. One cannot treat people, not to mention a whole class, as a means even if it is designed to serve some humane and distant end.

The peasants were expected to support the Bolsheviks and help to make the October Revolution a political reality. Together with the working class and the socialist intelligentsia, they had to drive away the capitalists and landowners and hold out in the life-or-death battle against the White Guard. Later they were expected to become caring and knowledgeable cultivators of land in order to save the socialist city from hunger, feed the nation, and help accomplish the tasks of the rehabilitation period. But hardly six or seven years passed when the wretched peasants began to be told to do something perfectly different. What they were now expected to do was hate their land and farms, suppress within themselves what had been created over thousands of years, with ease and mirth give up their horses and cows, and with their own hands destroy their peasant's world and way of life and work. They were told to step off the road of history and not interfere with the country's progressive development toward class-free, socialist homogeneity.

Later, the majority of those who had been unlucky enough to stay on the land, which their ancestors had defended with their blood, were forced to pay tribute for the superindustrialization and accept strokes on paper instead of pay days. They had to bear the abuses of men like Borzov, secretaries of local party committees who would force grain out of the peasants. The peasantry was denied many, far too many, boons of socialist life. The absolute majority of collective farmers, who made up about half the work force in the 1930s and more than one-third in the 1940s and 1950s, were not entitled to annual paid leaves or sickness allowances. They hardly ever used free or cut-rate holiday accommodations. Women farmers were denied paid maternity leaves, and hardly any of the collective farmers received retirement benefits.

In the meantime, nobody owed anything to the farmers who, because of the patriarchal Russian capacity for tolerance, bore every trouble that came their way. Far too many people in the socialist city absolved themselves from any moral scruples and duties before the suffering peasantry.

Most citizens, including the children and grandchildren of the socialist intelligentsia, believe that this is the way things should be and that they owe no apology to the peasants; that it is a historical necessity to erode the Russian peasantry and promote the progressive process of urbanization and turn the patriarchal peasant into a socialist worker. In England, they argue, the industrial revolution was attended by the atrocities of enclosures, while we in Russia could not avoid the excesses of collectivization on our road of industrialization. Over the sixty-odd years since Lenin's death, many a theoretical trick has been invented to absolve the socialist townsfolk from any guilt before the village and the peasant, many a trick persuading the townsfolk that they enjoy some innate, caste (there is hardly a better word for this) supremacy over the peasant (and, later, over the collective farmer). There was the notorious theory about the lower and higher forms of property whereby the townsfolk engaged in state-controlled production were declared to stand on the next rung of the historical ladder above the peasants, burdened as they were with what Stalin viewed as the transitional nature of cooperative property.

There was the theory about the absolute superiority of worker culture and worker morality over peasant morality. For more than half a century the peasants have been abused for linking their lives with private subsidiary farming, that last "harbor of private property" and the attending illness of private enterprise.

For this reason, I am deeply convinced, no complete perestroika or free ego or our society's moral health is possible until we morally and theoretically overcome this caste adversity of socialist city toward socialist country. We must go the whole way not only for the sake of elementary human justice and for paying due tribute to the farmers' part of our Soviet *we* but, primarily, for the sake of saving the moral health of the remaining nonfarmer part of the nation. No moral or spiritual progress is possible in a society one part of which is convinced of its primordial political, moral, and spiritual supremacy over another. In this respect, Christianity stands much higher than primitive sociologism, for it recognizes the primordial spiritual equality of people hallowed by Christ's love and suffering.

Our socialist townsfolk, however, especially if they have received a higher education, will not admit that the farmers are their equal as human beings, that the farmers owe nothing to anybody, that they too would like to be free and live their lives as they please, and that they have no less right to this country and its wealth than the townsfolk blessed with a higher form of property. Townsfolk cannot begin to understand that socialism will be true socialism only if all working people accept it of their own free will, each for his or her own motivation, or that their putting up with the new mode of work does not at all mean that they have accepted it with their hearts.

The sin of idolatry, of subservience to Varlaams, Stalin's despotic flunkies, is steeped in guilt before the peasant. Only those could be fond of Stalin as a leader who refused to see the peasants' tragedies and the horrors of the famines and who regarded each peasant as a potential kulak— a bloodsucker. That is why we are now repenting of having sinned against the peasantry and why we are now trying to overcome our adversity toward the village and rural people. It is justly believed that until we come to love the countryside, we will not love ourselves or our country and we will not be free in our judgment and our social choice. This is no exaggeration.

One's attitude to land, to soil, to the farmer is as much indication of one's humanity as one's attitude toward a child or a woman. For this reason, prejudice against the farmer and the inability to assess the farmer's role in public life were bound to lead to the darkening of reason and to many blunders in economic and social policies. Disregard for the peasant resulted in disregard for the agrarian sector and, later, in the problem of soil and land. Over dozens of years we failed to grasp the simple truth that the steady growth of food prices, rooted in the farmer losing interest in his or her work, has been the chief obstacle to the development of the socialist city. We failed to realize that our premature, unprepared, and, more important, ill-conceived collectivization, which did not accord with peasant mentality, was the chief obstacle to the nation's economic progress.

A nation ill-disposed toward its farmers is a sick nation, a doomed nation, a nation without a future. The share of the rural population in the total population does not matter. As in a litmus test, people's attitude toward the countryside reveals their attitude toward their ancestors and history, toward their national culture. Ideologies superseding one another have always been tested for their health and prophetic insight by the way they looked upon farm work.

Those who destroyed the countryside and country life invariably destroyed national culture. In this case the worst damage was suffered by countries that had not managed to create urban, burgher culture supplementing village culture. This, obviously, is the root cause of the great losses that Russian culture and Russian memory have suffered from the forcible erosion of the Russian peasantry. The thing is that "the memory of the Russian people was not only church or monarchic memory, but primarily peasant memory." In the opinion of G. Popov, a noted Soviet economist, this is the reason why the model of socialism that won out in 1929 and placed the main hardships involved in the building of socialism on the peasants' shoulders, was bound to result not only in the peasantry making sacrifices but also "in the destruction of the former foundations of peasant life and of every reminder of the past, the successes and achievements of the past."[17] In the last years of his life, Lenin called for an alliance with the majority of peasants, having departed from his original concept of maintaining an alliance only with the poorer peasants. Stalin and his entourage, however, took a different road. That the past culture rooted in the Russian peasantry was going to be denigrated was now a foregone conclusion.

A Justification of Initiative

Despite the mystical belief that 3 is a lucky number, I would pick the fourth year of perestroika as the period of the most significant changes. In terms of the truth spoken openly, thoughts freely expressed, and emotions shown without inhibition, the harvest of the year 1989 was so impressive that it takes your breath away. When I reread that year's newspapers and magazines, I cannot believe it's all true. Did all those things really happen? Do we begin to regain our dignity? Do we begin to think as normal people do? Do we now have the right to say that black is black and white is white? What we were afraid to touch upon and think about, even in our heart of hearts, is now set out in print and freely discussed. But even more striking things are taking place. Some sort of a modus vivendi has been gradually established between the truth and the political and ideological structures that have evolved in our society. Just think that Aleksandr Solzhenitsyn's *The Gulag Archipelago,* Alexei Gorki's *Untimely Thoughts,* V. G. Korolenko's *Letters to A. V. Lunacharsky,* Vassilli Grossman's *Forever Flowing,* Mikhail Prishvin's *The Year 1930,* which contains most profound ideas, and finally Vladimir Soloukhin's essays *Reading Lenin* have now all been published. One even gets the impression that this is too much of a good thing and an attempt to deal with the past quickly and mercilessly. It is an attempt to do away with our past beliefs. The pendulum has now swung the other way. For decades it has been standing still in the position of left-wing revolutionary extremism, but now it has begun to swing rapidly to the right. So far this movement toward the right can be regarded as great intellectual progress in the specific conditions that exist in our country today.

We have finally mustered enough courage to speak out honestly about the classics of our philosophy and for the first time in seventy years dared put in question the ideals and motives of the October Revolution. Many people have realized that the messianic spirit and internationalism of the October Revolution have been catastrophic for Russia's identity and centuries-old civilization. We have realized that Lenin decided to go ahead with the socialist October Revolution guided by a utopia. Now we know that the only way to prevent the rise of Stalinism was to abandon the platitudinous Marxist truths, which, after Lenin's death, triumphant revolutionaries could no longer abandon.

Today, we find it awkward to go on playing the old cunning game and pretend that all the atrocities and trials of the past years were the result of Stalin's evil character and his lust for power. Now it would be useless to argue that the reprisals, which he had personally ordered, had nothing to do with the terror of the Civil War and that all the ills of our revolution and the setbacks we suffered in the building of socialism should be blamed on some dirty individuals who "contaminated our pure idea."

An article by V. Kozhinov, entitled "High Boots Made of Shagreen Leather," exemplifies the attempts to overcome the deficiences of the pre-perestroika Staliniana. I think the author deserves full credit for a very honest assessment of the "revelatory publicistic writing." He admits that the latter represents some sort of a "euphemism" for a more serious conceptual criticism or some sort of a carefullly planned maneuver. He should also be commended for dotting all the i's and crossing all the t's for the first time. What he did was to point out the tragic gap between the hopes of our revolution and the bitter fruits our people tasted. It is true that we have failed to merge our revolution with democracy, and in this respect the twentieth century has been fruitless for us in terms of democratic gains for our people. On the threshold of the twenty-first century, we find ourselves lagging behind many civilized nations and are forced to start from scratch. But the most tragic thing is that everything we lived and broke our backs for was an illusion, even though in the name of it we deprived innocent children of milk and even their daily bread. "The period of social mythology and Utopias lasted for almost seven decades," writes V. Kostikov (see *Ogonyok*, 1989, no. 32:12–13). Today we have become increasingly aware that there is absolutely no alternative to the mechanisms existing in a civic society. Characteristically, the concept of renovated socialism itself has been essentially associated with the democratic achievement of European civilization. Mikhail Gorbachev's article "The Socialist Idea and Revolutionary Perestroika" marks a watershed in our offical ideology. It proclaims that we reject the past metaphysical opposition between socialism and capitalism and no longer draw a distinction between socialist values and the so-called bourgeois values.* When we say that the simple standards of morality and justice, personal rights and freedoms, and the laws of commodity production represent universal principles of life and belong to all human civilization, by the same token we reject our past belief in the possibility of a different non-Christian morality, noncommodity economy, and nonbourgeois democracy. There can be no alterntive to universal human morality, because everything that opposes it is inhuman. The only alternative to life is non-life, that is, chaos. These are the major conclusions to be drawn from the history of our state.

---

* In his article, Mikhail Gorbachev writes, "Taking into consideration the fact that we are part of human civilization and are responsible for preserving it helps overcome confrontation. But in the heat of our head-on confrontation with capitalism we clearly ignored the importance of much that mankind has worked out over centuries. Not only the simple norms of morality and justice but also the principles of adjective law, i.e., equality of all before the law, the rights and freedoms of the individual, the principles of commodity production and equal exchange, based on the operation of the law of value, are among such achievements of civilization" ("The Socialist Idea and Revolutionary Perestroika," *Pravda*, November 26, 1989). Daily Review. Published by Novosty Press Agency (APN). Translations from the Soviet press. Special supplement, vol. 35, no. 34, Wednesday, November 29, 1989, p. 16.

But suppose we had sobered up and realized that an impossible thing was impossible in principle and that there was no alternative to modern civic society other than a dead end and stagnation, which destroyed human dignity and natural human relationships. Still, it would be naive to hope that this would have put an end to left-wing extremism once and for all. Left-wing extremism will not go away, because it is impossible to overcome the contradictions of traditional civic society itself, which divides people into the lucky ones and the unlucky ones, the strong and the weak, and the rich and the poor. It is just as impossible to overcome the feeling of transcendency that constantly pushes humanity beyond the limits of experience. In the final analysis, it is impossible to overcome the messianic sentiments of the ambitious intellectuals who have chosen politics as their main occupation and are trying to use the dissatisfaction of the unlucky ones for their own egotistical ends. But today, on the eve of the twenty-first century, our past history and the lessons of the socialist transformation in the life of society in Russia have helped to strengthen our common sense in the struggle against utopian senti-ments. We have learned from our own experiences that miracles simply do not happen. All attempts to do the impossible both in Russia and in other European socialist countries (that is, to suppress the initiative and the freedom of the producers, to destroy their sense of property and their attachment to land and implements of work) have proved an utter failure. No one can change the natural course of history.

In the history of socialist construction, all attempts to use poverty as an incentive to work have been doomed. Humanity finds it hard to recon-cile itself to playing the role of a cog in the machine. Human beings have a gut reaction against humdrum, compulsory, and forced labor. In prac-tice, combining the idea of the free and creative development of personal-ity, the human ideal of Marxism, with the Marxist idea of plan and total suppression of economic initiative from below proved difficult. The pov-erty of individual citizens does not add up to a rich state. Gradually, we are beginning to appreciate again the wisdom of an old popular aphorism that a state becomes wealthy through the diligence of a master, his confi-dence in himself and his affluence.

However, if one takes a look from a broader historical perspective at what has happened to us, at the results of our plans for the total socialization of production and our efforts to suppress the market and the independence of the producer, we should probably be glad rather than sad. It is hearten-ing that humans, as creative and free beings, could not reconcile them-selves to the role of a cog in the administrative machine; they rejected the system of all-embracing guardianship, of total uniformity, and the bans being forced upon them. Therefore, the old order was rational and should not be razed to the ground. Therefore, humanity's history—the work, thoughts, and initiatives of hundred of generations, including generations of peasants, that came before us—was not in vain. Our forebears were not always wrong, not all the methods of work they discovered were false, and not all their principles of living together were misguided.

History and life have cut down to size all those overly ambitious people who believed they were visionaries and were destined to see more than other people.

Making an objective assessment of the situation, we are led to the conclusion that our failures—the fiasco of the former mechanistic approach of life under which the socialization of production and administer-and-command methods were a panacea for all troubles; the unsuccessful attempts to impose new "sophisticated" methods of organizing labor—have only strengthened the positions of real humanism and demonstrated that the barrack socialism of Stalin was against human nature. Humans are indeed free and creative beings. They tolerate no violence against themselves nor any offense to their dignity.

According to a famous Soviet playwright, a person who is not his or her own master can never be and will never be his or her own master. We must recognize once and for all that our long drawn-out struggle against the psychology of the proprietor and for the psychology of a non-proprietor was born of stupidity and was itself the greatest of all stupidities. Today, we have to admit that we did not understand the fundamental significance of private property in the development of human civilization. For all practical purposes, the struggle against private property has resulted in the destruction of the economy and the life of society.

I believe that a reassessment of the role and significance of private property and entrepreneurship in the life of society on the part of the educated, sober-minded and, as a rule, more qualified sectors of the public represents the most notable sign of the changes taking place in the minds of Soviet people. This is truly a watershed. Indeed, this marks our return to Europe and to the mainstream of human civilization. Before the revolution in Russia, a negative attitude toward private property was a sign of intellectual development and a free mind. But today a scholar who denies that private property and capital perform a civilizing function and does not question the necessity of its destruction cannot really be called a serious intellectual. All of a sudden it has become clear to many people that the traditional Marxist approach to private property, as something that is doomed by the verdict brought in by history itself and must be suppressed, was largely one-sided.

Yes, it is true that private property and capital divide people and inevitably breed conflicts and envy. Private property can make a man heartless and materialistic. But as it has now become increasingly clear in our society, private property helps to uplift large numbers of people and preserve their sense of dignity and their honor. Property gives economic and, consequently, social security. It breeds citizens who are sure of themselves and have something to protect and be concerned about. Private ownership of farm implements, a field washed with one's own sweat, and the ability to enjoy the fruits of one's own labor turn simple humans into beings who are motivated, thrifty, and enterprising. By its nature, private property is incompatible with mismanagement, idleness, and foolhardiness; all by itself it promotes accumulation and is opposed to wasteful consumption. Property is the material foundation of continuity in human history. It makes people concerned about their successors, those they can trust to preserve everything they have worked for all their lives. At the same time it breeds and nurtures children's respect for their parents. A poor person finds it difficult to become a good spouse and also a good parent. A poor man or woman cannot protect the dignity of his or her family.

There is no question that private property is a mixed blessing for society. In itself it represents the drama of human existence. But has anyone proved that the drama of human life will end or that humanity will resolve the eternal problems of existence, something young Marx dreamed about? The old, naive, and romantic rejection of private property is gradually abandoned together with the belief in the ideal and conflict-free human existence, which has Marxism as its source. People in this country begin to realize that the desire to eradicate social evils is utopian and that the most reasonable thing to do is to try to make them the lesser. We have realized that, and we have become scared. If private property breeds clever and thrifty people, then its opposite—state property, that is, nobody's property—breeds idle fools, insanity, and absurdities, which make the world shudder.

These principal lessons of our economic activity are even more important for us, the Russians, for those who associate themselves with the overwhelmingly peasant population of our country. Over a long period of time, ever since the time of the Narodniks (populists), an attempt was made to convince the Russians that they were not masters by nature, that they, as one Soviet publicist wrote quite recently, did not have enough energy to become free and independent producers of goods, that they preferred the total irresponsibility of collective work to economic responsibility. However, with an objective look at the facts, the entire economic history of the postrevolutionary village attests to quite the opposite. The Russian peasants, just like all normal people inhabiting the planet Earth, resent impersonal, compulsory work on land that does not belong to them. As early as the 1870s, in his letters from the village, one of the ideologues of the Narodniks, N. A. Engelgardt, wrote that the peasant prefers "to act on his own." He, indeed, loathes doing something when he works in an impersonal group, in such a manner that it is impossible to register the work for his family, not because he is an individualist, but because he, just like any other sane man or woman, wants to see the fruits of his labor, to enjoy them as a creative being, to free himself as much as possible from guardianship, those "watching eyes." He wants to feel that he is independent. It is true, he was ready to join with others in helping those who were left homeless as a result of a fire; he was prepared to assist widows and to look after common land. But why should people interfere with one another in such a serious business as working the land?

Our peasants worked efficiently and with joy only when they felt they were masters on their land, free, independent, capable of making their own decisions and doing what they wanted with what they themselves had produced. That is why under the NEP, when a private producer or a family worked the land, the rates of agricultural production outstripped by far those that could be attained by the forcibly organized *kolkhozes* (collective farms). That is also why, throughout the sixty years that *kolkhozes* have existed, the efficiency and productivity of labor on private plots have been much higher than in *kolkhoz* fields or on a *kolkhoz* farms. This is also why, as was recently stated by Gorbachev at a conference in the city of Oryol, when a farm or a field is leased to a family, as a rule, the productivity of labor increases twofold. By no accident, the small plots of land, retained by families and accounting for only 2 percent of all the land, provided most of the food for the country in the first twenty-five years after collectivization. The tragedy of our situation is that it has taken us sixty years to learn what has been evident for a long time. The founding father of the Russian Social Democratic movement, G. V. Plekhanov, pointed out to the Narodniks, who were long-standing and ardent champions of collective work on the land—to Tikhomirov, to name but one—that Russian peasants demonstrated amazing industry when they worked their private gardens and plots of land, that they took good care only of those lands that their families had retained over a long period of time. Plekhanov also warned that in Russia, despite all expectations, collective work in the field would hamper the progress of agriculture.

The last one hundred years of economic development of the Russian village explode the myth that the Russian people are infantile by nature and prepared to sell their souls to the devil to free themselves of the need to think and of personal responsibility for their work and well-being. Today, we can see that peasants have never accepted collective work on the land when forcibly imposed. When compelled to work, stronger and more capable young people, blessed by their parents, left, while the majority of those who stayed in the country, with a few exceptions, of course, went through the motions of working, saving their strength for subsequent work on their private plots.

Yes, it is a frightening admission for a weak person who has lost the habit of independent thinking, but it is impossible to escape it. It is true that for a long time we lived in a state of some sort of general aberration and for that reason did not see the eternal absurdities surrounding us. It is, of course, quite possible to blame it all on the people who had a genius for this kind of aberration in the building of this new world, but this does not really change anything. Even the aberration of a genius will be an aberration, and in the final analysis it always turns into evil. In his journal, Andrey Platonov wrote down the following observation: "A new world really exists, because there is a generation of people who genuinely think and act in the manner of orthodoxy and in the manner of a 'poster' brought to life."[18] It is true, though, that early in 1930 Platonov warned that such a state of universal Marxist orthodoxy was only possible as a local phenomenon. This is what he wrote in his notebook: "That world . . . is local as a geographical country and it exists alongside other myths. This myth will never be and cannot be universal."[19]

Andrey Platonov was right, because the instinct for self-preservation cannot disappear in all nations all at once. An aberration of genius is the loss of the chosen. But everything hangs by a hair. If there had been an open hearing in the court and all those who still preserved the ability to think and see clearly had begun to speak only to themselves, then the world depicted in Platonov's *Foundation Pit* would have crumpled under the pressure of common sense, because from the very beginning that world was woven from the wildest and most inconceivable contradictions.

Thousands and even hundreds of thousands of people, primarily children, were starving to death in cities because there was not enough bread. But at the same time, these same dying people banded together in military patrols to keep away the traders who carried sacks full of bread to sell to the city folk in the marketplace, and that meant to keep away life and open the door to death. All those atrocities took place because of the mystical belief in another and happier world where there would be no profiteers, traders, commodity exchange, and greedy people like Kostylev.*

---

* Kostylev is one of Andrey Platonov's characters.

During the Civil War, when starvation drove people insane and turned them into beasts and when prominent and not-so-prominent Russians died off like flies, the Council of People's Commissars used top government officials as its mouthpiece to launch a drive against private plots of land, chickens, and vegetable gardens.* Until the 10th Party Congress the Bolshevik leadership was truly in a state of aberration that suppressed common sense and the beginnings of economic thinking.

Only insane people, totally blinded to the realities by the fairy tale about a future kingdom of universal equality, could reconcile with the absurdities of this War Communism aberration.

One absurdity was piled on another, and the narcotic intoxication acquired a global character.

Self-taught people set themselves the objective of attaining the unattainable, something nobody had done before—to subordinate millions of economic links to reason and a unified plan and to establish order in the national economy similar to the order at an exemplary capitalist factory. But those people lacked systematic education. They were skilled in the only occupation of revolutionary struggle and did not have any notions about the fundamentals of contemporary industrial production organization or concrete economic knowledge.

Having set themselves the objective of turning Russia into a civilized country, they applied themselves to eradicating educated people capable of independent thinking, the Russians who taught kindness and reason to others. One sector of the intelligentsia after another was mercilessly exterminated. All those who, unlike the author Maxim Gorky, refused to regard the day-to-day atrocities of collectivization as the greatest beneficence and could not agree that the economy of queues and total shortages had advantages over the economy that puts the consumer at the center, were liquidated. The revolution set itself the objective of surpassing the labor efficiency in the capitalist world and introducing a more rational and effective production organization. But it used all its power to eliminate good and cultured workers, that is, those people who were knowledgeable, skillful, and thrifty and could help speed up economic progress.

The greatest absurdity was the reliance on the poor in an attempt to

---

* In March 1919, when starvation was at its peak, V. I. Lenin displayed his usual passion in protecting the law that said that "no worker or office employee in a state farm shall have the right to keep his own livestock, poultry, or vegetable plot." He further argued that the measure was justified in order "to introduce labour in common on a common farm. If private vegetable plots, animals, poultry, and so forth were permitted again, we should revert to the small scale economy that had existed hitherto. If that were the case, would it be worthwhile to have all this bother? Would it be worthwhile establishing state farms?" (V. I. Lenin, Collected Works, 29: 43–44).

turn the poorest sectors of society into a demiurge of history and the creator of the kingdom of beauty and reason. But poor, suffering, and downtrodden people could not, no matter how hard they tried, create beauty,
because first and foremost they wanted to satisfy their desire for vengeance. They wanted to destroy the world they hated because it was beautiful. The people who destroyed the beauty of the old world, its palaces,
libraries, and cathedrals, could not become the creators of a new and
hitherto unseen beauty. Only an insane person could believe that the
poorest sectors of the city and countryside population could become the
vehicle of reason and beauty. It is not entirely unexpected that there is a
striking dearth of reason and beauty in the post-October history of our
country. And it is not only functionalism and constructivism of the twentieth century that is to blame for it but our people themselves, who are no
longer sensitive enough to create beauty.

A poor person hates to be reminded of the causes of his or her poverty
and hates those who work day and night to break their chains. He or she
hates those who are their own masters and are good workers, because
they remind the poor person of his or her own inadequacy and stand
head and shoulders above the mass of the poor and the average. For
example, a poor farmer finds socialist transformations heartening not
because they will bring him or her reason and beauty but because as a
result only "average people he or she likes" will remain in the village.

As Andrey Platonov has shown in his novels *Chevengur* and *The Foundation Pit*, the life of the poor and their lack of knowledge and education
make them generally incapable of concentrating for long, taking a broad
view of the world land, or, more important, thinking independently. All
workers potrayed in his novels are afflicted with one and the same
disease—they are not accustomed to thinking. For example, one of the
protagonists in *The Foundation Pit*, the socialist worker Chiklin, "could
think only with difficulty which made him very sad, and although this
was something he did not like, he only had the ability to feel and be
excited without words."[20]

The absurdity of our revolution consisted in that it entrusted the destinies of the nation to the unfortunate people who, due to their poor education and their unhappy and bitter life, were ready for that mission least
of all. Poor people are poor because there is nothing for them in this
world. They have no solid ground under their feet. They lack prudence
and common sense. They can believe anything you want, and they can be
carried away by romantic dreams. But this is not their strong point but
rather their misfortune. And again I cannot help recalling what Andrey
Platonov wrote about Communist activists' love for the poor who, "hav-

ing partaken of simple bread, desirously strove for an invisible future, although the earth for them was empty and dreadful." For Platonov, this was primarily a sign of moral deficiency.

Today, we have realized that the society we have created and lived in is far from being one of collectivism, unselfishness, and altruism. There is also egotism lurking behind all our history, our dramas, life-styles, and notions. The only difference is that the egotism of the old society, which was ruled by strong people of noble birth, was replaced by the egotism of the weak, the egotism of the average, and the egotism of the stupid. The total prohibition of individual initiative and thrift, the experience of the struggle against everything stamped with individuality, the suppression of talent, the clampdown on the intelligentsia, and, finally, the selection of top officals based on their class identity represent a practical implementation of the egotism of the average. For decades our institutions were used for only one purpose—to ensure a comfortable life for mediocrities, so that nothing would remind them that other people had ideas and talents and wanted to find truth in this world. To not disturb the peace of mind of our uneducated leaders we ignored many achievements of our own culture and for decades maintained a ban on the best sociological writings, including the works of Georgy Plekhanov. For that purpose we used the iron curtain of *spetskhran* (special repositories in public libraries closed to ordinary members of the public) to isolate ourselves from the cultural and intellectual developments taking place both in the West and the East. Probably, it was for that same purpose, to ensure total independence from people with brains and reassure him of his own genius, that the great mediocrity Stalin systematically exterminated the few Russian intellectuals who still preserved the ability to think. Incidentally, Stalin had his own logic. Suppose Andrey Platonov is right that the society that emerged in the wake of the revolution could exist only so long as the overwhelming majority of the population preserved their faith in the Communist Garden of Eden and so long as its consciousness would remain in a state of narcotic hibernation. If this is all true, then the struggle against those who still retained the ability to think and their common sense became the main condition for the preservation of the revolutionary gains.

The state we created was the first kingdom of mediocrity in the history of humanity, and mediocrities ruled the roost in our society for decades. Unless we understand this, both our postrevolutionary history and the current political struggles are bound to remain obscure. The principle of antiselection has never been practiced anywhere else on such a large scale or for so long. Never before in the history of humanity was it so easy to become a leader and acquire power over other people. After the revolution, the mere fact that a person belonged to the working class or the poorest sectors of society or was a member of the Bolshevik party gave him or her unlimited power over other people. At a later stage, during the Stalinist era, personal loyalty to the leader of all nations gave that power. Until perestroika was launched in 1985, a person's competence, qualifications, or abilities were never really taken into account.

In a sense, Stalinism and its political experience have a universal historical significance. For the first time, the revolution in Russia and the Marxist teaching on the class struggle made it possible to abstract from the fact that people have unequal abilities. For the first time, it was possible to give political and moral satisfaction to the weak not gifted by nature, with no willpower and unable to defend their dignity in work or open competitive struggle.

Collectivization as conducted was, above all, a justification of laziness, mediocrity, careless and wishful thinking. First of all, collectivization made it possible to ignore such an unpleasant fact of Russian history as the existence of a "lazy peasant"; it provided peace of mind to bunglers and those who did not love the land. Moreover, this was achieved at the price of eliminating all those who were a reproach, an irritant with their diligence and excellence. For the first time in human history, not a bungler was punished, but a master, the one who through his work tried to pull the country from the quagmire of a devastating economic crisis. In this case, the dignity of those who were disadvantaged by circumstances (of course, individuals are not to blame for being unable to do things that others can, for having been born weak) was protected by the censure, punishment, and condemnation of the strong. Mikhail Sholokhov revealed the secret and profound motivation for collectivization in his novel *Virgin Land Upturned*. Makar Nagulnov, one of the main characters in the novel *A Staunch Communist*, personifying the Communists in the village, hates a Red Army partisan, Tit Borodin, primarily because he works day and night like one possessed and has become one with his plot of land.

The idea of overcoming people's innate inequality through the elimination of the most talented is not new. The radicals of the French Revolution (in particular, Gracchus Babeuf) declared that talent could be sacrificed in the name of equality. But Stalin was the first to implement this idea in practice in the period of "dispossessing the kulak."

Unfortunately, even today when the horrors of forced collectivization and its devastating consequences are spoken about openly and without fear, we rarely grasp fully the philosophical essence of what we have lived through. It is probably time to give some serious thought to the problem of inequality, caused by the fact that people naturally differ in intelligence, will, and endurance. N. Amosov, a prominent Soviet surgeon and a scientist, is probably right when he states that, in every population, strong people with a strong desire to work on their own, for themselves, account for about 5 to 10 percent. Compare this with the fact that real, not invented, kulaks in Russian villages represented about 4 to 5 percent. Everywhere throughout history these people were the driving force of economic progress. However, at the same time, this type of personality is usually associated in society with predatory instincts: greed, ruthlessness, heartlessness; the success, prosperity, and affluence of these people humiliated not only total failures but also "middle peasants." This makes it possible to understand why such workers are hated so much. The resistance to the pressure of the strong is justified if one is guided by the interests of those whom they are constantly running down. Indeed, why should the strong, a minority, impose their work ethic and standards of life onto the overwhelming majority while at the same time profiting from other people's misery and weakness? This question reflects a fundamental injustice of human life. When, during the Civil War, Lenin castigated the kulak as "the most ruthless, uncouth, and savage exploiter," he gave expression to the feelings of the poorest peasant masses hating that successful type of worker who stopped at nothing to ensure the prosperity of his or her farm.

As is known, we redressed that injustice in a rather simple manner. Russia revolted against the degrading situation in which some ate meat while others scrambled for bread; it removed that problem, albeit for a time, by getting rid of the strong and talented people whose wealth and prosperity made the life of the majority intolerable. Thus, we just physically eliminated good and prosperous farmers in the village during a number of campaigns spaced over a process that began in mid-1918. Those who stayed alive left for the city. We openly and deliberately sacrificed the interests of economic progress to get rid of the intolerable and insulting Russian inequality and injustice.

Obviously, however, the way that was chosen in Russia to resolve this basic conflict between efficiency and equality cannot be claimed to be a universal method, particularly at the current stage in the development of civilization when we can see clearly what the Communists of the 1920s and 1930s neither saw nor understood. For example, it has become clear that the individualistic genotype who causes such injustice and is capable of working like one possessed is also the principal creator of a nation's wealth and that any attempts to drive this person off the face of the earth usually results in a radical weakening of social vitality. The present disastrous situation in agriculture is largely the consequence of former simplistic methods of resolving the conflict between efficiency and equality. Society has to pay a particularly heavy price when its policy runs counter to the principle of the survival of the fittest, no matter how humane are the considerations used to justify it.

If we take a look at the October Revolution and the postrevolutionary history from this point of view, many things will become much clearer and ridiculously simple. Why did the leadership of the Bolshevik faction hate the liberal intelligentsia and the leaders of the Constitutional Democratic Party so much? Why did they use foul language referring to their "brains"? I think that the root of this intolerance lies not only in the political motives and the antagonistic outlooks of these two sections of the Russian intelligentsia, which opposed each other from the outset. I am convinced that the Bolsheviks had a personal antipathy to the intelligentsia, who identified with the *Vekhi* (Landmarks) magazine.* They were rankled by the intellectual and spiritual superiority and the encyclopedic knowledge of the liberal intelligentsia. For example, with all due respect for the literary and political talents of Lev Trotsky, it is impossible to ignore the fact that his level of knowledge was far below that of an undistinguished professor at a provincial college. This probably explains why the leadership of the country seized every political opportunity and used every little pretext to expel all prominent liberal intellectuals and scholars from Soviet Russia in 1922. But even in exile they helped sustain the faith in the power and vitality of Russian culture.

The old Leninist guard were themselves doomed to fall victim to the intellectual inferiority complex, the envy of and the hostility to the talented and knowledgeable on the part of the uneducated majority. As it turned out, they had been playing with fire. They had called on the poorest sectors of the city and countryside population to help the world proletarian revolution. They had appealed to the embittered people who had failed to learn how to work or think properly and wanted to avenge themselves on the talented, noble, clean-washed, and well-dressed intellectuals. In doing so, they had sealed their own doom, and nothing could prevent their violent death.

When they returned to Russia from exile and began to teach a Budyenny, a Voroshilov, a Koganovich, or a Yezhov† that morality and law were false bourgeois notions and that the Russian bourgeois intel-

---

* *Vekhi* was a collection of articles published in Moscow in 1909 by a group of publicists and philosophers associated with the Constitutional Democratic Party.
† These were Bolshevik leaders renowned for their ruthlessness.

ligentsia was "rot" or "shit,"* they were already digging their own grave. After vengeance had been taken on Russia's ruling classes and those intellectuals who could not agree with leaders of the October Revolution, the party intelligentsia inevitably became the object of hatred, too. They had given power to the person with a rifle and taught that person to think that he or she was nobler and cleverer than educated people. They had taught that talent and knowledge meant nothing in the revolutionary epoch. By the same token, they had created the moral atmosphere and formulated the ideas that could be used to justify violence against themselves. The ideas and morality they had instilled in the minds of the poor and the proletariat in 1917 were later used against them by Stalin, who did not really have any class identity. In fact, Stalin did not invent anything new. He did what Lenin and Trotsky did in 1917, that is, directed the bitterness of the poorest majority against the person with a pince-nez, or the minority. He organized a redistribution of the riches, that is, the modest privileges of the Leninist guard. That was the inevitable consequence of the union between a small number of the revolutionary intelligentsia and a large number of the poor in the city and the countryside.

Our awakening came when for the first time we saw humanity for what it really was and stopped deceving ourselves. Stalin's demystfication inevitably led to the demystification of all the other revered leaders of the October Revolution and their motives.

For decades we did not want to recognize that much in humanity cannot be squeezed into the theory of class struggle and the class nature of morality, as it evolved historically; that along with the antagonism between the exploiters and the exploited exists the problem of a perennial conflict between hard-working and indolent workers, between talent and mediocrity, between good and evil people, between those who have found their place in life and those who are still searching, those who have deceived themselves and those who have simply never reflected on life. There is also the perennial problem of mediocrity, envy, greed, the lust for power over the people, and even unprovoked cruelty and aggressiveness. A heavy price has been paid for crude, imposed atheism. Not only have we destroyed churches, offending thereby the dignity and feelings of believers and violating people's sacred rights, but, along with this, destroying many centuries of people's culture and the ways they have

---

* In September 1919, Lenin wrote to Gorky, "The intellectual forces of the workers and peasants are growing and gaining strength in the struggle to overthrow the bourgeoisie and its henchmen, the intellectual lackeys of capital, who imagine they are the brains of the nation. Actually, they are not brains but sh— —" (Lenin, *Collected Works*, 44:284).

learned to restrain the beast in humanity. We deceived ourselves, having convinced ourselves that humanity was all-powerful and that we could endure anything. So far, our history has been a convincing proof of the opposite, demonstrating that humanity is weak. Humanity is weak when tempted by power, weak when tempted by flattery and subservience. Humanity is most vulnerable, as Brezhnev's era has demonstrated, when tempted by gold. Humans lose their souls to this temptation even when they are unable to buy worldly goods and pleasures. Human beings are prone to money-grabbing. But the history of humankind has not known a more preposterous manifestation of money-grabbing than that of our socialist mandarins. As we now know, even Erich Honekker, a romantic Communist who spent ten years in Hitler's concentration camps, valued power and privileges most of all in his old age.

Very many Bolsheviks, leaders of the October Revolution, in the heat of the power struggle, defending their ambitions and individual preferences, forgot their *raison d'être* and those millions of people they involved in tearing down the old regime. This is a tragedy, a historical drama. At no other time so much as in the years of the relentless and total struggle against the egoism of an individual has it become clear how low a person can fall.

When all the dams holding back humankind's violent instincts burst, when it was stated that nothing was a crime and that there was only one necessity—to build a classless society—we as a people, as a society, became spiritually unprotected.

In fact, every one of the evident absurdities of our economy and political system today emerged because we stubbornly did not want to see humanity as a product of nature and history. We did not want to see the internal contradictions of humans, that they combine the most diverse needs. For example, on the one hand, humans want to assert themselves, to compete and be leaders, but, on the other hand, they need companionship and bend to the authority of the strong individual or group.

It was indeed absurd when attempts were made formerly to attain a higher Communist morality, "the highest manifestation of intellectuality," through the destruction of universal morality, by voiding humanity's soul of mercy, compassion, respect for parents and forebears, and by freeing humankind from historical memory, guilt, and personal responsibility.

It was indeed absurd when we, and others, tried to stimulate efficiency and excellence with equal and meager pay. Stalin's attempt to revive the feudal system of attaching peasants to land in the twentieth century was proof that he was out of touch with the times. The word *absurd* also applies to our numerous attempts to deal with the problems of organizing production or of educating people to work conscientiously, of infusing them with enthusiasm, or of constructing the entire economy and all economic activity on moral and spiritual impulses. How can peasants be expected to work diligently when every year they are stripped of all they produce, when they are deprived of independence and have no voice?

This practice of organizing and stimulating labor came into collision with common sense and the experience accumulated over centuries. Throughout history, every nation saw that equal remuneration for unequal work bred laziness, destroyed excellence and the desire to work. But we defended that principle as an achievement of socialism, denouncing those who did not keep in step with the others but strove for personal success.

I believe something was unnatural and, in a sense, even false in our former attitude toward humanity. On the one hand, we say that humans are born kind, pure, that they are inherently gregarious beings who want to do good, and that only adverse circumstances and "bad" economic relations can make them wicked. On the other hand, however, we did not believe or trust humanity; from childhood we deprived human beings of the right to make choices and instituted numerous bans and limitations. Fortunately, organizing life in society as if it were a barracks or, more precisely, a monastery is impossible. Yet, because of this contradiction, we lose twice over.

First of all, by telling people that they are angels, that they have nothing to be afraid of, we freed them from self-discipline, made them lose interest in their own soul and the motivation for their actions. This resulted in moral and intellectual infantilism, an inability to distinguish between good and evil.

At the same time, by smothering people in regulations and guidelines, we exacerbated moral infantilism, since human beings deprived of choice are not responsible for anything.

In not a single case known to history has someone successfully forced people to work creatively or demonstrate initiative. However, despite this self-evident truth, for a long time we continued to crack down harder, staking our success, as has been stated above, even on the courts as a means of strengthening discipline, on various forms of noneconomic coercion to make people work well. It is true, though, that we still have people today who actively oppose a radical economic reform and believe there is only one way to treat the Russians. They believe, for example, that only by cracking a whip or scaring people with jail is it possible to develop advanced robotics.

Over many long years, our production was based on the most unnatural forms of organizing labor and maintaining discipline. Stricture, reprimand, dressing-down, and intimidation were common practices. The latter introduced nervousness and tension to the production process and posed a constant risk of failure. Some people burnt themselves out at work, consumed by enthusiasm; others were devoured by fear. Even now the degrading system of coercing people to work by various forms of intimidation still predominates in the village: "You won't get this; that will be taken away; etc."

Again, let me repeat that we should not be sorry if we have failed to change humankind's nature; rather, we should find it heartening. It follows that Mikhail Bakunin* was right when he predicted that life and society would never be forced to comply with a priory scheme or an unnatural idea. Violence can help a utopian idea establish its domination over vast areas of human life. It can bridle humanity's passions and keep humankind down for a very long time, but it is not all-powerful. Fortunately, pure and complete totalitarianism is impossible. It is incapable of controlling humanity's thoughts, once they have germinated in the mind. Totalitarianism cannot change the profound relationships between parents and children. It is impossible to make all children denounce their own parents, as Pavlik Morozov did. It is impossible to force a mother to put her child in the care of public nurses or Communist boarding houses in accordance with the instructions of Marx and Engels. It is impossible to force people to stop being concerned about themselves or their relatives and make them think only about strangers. People will never totally renounce their identity in accordance with the dictates of Communist morality. It is impossible to force them to think in the same way and see the world only through the eyes of official propaganda.

Contrary to what Marx and Engels asserted it is not true that religion is an opiate and a sign of a downtrodden and bestial creature. Religion has helped human beings to realize they have souls and consciences. The search for God develops the mind and the heart as nothing else. The destruction of God created gods out of ordinary people and gave rise to an abhorrent belief in the wisdom of leaders. This offends human dignity and blunts intelligence. During the epoch of leader worship, as at no other time, humanity slid down to truly abysmal depths.

Now we have realized that, contrary to what authoritative sources say, humanity frequently sets itself objectives it cannot attain. The price for this is a sea of blood shed by innocent people, interminable suffering,

---

* Mikhail Alexandrovich Bakunin (1814–1876) was a Russian petit-bourgeois revolutionary and ideologist of anarchism and Narodism.

and pain. An idea independent of the laws of time and space soars in the clouds. It perverts the mortals squeezed into their material existence. We have realized that an attempt to achieve harmony between the beauty of an idea and the beauty of the world is an insane enterprise. But it would be equally wrong to say that a beautiful idea has no right to exist because it can never be implemented in its pure form. It has turned out that the proletariat, its party, and leaders are not always right and that it has never held the monopoly of the truth.

The prophets of communism were wrong when they taught that laws, morality, and religion were nothing but a bourgeois prejudice and that spiritual good and material prosperity were assured for those who did not believe in the eternal principles of morality. It has turned out that it is impossible to uplift human beings spiritually and cleanse them of the old slime by involving them in the plunder of the plundered wealth and the expropriation of the expropriators. The slogan "Plunder the plunder" could only provoke a pogrom leading to another pogrom. Evil means immediately defeat the most noble ends. One act of violence or vengeance can only lead to another act of violence or vengeance and exacerbate the pathological condition of society. Violence can never serve as a lever of history and a midwife of a new life. More often than not, violence is an indication that society is intellectually sick and its healers are intellectually sick, too. The fiercer a revolution is, the greater is the aberration of revolutionaries and the more difficult it is to bring society back to normal life. The cause of revolution is doomed if in its name innocent children are shot by firing squads. Not surprisingly, the murder of the innocent children of Tsar Nicholas II is now considered as repulsive as Stalin's harassment of the children of the Communists subjected to reprisals. Poverty can hardly serve as a guarantee of good intentions and unselfishness. To the contrary, it breeds hate and enmity. A poor person is least of all prepared for creative work.

The struggle against private property has not put an end to old crimes. Rather, it has generated new crimes, which are even more difficult to identify and eliminate. A society where everything is unified and fashioned on the same pattern is genetically, politically, and philosophically undeveloped and ultimately declines, yielding ground to the forms of life and production that are right and diverse.

It is not true that violence is a midwife of history. It is not true that only things born in blood are lasting and can bring people happiness and peace. George Sand's* alternative—a bloody struggle or nonbeing, which

---

* George Sand (1804–1876) was a French novelist.

brought to life Marx the revolutionary—turned out to be false. Violence and suppression of the so-called nongenuine interests to satisfy other interests, which the revolutionaries believed to be genuine, cannot in itself resolve any social problems.

Most frequently, violence is directed against the past. In its turn, this leads to the destruction of material, spiritual, and cultural foundations of society. After a revolutionary upheaval, nations remain sick for a long time. Violence done by one person to another and participation in the so-called revolutionary renewal of life can only embitter a person's soul and habituate him or her to crime. Andrey Platonov was right again—it is impossible to build a new world without breaking your heart.

Coercion drives diseases inside social existence and frequently makes them irreversible. Violence and ruthlessness can breed only violence. No one, not even God, has the power to compress time, speed up the course of things, or form an unnatural graft on the tree of life. Only coordination of diverse interests, interaction, consensus, dialogue, and reconciliation can ensure durability of existence, stability, and genuine protection of personality. It is not true that the proletariat does not and must not have a homeland. No one has the right to deprive a person of the greatest joy of belonging to his or her people and homeland. Every person needs to know his or her own ancestors, the beliefs and traditions of his or her land. They need to know they are a necessary and important link in the eternal life of their species. A nation's spiritual comfort must never be bought at the price of another nation's suffering, heartbreak, and alienation of its national identity. Attempts to destroy national consciousness and national identity always result in universal woe, particularly in great nations. If a nation loses its national identity, this always leads to pathology. It becomes a threat to itself, to its neighbors, and to all humanity. But sooner or later, even a crippled nation, which has survived the disease of self-genocide or self-destruction, begins to feel the need to understand itself, its provenance and destiny in this world. Only a person who is proud of his or her language and the shrines of his or her ancestors can have respect for the language and the shrines of other nations. Cosmopolitism is not an asset but rather a disease that afflicts the soul of an unhappy person who has nothing to lean on. A person who has no homeland cannot belong to all humanity. The so-called man of the world is a suffering man, who has failed to find his idenitity. A person who does not feel the pain of his or her people cannot feel the pain of all humanity. It is necessary to expose nationalism as being spiritually defective. In effect, it represents a variety of national arrogance and chauvinism. But at the same time it is necessary to oppose any attempt to resort to "innocent" lies in the question of the nationalities, to deprive a nation of the right to be a nation, and under all sorts of pretexts prevent the revival of long-suppressed national feelings. No nation has the right to resolve its own national problems by infringing upon the national interests of other nations. It is wrong to try to overcome the dramas and historical injustices of one's own history by new injustices, dramas, and tragedies. It is impossible to attain freedom by suppressing the freedom of both neighbors and strangers. No objective can justify the sacrifice of personal rights and freedoms and the denigration of another person's dignity. No ends can justify criminal means, and a crime will always be a crime.

We should be happy that our intellectual hibernation is over, that the philosophy of psychopathic and misanthropic ideologues, dressed up as Communists, has been exposed. We should be happy that we have recognized that humans have the right to be themselves, not to be ashamed of their passions, to strive for personal success, but, at the same time, to fear loneliness, approaching old age, and death: Humans have the right to be by themselves when this is the wish of their souls, and they also have the right to feel pity, to show compassion and mercy.

If life were not immune from stupidity, hate, or the influence of evil, it would have perished a long time ago. But it goes on and develops, periodically allowing people to celebrate intellect, truth, and justice.

Sooner or later, even in Russia, everybody gets their due and everything falls into place: Mediocracy demonstrates its mediocracy; flattery, obsequiousness, and immorality are condemned and despised by the public; while talent, honesty, and intellect take up their worthy places in public life. The present triumph of common sense and the victory of humanism and morality are the greatest intellectual successes of perestroika, proving that the moral choice made by people some time ago, when they discovered they had consciences, was not doomed. In the final analysis, good is stronger than evil, and intellect is stronger than militant stupidity.

What has now taken place was inevitable after we had the courage to say to the whole world that Stalin was a criminal and that his policies brought untold suffering to the peoples of Soviet Russia. When we had finally mustered the courage to say what we did, we thereby rehabilitated our moral feeling and set it free from the prison of stereotypes based on class identity. We were forced to agree with the wisdom of the Christian commandment "Thou shalt not kill." Many writers, historians, victims, and witnesses of Stanlinist reprisals who denounced Stalin's crimes did not know what they were doing. They thought that by condemning the executioner, who had been lying from what they believed was "inner conviction," they would uplift his victims both politically and spiritually, that is, all those who had been forced to lie under the pressure of circumstances. They thought they would be able to prove that the martyrs of the 1930s knew the truth we so badly need today. They hoped that the dictatorship of the conscience would use all its power against Stalin and leave all the other leaders of the revolution in peace. They hoped that it would justify the dictatorship of the proletariat, which they found difficult to reject for personal reasons. They probably hoped it would be possible to pass the judgment of history on Stalin's terror without condemning the terror of *prodrazvyorstka* (the system of requisitions) and terror as a means of coercing Russia into happiness. They thought that it would be possible to condemn Stalinist reprisals against the party and nonparty intelligentsia without condemning those leaders of the revolution who had been seized with the insane idea that people themselves were the main obstacle on the road to happiness and that they had to destroy themselves in the name of their own happiness.

But it was all in vain. In recent months we have realized that in philosophical disputes the law of the excluded middle is immutable. It is either the class identity alternative, which provides a moral justification for everything in the name of communism, or the moral principles. There is no question that all those politicians who stand behind Nina Andreyeva's manifesto and have not yet abandoned their positions were far more shrewd than those who tried to expose Stalin's crimes and at the same time justify the inevitability and necessity of Red terror.

Today we have every reason to say that the public has much more confidence in those writers who speak in the voice of conscience and assert that the torture of millions of people and violence against innocent victims cannot be justified and must be condemned as a crime. By contrast, the public is less inclined to believe those writers who put a heavy emphasis on violence as the most reliable means of attaining justice. Most people do not believe that Russia could only overcome chaos and dislocation by going through all the destruction of the Civil War, bleeding itself white and liquidating all those who could think and work better than others, that is the best intellectuals, farmers, and workers. Today we see growing support for the moral philosophy that upholds the value of human life. Increasingly, people refuse to believe that only repeated waves of terror could take the ship of our state off the sandbank and into clear waters. I regard these developments as proof that our society and our nation are regaining the ability to see and think clearly.

The most important conclusion to be drawn from our tragic history and the experience of the transformation of human life consists of realizing that even in Russia—an unhappy, sickly, and dislocated country—life could not be defeated. The artificial and invented forms of life have not prevailed, destroyed humanity's natural habits, or impeded the natural course of events. In fact, artificial and invented forms of society and production organization were preserved for seven decades only because they existed side by side with unartificial and uninvented mechanisms of life. Alongside vast expanses of *kolkhoz* and *sovkhoz* fields, forcibly taken way from farmers who generally went through the motions of working them, there were their small private plots, where they worked, putting their heart and soul into it, and provided both themselves and city folk with vegetables, milk, and meat. We won the terrible war against fascist Germany also because Stalin had enough intelligence not to take away farmers' private plots of land.

The artificial invention would have crumpled a long time ago but for our vast natural resources, the patience of our Russian people scared into submission by the atrocities of the Civil War and Stalinist terror, and the fear of losing the little they had left. The developments of recent months in Prague and East Berlin have shown that everything artificial, imposed by force, and not freely accepted by people can be rejected in a matter of a few days. It is true, though, that both in Czechoslovakia and East Germany there were far fewer artificial and unnatural things than in our country. Their traditions, institutions, and values of civic society were far more developed and had far greater vitality. In fact, artificial things in their countries did not really stand a chance. The comparative vitality of these countries, as well as Hungary and Poland, is explained, among other things, by the fact that their ruling Communist parties have long reconciled themselves to their impotence and renounced all attempts to achieve total harmony between Marx's forecast and the real structure of production. A cease-fire between artificial and nonartificial things was established a long time ago. But even in the conditions of Russia and despite the trusting Russian character, the artificial has not succeeded in getting a stranglehold on the life of society. People reconciled themselves to those artificial things and learned to live with them, but few took them seriously. Few people regarded Stalinist crimes as a benefaction, and few believed that everything that served the cause of strengthening communism and the socialist state was morally justified. If it were different, as a nation we would never have cleansed ourselves spiritually of the Stalinist slime.

For example, no one really took the Communist propaganda of altruism seriously. Everybody, with very few exceptions, realized full well that our life made concern for one's own self and one's relatives the most important thing. The natural things that had existed for centuries manifested themselves in most diverse forms but most frequently in the forms that were unnatural and pathological. It was the inevitable moral price for living in an invented and unnatural world.

While the official propaganda drove home the message that Communist motives for work would soon and inevitably triumph, in the early 1960s the number of freeloaders or petty thieves who stole public property grew rapidly. What the state did not pay the farmers for their hard work, they took without permission and carried home everything they could lay their hands on.

During the Brezhnev era, the gap between the dictates of the Communist theory and actual life manifested itself most clearly. This period we usually refer to as stagnation, but in fact it was not stagnation in the precise sense of the word. It was a period when common sense scored one triumph after another—people saw that the emperor had no clothes. The prophets preaching the Communist dogma revealed themselves to be ordinary liars, mouthing Marxist phraseology to protect their own mercenary, most primitive, and unimaginative egotistical interests.

Our experience has proved impossible to be impossible. Natural things ultimately triumph over unnatural things. This conclusion has a universal significance. Only now the hidden and true meaning of our history, which began in October 1917, has been finally revealed. But our experience is just as important for us. If natural things in our country have finally triumphed over artificial things, then we still have hope of returning to the mainstream of history.

NOTES

1. Lenin, *Collected Works*, 32:226.
2. Ibid., 344.
3. M. S. Gorbachev, *Toward a Better World* (New York: Richardson & Steirman, 1987), 256–57.
4. *Tribuna Ludu* (in Polish), April 17, 1988.
5. K. Marx and F. Engels, *Collected Works* (London: Lawrence & Wishart, 1975), 23:423.
6. F. Burlatsky, "Problems of Present-Day Socialism" (in Russian), *Questions of Philosophy,* 1988, no. 11.
7. Yu. Chernichenko, *Literaturnaya Gazeta*, April 13, 1988.
8. V. Belov, *Pravda*, April 15, 1988.
9. V. Bashmachnikov (in Russian), *Znamya*, 1987, no. 3:206.
10. K. Kautsky, *Bolshevism in an Impasse* (in Russian) (Berlin, 1930), 101.
11. A. Chayanov, *A Brief Course in Cooperation* (in Russian) (Moscow, 1925), 5:12–13.
12. V. Bashmachnikov (in Russian), *Oktyabr,* 1987, no. 12.
13. *The 14th Congress of the Communist Party of the Soviet Union (B), Shorthand Account* (in Russian) (Moscow-Leningrad, 1926), 53.

14. V. Belov, *Pravda*, April 15, 1988.
15. M. Bakunin, *The Whip-German Empire and Social Revolution* (in Russian), *Selected Works* (Petrograd-Moscow, 1922), 2:50–51.
16. Bakunin, *The Whip-German Empire*, 51.
17. G. Popov (in Russian), *Znamya*, 1988, no. 1:189.
18. Andrey Platonov, "A Wooden Plant: From the Notebooks, 1927–1950," *Ogonyok*, 1989, no. 33:14.
19. Ibid.
20. See A. Platonov. *Juvenile Sea* (Moscow: Sovremennik, 1988), 109.

CHAPTER 8

When and Why
Did We Betray Humanity?

Stalinism is the most concentrated and consistent manifestation of the technocratic attitude toward humanity. It is a negation of freedom of choice and the intellectual autonomy of the individual. Probably few other periods in the history of humankind held the individual in such low esteem, treated the individual's sufferings with such indifference, and so openly flouted the fundamental intellectual values of human life. The fear and hatred generated by Stalinism not only made humans callous in spirit and blunted the moral sense but also resulted in crude social thinking. Absolute power over people, their lives and work, gives little incentive to discover what those people are and what they think or feel, to comprehend the eternal and fundamental problems of humanity's existence. A person whose destiny is fully in your hands, who is obliged to obey without question your every order is, in fact, no longer a human being but a thing, an object for the exercise of the will of an omnipotent ruler.

Is it any wonder then that people devoted to Stalin today still come down with indignation on all those who champion the right to intellectual autonomy of the personality and who dare speak about moral sense and the freedom of moral choice, of the right to an independent judgment or opinion? A wronged soul revolts not against its oppressor but against the one who reminds it of its defect. It does not want the truth, which it is unable to embrace once again; it has grown lazy and does not want to shoulder the responsibility of an independent choice or free judgment.

The most terrible legacy left by Stalinism is hardened souls. Over a short historical period we succeeded in producing a peculiar breed of people. They are unable to act according to the spirit or to have compassion for the grief of others. As Yuri Karyakin, a Soviet publicist, wrote, they pity no one. It is possible that all nations in all times have had an excessive amount of such people with dead souls. However, in our country they are somehow special.

Very recently, riding on a bus out of town, I had to hear a confession of the man who sat next to me. He was a stocky, confident, sixty-year-old. In the past he had been secretary of a regional party committee in rural Byelorussia. For one hour he tried, in perfect earnestness, to convince me that people like Shalamov* had been better off than those who had been free, building socialism. Political prisoners, my companion argued, worked in the open air, doing manual labor, with board and lodging provided. "That is why they live so long," he said with regret. On the other hand, we, who were free at that time, die of heart attacks. He believed it was all extremely unjust.

Even the most vivid imagination would probably fail to come up with such a way to justify Stalinism. But apparently such reasoning is possible. A mind devoid of compassion and unmoved by the pain of others can be highly cunning.

I am deeply convinced that, in intellectual and moral terms, the 1930s and 1940s represented a leap backward, an unqualified regression to the precivilized state of society. Morally and legally, Stalin pushed the country back hundreds of years. Today, this has become clear. At no other time in Russia were the concepts of life, humanity, or humanity's inner world so crude and primitive as in the years when Stalin ruled supreme. At no other time was animal individualism so rampant. At no other time were people so turned in upon themselves—so obsessed with their selfish interests—as in the era of ostentatiously proclaimed collectivism.

At no other time in the history of Russia did so many fallen people act against their consciences and violate their souls to save their flesh and to avoid finding themselves behind barbed wire. We, however, live in different conditions today and enjoy—unexpectedly and, in many cases, undeservedly—the rights of free people, the right to preserve our dignity and not live a lie. So we probably should not reproach that miserable generation for having sacrificed their good names and their natural spiritual impulses to save their lives. It is unrealistic for everyone to give up their lives to retain their dignity and to preserve their consciences. When no one exists, personal dignity becomes pointless. That is why I believe that only those who managed to preserve their human dignity have the right to judge the people who lost theirs under similar circumstances. Our very youthfulness forbids us to pass judgments on those who came out

---

* Varlam Shalamov, a poet and an author, spent twenty years in Stalinist prisons for his political activities.

of that hell with crippled souls and who want to contribute what they can to the moral rebirth of their people. We should ponder and try to understand what has happened to all of us and why. For this reason, revealing the intellectual sources of Stalinism is today's top priority.

How could it have happened that in Russia millions of people simultaneously forfeited an inalienable human right—the right to their unique lives—and found themselves hostages of an ambitious despot who at his own whim determined who should be the first to perish and who should follow, who should be thrown behind bars and who should stay free? Even the cruelest tyrant of the most barbaric Eastern autocracy did not have such power over his subjects as did Stalin. History has seen it all: the vandalism of the victors destroying at the same time the culture and the population of defeated countries; the madness of civil and fratricidal wars and of ruthless religious fanatics. However, no one has ever before seen this all come together as it did in our country.

The temptation is still strong to explain away the horrors of Stalinism by reference to the intellectual and moral defects of Stalin's personality. Very many authors who write on the subject are still unable to resist the simple and, at first glance, obvious explanation of the source of Stalinism. Since the terror ended in 1953 after the death of Stalin, then the causes of it lay in that horrible, perverted personality. As has been the case more than once in history, here the superficial and the obvious concealed the inherent and genuine cause of the imminent transformation in our life, namely, the awakening of the moral sense in people exhausted by violence and suffering. The true representative of these people was N. S. Khruschev.* People

---

* I believe that Yu. N. Davydov spoke more truthfully than anyone else about the causes of the birth and death of Stalinist terror in his still-unpublished article "Totalitarianism and Bureaucracy." In his view, Stalin's system of terror began to come apart on the eve of the death of Stalin when people laying claim to the position of the leader began to clarify their relationships and were forced to put off upcoming repressions planned by yesterday's "leader" and, subsequently, to scale them down altogether. Davydov writes, "That dealt a devastating blow to totalitarianism the significance of which those who dealt it clearly did not quite comprehend. As it . . . could not exist without more human sacrifices, it was a must to create an emergency situation in the country, the only situation ensuring 'normal' functioning of the totalitarian and bureaucratic system."

Developing his ideas, Davydov believes that, proceeding from this point of view, "it is worthwhile to take a fresh look at the *historical* significance of the 20th Congress of the CPSU and the report by Khruschev on Stalin's Cult of the personality. The disclosure of the horrible crimes committed by Stalin was not the only issue. By calling them *crimes* the leadership of the party and the state publicly renounced mass repressions, without which totalitarianism is unthinkable as a matter of principle. Totalitarianism without such repressions—without the possibility of such repressions constantly present even during brief respites between them—is no longer totalitarianism. Even when the tentacles of a totalitarian structure entangles the political, economic, and cultural life of the country, this is no longer totalitarianism but authoritarianism."

remember that time—late 1952, early 1953. Ordinary people were tired of suffering, of fearing everything. They were eager to live normal lives. It was a time when many, many people rejoiced to be rid of the leader they hated.

Seemingly, those to whom the death of Stalin brought liberation and hope find it very difficult to separate in their minds these two facts, namely, the demise of the leader and the end of the terror he unleashed. This alone helps explain why right up to this day even serious scholars embark on the simplistic road of personifying the evil of Stalinism and believing that the causes of Stalinism are rooted primarily in the soul of the scoundrel who headed the party leadership after the death of Lenin. For example, G. Pomerants's essay "Mother's Question" is marked by a penetrating intellectual purity, despite his starting assumption that the same brush tars all revolutionaries who agreed that "all actions are permissible" in order to attain a noble goal. Yet, all of a sudden he begins a traditional "exposure" and with characteristic passion attempts to prove that the Russian revolutionary movement did not know anyone greater than Stalin, that compared to the dirty and disgusting personality of the member of the underground Koba (Stalin's underground alias) all Trotskyites were saints. The author of the essay writes,

Just like all provocateurs, Stalin knew how to be both—in the midst of revolutionary ideas and actions and, at the same time, on the sideline, as it were. He had a good command of the language of the revolution, and, believing in nothing, he used this or that idea, depending on which was more profitable. He saw his comrades from the inside, he knew their weaknesses and skillfully pitted Zinoviev against Trotsky, and Kamenev against Rykov. He organized the murder of Kirov and shot two others of his rivals for that. What Azef, what Malinovsky could have done more? Stalin was the greatest provocateur of all time and of all peoples. He is unrivaled.[1]

Contrary to the reader's expectations, essayist I. Klyamkin was also carried away by the personification of Stalinism. Previously he firmly believed that the "bloodbath" Russia had endured was inevitable and a logical outcome of its entire history, starting with the time of Peter the Great. However, in his new article, entitled "Why It Is Difficult to Say the Truth," he has changed his line and tried to reveal the human and personal dimensions of what happened. He has attempted to demonstrate the constant role of coincidences that, in his view, helped not the greatest but the most perfidious. Klyamkin believes that a lot could have been avoided if the old guard Leninists had not betrayed their moral principles, if in the name of salvation they had not embarked on the path of lies that helped the scoundrel. The author writes, "I am interested to know why these preposterous coincidences in our circumstances led to such a catastrophe, one that did not result from political deceit, even when such deceit was not considered to be reprehensible."[2]

In Klyamkin's view, all that has happened to us is a coincidence because those who lost to Stalin may well have resisted the lie since, essentially, they were servants of the truth and, compared to Stalin, they were whole and moral personalities. Klyamkin insists,

I am convinced that almost all of them were and remained the servants and champions of the idea and in terms of their intellectual and moral development belonged to a category of people different from Stalin. He had the source of the lie inside him. In such leaders of the day as Kamenev, Bukharin or Rykov, the lie developed and was constantly nourished by their false and ambiguous position, in which after the end of the Civil War the Old Guard of the party found themselves.[3]

It is hard for me, as a reader, a philosopher by education, and a Russian, to accept that my people from the very beginning were doomed for self-destruction, for the Stalinist mincing machine, for the *kolkhoz* system. I find more appealing the nonfatalistic treatment of our Russian history that devotes a proper place to freedom of choice, to coincidence, and recognizes their force and influence on what happened to us yesterday and what is happening to us today. It provides the possibility to believe that everything could have happened differently, without these senseless sacrifices. Such a view of history enables us to see its real and living actors with all their individual characteristics, preferences, and thoughts. Such a view makes it possible to see how much we have let slip through our fingers, how much people and countries pay for light judgments and for the laziness of the mind and spirit.

I am convinced that the worst happened, that it was simply impossible to think up a solution to our problems and contradictions more horrible and preposterous than Stalin's. It is also true that it is simply impossible to imagine a man more malevolent, cynical, treacherous, and mean than Stalin. In terms of personal decency, Stalin was indeed no match for the majority of Leninist guard. It is also true that Stalin's competitors for leadership in the party (such as, for example, Trotsky, Zinoviev, and Kamenev), who could hardly be suspected of being provocateurs, were in fact capable of just that. As early as 1918, Gorky pointed out that Jews "fought for the political freedom of Russia . . . much more honestly and energetically than many Russians, because Jews produced significantly fewer renegades and provocateurs."[4]

I am also inclined to conclude that if any other of Lenin's comrades, any leader of the October Revolution, were to have taken Stalin's place, then we would have reached the end of the twentieth century with fewer losses; we would have been able to make our life in Russia more dignified, attractive, and respected by other peoples. Instead, the worst happened. Even Trotsky, a champion of the "gun-down and crack-down" policy, would not have wreaked such havoc. Even if he had succeeded as early as 1924 in convincing Zinoviev and Kamenev of the danger facing the party and won over those people close to him in their vision of the world and Marxist orthodoxy, he would not have destroyed so thoroughly the foundations of life in Russia as did the "nationalist" and "Russian chauvinist" Stalin.

It is beyond doubt that Trotsky, just as Stalin, would have wrung the neck of the NEP and would have resorted to forced collectivization.* Both his character and his treatment of Marxism would have undoubtedly led Trotsky to introduce a military-style organization of production in the country. Personally, I am unable to find in the works by Trotskyites (and, above all, in the writings by Trotsky and Preobrazhensky) proof that they insisted on the difference between state-owned production and its real socialization. I see no proof that they, as Pomerants writes, were against forced socialism.†

However, we still have reason to believe that such educated Trotskyites, as well versed in economy as Preobrazhensky, would have implemented the idea of total centralized control over production, the idea of edging out the market and the law of value with fewer material

---

* In October 1929, in Constantinople, in an article entitled "The 12th Anniversary of the October Revolution," Trotsky writes about the same thing Stalin spoke about in his report "On the Right-Wing Opposition" at the April Plenum of the Central Committee in April 1929. In emigration, Trotsky also insisted that socialism was incompatible with production on land owned by peasant families. In his article, Trotsky claims that "dispersed agriculture would pose serious difficulties for the socialist restructuring of agriculture in Russia even if the proletariat came to power in more advanced countries. These difficulties are many times over more serious now when the country of the October Revolution is fully on its own. In the meantime, an extremely slow pace of socialist restructuring in its turn leads to the peasant units becoming increasingly more fractional, and, consequently, makes them more consumption-oriented. This is one of the reasons for the lack of agricultural products."
† Pomerants writes, "Stalin with his iron logic deliberately put all human feelings out of bounds, thereby depriving of their arguments all his opponents who disagreed with his plan for the construction of socialism in one individual country. . . . Public property is the basis of socialism. Trotskyites learned that very well. However, they did not agree that state property equals public property and that everything boils down to this. To them socialism with an army, police, intelligence and counterintelligence, prisons and camps seemed a parody of common sense, a square circle of sorts. Heretics questioned not the possibility of industrialization, but something quite different. Not only did they have no doubts, they were absolutely certain that a society with tyrants is not socialism. A classless society signifies an end to class struggle. In a class society a crackdown can be increasingly more severe. However, heretics did not believe that such a society was socialist. They had romantic perceptions about socialism" (Pomerants, "Mother's Questions," 20).

and human losses.* In the final analysis, even if the initial idea is utopian, a clever person will implement it with fewer losses than an egoistic fool.

I do not believe that Trotsky, who acquired power under the banner of democratizing internal party life and fighting party bureaucracy, would nevertheless allow himself to be removed from his position democratically. In my view, that proposal belongs in the realms of fantasy.†

In my view—which is in itself the alternative to which Pomerants appeals—it is artificial either to feel the need for democracy and to protect the rights of the individual Communist or to be close to the people and the party. The fact that Trotsky, in his words (and this corresponds to reality), "knew the country insufficiently and regarded it only as a reserve and material for the construction of socialism" does not imply that he held values of democracy above all and was prepared under any circumstances to live up to them. I am deeply convinced—and this can be easily proven—that a revolutionary unable to see in a working peasant, in a *muzhik*, a person equal to himself or herself in political and intellectual merits cannot be called a democrat. The concept of *democracy* does not correspond to an assessment of the worldview underlying the actions of Trotsky and all the left-wing leaders of our revolution. It is preposterous to consider as democrats and champions of the equality of people those political leaders who regard 85 percent of the country's population as second-rate citizens and who sincerely believe that history granted them the right to make decisions at their "theoretical" discretion, decisions affecting the destinies of millions of people. These revolutionaries regard the country as the dung heap of history and material for the construction of socialism. Without a flicker of doubt they take decisions affecting the destinies of millions without asking them anything, with no regard for their interests or aspirations. And with even less care, when need arises (particularly when it is a "historical" need), they sacrifice the rights and interests of individual members of the party.

I repeat that I agree that Trotsky, unlike Stalin, could have put to better

---

* Despite what Pomerants writes, Preobrazhensky, the chief theorist of Trotskyism, was not only a champion of the rigorous version of the class approach but also an ardent supporter of total state control over production. For example, he wrote, "Socialism wins when the state economy is tightly organized, when it operates as one unit, joined to the political power in conditions of free competition being systematically curtailed and almost eliminated" (E. A. Preobrazhensky, "The Principal Law of the Socialist Situation" [in Russian], *Bulletin of the Communist Academy*, 1924, book 8:100).

† Pomerants writes, "With the preservation of democracy inside the party, the risk of a temporary victory by Trotskyism was not all that great. One congress would adopt a program to mount an offensive on the kulak while another would have abandoned it (as was the case with labor armies). Preserving an order under which it is possible to criticize mistakes is more important than individual decision, whether correct or not" (Pomerants, "Mother's Questions," 22).

use the Russian peasantry, doomed to become raw stuff for the construction of socialism. Unlike the "leader of all peoples," Trotsky had common sense and a liking for the technology for implementing political decisions. However, it is hard for me to believe that Trotsky, having taken up the position of supreme leader of the party, would have voluntarily abandoned that position when principles of democracy demanded. Pomerants himself writes that the Bolsheviks formed a party that strove to have an uncontested leader. Hence it follows that the very psychological organization of that party prevented a frequent change of leaders. A general secretary who may lose power at any moment will never be perceived as an uncontested leader, taking the country and all humankind to a great historic goal.

Recall Trotsky, the hero of the October Revolution!

Recall Trotsky, who in the fall of 1917, in the name of preserving the power of the proletariat, burnt all the bridges that could be crossed to return to a parliamentary democracy in Russia.

Recall with what flair and decisiveness on October 25 at the 2d Congress of the Soviets he rebuffed Menshevik Martov, who lashed out against the overthrow that had just taken place. Trotsky argued that

the uprising of the masses of people required no justification. What happened was an uprising and not a plot. We tempered the revolutionary energy of the workers and soldiers of Petersburg. We openly molded the will of the masses, directing it toward the uprising and not a plot. . . . The masses of people walked under our banner and our uprising triumphed. And now we get suggestions to relinquish our victory, to agree to concessions, and to conclude an agreement. Who with? This is what I ask: who should we conclude an agreement with?* With those miserable little groups who left this place or who come up with this proposal. Yet we saw them in their entirety. There is no one in Russia behind them any more. An agreement has to be concluded with them, as between equal sides by millions of workers and peasants, represented at this congress, whom these miserable people are prepared not for the first or last time to trade in exchange for the mercy of the bourgeoisie. No, agreements will not do here. To those who left here, and to those who come up with proposals, we must say: you are few and pathetic, you are bankrupt, your role is over and you should go where henceforth you should belong: in the dustbin of history. . . .⁵

I believe that if what did not happen were to have happened and if Trotsky had replaced Lenin as the supreme leader of the Bolshevik party,

---

* This is a reference to a proposal by Martov for the 2d Congress of the Soviets to adopt a decree on the need for a peaceful settlement of the crisis through the formation of a generally democratic government and to elect a delegation for negotiations with all the socialist parties.

he would have protected with even more flair and decisiveness what he believed to be, not without reason, his natural rights to the position of a leader.

However, it seems to me that Pomerants did not make a very happy choice in selecting that character to illustrate his point about it being possible for events to have taken a different turn and for our historical drama to have had a different ending. Reading articles and statements made by Bukharin in the late 1920s is a frustrating experience. All that he says is so reasonable and practicable. To be honest, among the remaining leaders of the October Revolution he was the only one to see the light (Trotsky and Zinoviev died blind doctrinaires, believing Marx's every word). He saw that the dogmatic hopes of achieving a high productivity of labor without competition and without the personal interest of the producer in the best possible results of labor were utopian and illusory.*

If only he, Rykov, and Tomsky had been decisive and politically flexible enough. If only the revolution had taught them what the underground operative and expropriator Stalin learned in his time. Then the shift in our revolution toward realism indicated by the dying Lenin could have taken place. Then we would not have had to travel the long road spanning six decades from the utopia of War Communism to common sense. If only it had been so!

Nevertheless, it is hard for me to agree that the worst happened because the meanest and the most perfidious won, because Stalin (unlike other leaders of the October Revolution) was no romantic, because the word *socialism* did not retain for him the heartfelt meaning, or because he was not "a servant of and a zealot for an idea."

Of course, this does not mean that I deny the influence of morality or of the moral and intellectual development of a politician and state leader on the domestic and foreign policy he pursues. It is just that my inner voice does not allow me to accept the claim that a fanatic dedication to an idea learned sometime in the past is a characteristic of the moral quality

---

* In his report "On the New Economic Policy and our Tasks" delivered at the meeting of activists of the Moscow Organization on October 17, 1925, Bukharin, in fact, recognized that the critique by the bourgeois economists of the nonmarket, the so-called destructive socialism, was justifed. Echoing the Austrian professor Mises, N. I. Bukharin writes, "The so-called destructive socialism of communists leads not to the development of production forces, but to their deterioration." Elaborating his point, he claimed that "it happened primarily because communists forget the vital role of private individual initative and private incentive. It is true that there are defects inherent to capitalism. However, capitalist competition leads to the development of the production forces that are urged on by capitalist development, and as a result of the growth of the production forces in society, the share of the working class also grows. Since communists want to organize production by decree, using a stick, their policy is doomed to fail and this is already happening" (Bukharin, *Selected Works* [in Russian] [Politizdat Publishers, 1988], 127).

of an intellectually mature personality. I am deeply convinced that the concepts "servant of and zealot for an idea" and "moral human" are not synonymous.

The more I study the history of the party, the history of the Civil War, the history of Stalin's era, and the more I read articles on the subject, the harder it is for me to believe that Stalin belonged to some special category of revolutionaries qualitatively different from that category of people we now group under the labels "the Leninist guard" or "the old party guard." All the evidence demonstrates that all of them who were capable of "not going soft," of bearing in their soul all the tragic consequences of the major tactical switch they chose in their life involving the transformation of the imperialist war into a civil war, were indeed very much alike and tarred with the same brush. They were all active participants in and organizers of the armed uprising on the night of October 24–25. They were not afraid of taking into their own hands the power that was there for the asking. They bore a heavy cross of personal responsibility for the revolution in Russian history that subsequently proved to be world revolution. They were all equally responsible for what happened in the country. They contributed equally to what we have achieved and to what we have failed to achieve.

This is beyond the understanding of those people who want to monopolize anew the history of the October Revolution, the truth about the Russian destiny. Those people find appealing the part of the old party guard who arrived for the revolution in a sealed railroad car from the West, who learned European manners, and who knew how to wear a bowler hat and a pince-nez. Those people believe that this part of the old party guard was fundamentally different from the part that met the February Revolution in Russia, became callous in soul and uncouth in manner, in exile and in Siberia. Incidentally, that same illusion about the two types of leaders in the October Revolution is reflected in Kozhinov's assumption that the Bolsheviks, who did not sever the link with Russian soil, who lived through the "peaceful respite" in prison and in exile in Siberia, loved that soil more than those who were in emigration. Those who stayed at home—people like Stalin, Yaroslavsky, Molotov, Voroshilov, and Sverdlov—were involved in the destruction of the traditional, patriarchal, and peasant Russia on as large a scale as the repatriates.

In contrast to us, both the repatriates and those who stayed in Russia and gambled on the October Revolution understood, particularly when the Civil War began, that they shared one destiny and one responsibility. They understood there was no turning back. Therefore, anticipating the

worst possible conclusion, they knew fear just like any living person.*
They had to push on till the end in their offensive on the past, on old Russia. They had to push on further and further, blasting to destruction the
social and economic basis for any possible restoration of the old order.
For them, ordinary mortals, all of that posed a risk and a threat of reprisals that this time would be directed against them.

Why do we want to ignore the fact that, as 1937 demonstrated, the
"Ironsides" with few exceptions (Tomsky and Pyatakov) were not so
tough after all and that fear visited them as frequently as other mortals?
Zinoviev and Kamenev would not have crawled on their knees, begging
for mercy before their execution, if they were indeed men of iron who
managed to rise above the weaknesses of ordinary mortals. We now
know that in the majority of cases, Stalin was also guided by fear for his
life. We are impressed by the assertive left-wing fanaticism of the old
guard who tried to reorganize within the shortest possible time the class
and economic structures of old Russia. But perhaps their motivation was,
in fact, far more trivial. Perhaps it was not at all their dogmatism, their
sacred belief in what Marx wrote about the future classless socialist society with no market or goods, but just simple fear for their lives. At the
14th Congress of the All-Russia Communist Party (Bolsheviks), Zinoviev
and Kamenev spoke against what they considered to be the rash economism of Bukharin, who allegedly did not know what he was doing when
he called on the party to reinstate the well-to-do and independent
muzhik.† Perhaps they were not concerned at all about the purity of
Marxism and socialism. Perhaps they were just afraid. Perhaps from the
depth of the unconscious they, like puppets, were moved by fear.

Of course, no one will now be able to clarify what was the real driving
force of the leaders of the left-wing oppositions and, subsequently, of
those remnants of the old guard who united around Stalin in a "crusade"

---

* It is known that Zinoviev, who was romantically left-wing and intolerant of the peasant
proprietor, was a man of weak will, an outright coward. Recalling the defense of Petrograd
in October 1919, Trotsky wrote, "Zinoviev was at the center of confusion. Sverdlov tells
me, 'Zinoviev means panic.' And Sverdlov knew people. Indeed, when the going was
good, when, as Lenin put it, 'there was nothing to fear,' Zinoviev climbed to the seventh
heaven very easily. However, when the going was bad, Zinoviev would lie down on the
sofa, literally and not metaphorically, and would lie there sighing. From 1917 on, I had an
opportunity to see that Zinoviev was never in a moderate frame of mind: it was either the
seventh heaven or the sofa" (L. Trotsky, *My Life: An Experiment in Autobiography* [in Rus-
sian] [Berlin: Granit Publishers, 1930], 2:158).

† Bukharin wrote in 1925, "In general, all peasantry, all its layers should be told: get rich,
accumulate and develop your farms. Only idiots can assert that we should always have
poverty; today we must pursue such policies as a result of which our poverty would disappear" (Bukharin, *Selected Works*, 136).

to reshape old Russia. We will never know what drove these people, who were well educated by Russian standards, to encourage the destruction of churches, to endorse a demeaning treatment of what was left of the old Russian intelligentsia. No one can say for sure what fanned their physiological hatred of the country and the peasantry.

However, many reasons allow us to suppose that, added to their romantic raptures over the construction of a new Russia and the creation of a new humanity, there was a selfish interest, perhaps an instinctive desire to protect themselves as far as possible. Pomerants has a point when he writes that no benefactor is without a second thought in the back of his mind.

It is no accident that both repatriates and those who stayed in Russia rushed to isolate Lenin and, eventually, to publicly pronounce him intellectually unsound when he proposed to seek a compromise with what was left of Russia. He had decided it was senseless and immoral to go all out to implement a romantic dream.

Perhaps it was not an evil spirit or blind faith that moved Zinoviev, Kamenev, and Bukharin when they trusted Stalin and gave him power. Perhaps it was the deep-rooted instinct of self-preservation and an unconscious desire to strengthen the position of "a strong man" who had the will required to preserve and safeguard the conquests of power. Perhaps the same instinct, that same unconscious gut fear, moved the "losers" when, against all logic, they began with all their revolutionary zeal to bolster Stalin's personal dictatorship.

Recall that, even after the murder of Kirov, few people in the old party guard supposed Stalin would go so far as to begin to eliminate physically his former political rivals. Speaking at the Central House of Artistic Workers in January 1988, Bukharin's wife, A. Yu. Larina, stated, "Stalin was trusted least of all, but even in 1936 no one could suppose that he would do what he did in 1937."

When I suggest that the overwhelming majority of the leaders of the October Revolution had some special subconscious ultra-left-wing motives, I am, of course, unable to substantiate my claim. The heroes of the revolution were remarkably tightfisted with confessions: They told almost nothing to their descendants about what they felt in their souls when they smashed what had seemed to be eternal, when they sent thousands and hundreds of thousands to die in battle for new power, when they signed thousands upon thousands of death sentences. The ultimate mystery of the revolution and our history died with them. Only Trotsky allowed a glimpse behind the cloak of this mystery. However, he did not do this so that we, his descendants, might become wiser but rather to appear better to us than he really was. He said nothing about the soul of Trotsky, the executioner.

However, it is not difficult to show how vain are the present attempts to separate "pure" leaders of the October Revolution from its "impure" leaders. We cannot limit our understanding of the October history to the level of the initial idea of Shatrov's play *The Dictatorship of Conscience.** It is also not difficult to prove that the instinctive desire, conscious or unconscious, to shake up and overhaul old traditionalist Russia as quickly as possible was the main reason and a precondition for the establishment of Stalin's totalitarian regime. However, we shall return to this theme in a subsequent publication. Let us now turn to the pure and the impure.

If a significant moral and intellectual gap had existed between those Bolsheviks who were educated in emigration and those who did not go to schools and universities, there would never have been the October Revolution. Given the facts, it is difficult to accept the attempts to explain the defeat of the repatriates by their alleged cultural incompatibility with the remaining uneducated Communist masses. It is difficult to agree with the claims that, for the Red Army commanders who fought at the time of the Civil War, these representatives of the intelligentsia with their pince-nez and beards constituted an alien class.

Do not forget that, in 1917, Trotsky, Zinoviev, and other members of the intelligentsia, the leaders of the Bolshevik party, unanimously and spontaneously found a common language not only with revolutionary sailors and commanders but also with the person with a gun, with the patriarchal and illiterate Russian peasant dressed in a military overcoat. On the other hand, Plekhanov,† even though he appears to be one of us, a Russian, also returned home in early April 1917 but never managed to gain a rapport with the masses. He was unable to tell the revolutionary hordes what went against his convictions, and he did not wish to flatter them. At the same time, the masses did not want to hear anyone who was not prepared to agree with them.‡

---

* Mikhail Shatrov's play *The Dictatorship of Conscience* was first produced in the spring of 1986. It contains a poignant critique of Stalinism. The playwright explains the phenomenon of Stalin by his betrayal of the ideals of the revolution and Marxism.

† G. V. Plekhanov returned to Russia early in 1917 after thirty years in emigration.

‡ The interest of the revolutionary proletariat of Petrograd in Plekhanov soon flickered out, particularly after his article entitled "On Lenin's Theses and on Why Gibberish Is Something Interesting" ([in Russian] *Unity*, [April 9-12, 1917] no. 9-11). In this article, Plekhanov lashed out against Lenin's appeal to a socialist revolution. Plekhanov wrote, "The proviso contained in the eighth thesis (not the 'introduction' of socialism, but control and all that) represents only a weak attempt of our 'communist' to calm down his Marxist conscience. In effect, he totally breaks with all assumptions of socialist policy, based on the

And Lev Trotsky was the perfect manager of everything. Nikolay Suk-hanov recollected the ease with which he could settle all the problems of the discontented masses at rallies, winning general favor and approval. For instance, he promised that

the Soviet government would send a soldier, a sailor, and a woman-worker (for some reason Trotsky never failed to mention the woman-worker at dozens of rallies) to every village: they would inspect the stocks of the well-to-do peasants, leave them as much as they needed, and take the rest free-of-charge to the cities or to the front. The working masses of Petersburg were very enthusiastic about these promises and prospects.[6]

A Menshevik, Nikolay Sukhanov tried to account for Lev Trotsky's enormous political success. In his view, it was quite understandable that all sorts of "confiscations" and "free-of-charge amenities" dealt out with truly royal lavishness were attractive and fascinating when promised by the people's defenders. They were irresistible.

Such was the source of the spontaneous and irrepressible development of this method of agitation . . . The rich versus the poor: the rich have a lot of everything whereas the poor have nothing; all shall belong to the poor, all shall be divided among the poor. You are told this by your own workers' party, by the party supported by millions of poor peasants and workers, by the only party which struggles with the rich and their government of land, peace and bread . . . Recent weeks have seen this propaganda bandwagon sweeping across Russia. Thousands of hungry, tired and embittered people have heard this verbiage every day . . . It was part and parcel of Bolshevik agitation even though it was not part of their official program.[7]

If it is true, as many journalists believe today, that Stalin had the upper hand over the Bolshevik intellectuals mostly owing to their measurable moral and ethical superiority over the heroes of the Civil War and the average party activist; if it is true that the Bolshevik intellectuals lost

theory of Marx, and with all his rear and artillery moves over to the camp of anarchies, who have always and without respite called on workers of all countries to carry out a socialist revolution, without inquiring as to what specific phase of economic development this or that individual country was going through. . . . Anarchism has a logic of its own. All Lenin's theses fully agree with that logic. The issue is whether the Russian proletariat will make that logic its own. . . . However, I am firmly convinced that that will not happen and that in Lenin's appeals to fraternize with the Germans and to overthrow the Provisional Government, to usurp power and so on and so forth, our workers will see precisely what they represent in reality, namely *an insane and extremely harmful attempt to sow anarchist discord on Russian soil*. The Russian proletariat and the Russian revolutionary army shall not forget that if that insane and extremely harmful attempt is not resisted immediately, energetically and resolutely by them, then it will uproot the young and delicate tree of our political freedom" (G. V. Plekhanov, *A Year in the Mother Country* [in Russian] [Paris, 1921], 1:27–29).

because they spoke a different language from the common people and, therefore, were not understood by the latter, then how could these same intellectuals have found a common language with millions of people in 1917 despite the fact that most of them were illiterate?

Why did the best orators of the October Revolution, who had touched the hearts of Russia's poorest and least fortunate class—that is to say the hearts of the intellectually least developed people in Russia—all of a sudden become so "helpless" when they confronted the same people, who were less numerous but who had already learned the rudiments of political and social awareness? It would seem to be much more difficult for an intellectual to deal with an oppressed slave than with the former slave who has freed himself and has become the master of his fate. There is an inner contradiction in the reasoning of those who speak about the tragedy of a morally and intellectually superior group of staunch Bolsheviks, the so-called Ironsides, beaten by a cynical villain.

But may we, after all, condemn Stalin for relying in his fight for power and an accelerated rate of socialist construction on the least educated, least intellectually developed part of society? For he leaned, above all, on poor peasants, second-rate farmers. He recruited his cadres, the Suslovs, among those who were fortunate enough to have been born in poor families, whose parents were either failures or bunglers. He actually acted in keeping with the established Bolshevik tactics, because Bolsheviks had always counted on the union of the most exploited part of the working class—that is, unskilled and semiskilled workers—with the poorest peasants.

By 1929, the challenges of the party had, of course, radically changed. But let us reason a little. If Bolshevik intellectuals, who had assimilated the ideas of Western civilization, could have believed in 1917 that poverty in Russian villages would be overcome only by means of collective grain factories and the socialization of peasant labor, then what's wrong with Stalin's belief in the same doctrine for his Bolshevik views that took shape in Russia?

One should bear in mind that Stalin had every formal ground to think in 1929 the way the party's old guard had thought in 1917. The fact that by 1929 every peasant's farm was poor allowed Stalin to resort to the already-tested method of relying on poor peasants. But why should we be surprised at that? Only some six years ago Konstantin Chernenko, general secretary of the Central Committee of the Communist Party from 1983 to 1985, was regarded as the proof of his social purity and doubtless virtue because of his farmhand family orgin.

I am not trying to excuse Joseph Stalin. I am not excusing at all his awful violence against the peasant. I am simply trying to show that, qualitatively, Stalin's thinking did not drastically differ from the thinking of those with whom he had fought for power after Lenin's death.

Pomerants writes in his essay that Lev Trotsky, the romanticist of the revolution, was the idol of sailors' rallies between 1917 and 1922. This is perfectly true. But, to be blunt, this fact does not compliment his morality and intellect. The Red sailors were embittered, morally unstable, and resentful. They were convinced that the revolution had allowed them everything. Their reasoning was as follows: "What has been done can't be undone and none can judge us." Therefore, their idol could be only a person spiritually close to them, also contaminated with hatred toward everything hated by them.

The Red sailors brought to the revolution, along with revolutionary energy and uncompromising struggle with the bourgeoisie and the old world, a lot of unjustified and unmotivated cruelty. Immediately after the establishment of Soviet government in Sevastopol and Vevpatoriya they started the massacre of the so-called "bourgeois intellectuals." They published a declaration of the "Special Meeting of the Republic's Red Fleet Sailors," which called for terror and reprisal. This declaration said,

We, the sailors, have decided: if the killing of our best comrades continues in the future, we shall avenge the death of each murdered comrade by killing hundreds and thousands of the rich who live in light and luxurious palaces and organize counterrevolutionary gangs that fight against the working people, against the workers, soldiers, and peasants who have borne the brunt of the October Revolution.[8]

Zheleznyakov, a Red sailor and a Bolshevik, the head of the guard that had dissolved the Constituent Assembly, said that it was pardonable to kill even a million people to secure the well-being of the Russian nation.

I am not discussing these facts in order to criticize and condemn these poor people, who were embittered by the war and all their previous existence and corrupted by the belief that the victors could not be prosecuted. Even Maxim Gorky, who was not afraid to call a spade a spade and to condemn the crimes of Red sailors, regarded them as spiritual victims of tsarism. He sent a message to the authors of this threatening declaration:

Your words that there can be no judge for you sound to me as half-repentance, half-threat. These works, Messrs. sailors, have fully preserved the triumphant spirit of the bloodthirsty monarchist despotism. You have destroyed its appearance but you have failed to kill its soul. And it lives in you, urges you to roar like animals, and deprives you of the human looks. You should [continued the author of *Untimely Thoughts*] remember that you have been educated by violence and murders. When you say "there can be no judge for us," you say this because you know that none was prosecuted or punished for massacre under tsarism. None was prosecuted for the massacre of thousands of people January 9, 1905; none was sued for the killing of workers in the Lena and Zlotoust mines; none was punished for the slaughter of your fellow sailors from *Ochakov*. None was prosecuted for all those massacres which were so typical of the history of the Russian monarchy. You were brought up in the atmosphere of these unpunished crimes and this bloody belching of the past echoes in your roar.[9]

I am reminding you of all these atrocities and tragedies of our revolution to urge all of us to be reasonable. We must have at least some idea of the views and the options of those party old guard representatives whom we are currently trying to ennoble in our search for the one to blame, and in our attempts to oppose them in every respect to Stalin, a murderer and provocateur. Indeed, the clever and mobile features of Lenin's fellows-in-arms, who are now often shown on television, look much more attractive than the trite, thoughtless, round faces of the Stalinist Guard. The appearance of Trotsky, Zinoviev, Kamenev, and Bukharin is, of course, much more appealing to us than that of Voroshilov, Budennyi, or Zhdanov. But we must be reasonable. The appearance, the language, and the European manners of Trotsky, Zinoviev, or even Lunacharsky* are not indicative of their intellectual values, to say nothing of their moral values.

Tastes differ. It is perestroika's historical merit that it has allowed people to express their likes and dislikes and to speak openly of their political interests and shades of opinion on the ongoing restructuring process.

Some people care most for the Lenin who urged the people to destroy as little as possible and to preserve as much as possible of the old Russia and the old popular (that is, peasants') life-style. For them *Stalinschina* means, above all, the destruction of the fundamentals and prerequisites of the people's life-style. In this connection we should mention, first of all, the name of V. Kozhinov, the author of the article "A Difficult Farewell."† V. Shubkin also gravitates toward treating *Stalinschina* as a purposeful and deliberate destruction of the fundamentals of civil society in Russia.[10]

---

* A. V. Lunacharsky (1875–1933), a prominent Bolshevik and V. I. Lenin's associate, was People's Commissar for Education.
† This author notes, "Stalinism resulted from 'the break' of the people's and human life-style which went beyond all necessary limits" (V. Kozhinov, "The Great Danger," *Nash Sovremennik* (1989), no. 1:159).

But other authors dealing with this subject, who today constitute the majority, gravitate toward the Lenin of the Civil War period. This Lenin believed that the objective of socialist construction in Russia was to crush Russian petite bourgeoisie, to completely destroy old calico (the cheapest cotton cloth), bourgeois Russia. This Lenin took pride in the fact that "we have acquired practical experience in taking the first steps toward destroying capitalism in a country where specific relations existed between the proletariat and the peasants."[11] Therefore, these authors believe that *Stalinschina* is accounted for by our failure to meet the objective put forward by Lenin, by our failure to subordinate the petit-bourgeois (that is, peasants', popular) Russia to the revolution, by our failure to carry through the important policy of "destroying old bourgeois culture."[12]

Tastes indeed differ. If some people love and worship Stalin, there is nothing wrong with some others' admiration for Lev Trotsky, the great "gunman" of our revolution. Everyone is entitled to choose one's own idol. Some people worship the Ironsides, while others worship the martyrs of the revolution who fell victim to the Ironsides' devotion to the ideal of the revolution.

It simply seems to me that it would be wrong to base our judgment of the revolution as a whole, its past and its future, on our personal deep-seated liking for some revolutionary leaders.

For instance, I fully appreciate Otto Latsis's belief that the staunch revolutionaries, the old party guard, were exceptional people; that they had both the experience and the moral strength to keep the country from leftist frustration and to secure economic, political, and cultural progress. This author asks a question: "Can several thousand people—the top-level party members—meet this challenge?" And answers it himself: "Yes, they can, provided they do not interfere with one another."[13]

But with all my respect for Otto Latsis's special liking for those who, as he puts it, "have taken all the key positions in the party and the state," I would nevertheless like to express my own opinion on the matter.

First, I doubt greatly whether these people who organized and guided the process of "destroying old bourgeois culture" could all alone, without the support of other social forces, revitalize the nation's cultural life and once again provide the conditions for cultural creativity and the pulsation of thought. It is noteworthy that the party's old guard did not see the problem; they had no insight into the need for the restoration of the rule of law in Russia or providing the conditions for free spiritual and intellectual creativity. These people—who during the twenties actively participated in the demolition of society's basic cultural institutions, including the Church, in the destruction of the centuries-old life-style and traditions—could hardly recognize these challenges and revive cultural progress with their intellects and hearts.*

Indeed, against the background of the cultural and intellectual poverty left by Stalin in society and in the party, both Trotsky and Karl Radek,† as well as Zinoviev and Bukharin, can be called the luminaries of intellect. But only against the background of this poverty!

Their thinking was, in fact, surprisingly flat and predetermined. They did not go beyond the same scheme of the class approach and arguments in favor of the uncompromising struggle of the new world with the old one. Look through Radek's book *Portraits and Pamphlets*. Does not his language remind you of Stalin's style? It is iron, moralizing, objection-proof, insulting human dignity—the language of a revolutionary tribunal. "Our artists," writes Karl Radek, a representative of the small group of Bolshevik intellectuals attacking Babel, Vsevolod Ivanov, and Pilnyak (Soviet authors), "are poor workers, they don't like to work. They were educated on the bohemian rules reinforced by the mess of the Civil War. They don't want to live in our village, they don't want to travel third-class . . . they like neither to go down into the mines nor to live in workers' settlements . . . They don't know either the true worker or the peasants of our days."[14]

I doubt that an intellectual like Karl Radek, had he remained alive, could have done more than Stalin did for the development of our culture. One who looks, of course, will always find something. Trying hard, it is possible to find a glimmer of spirit in Karl Radek, too. But sensibly speaking, it is hardly possible to prove that he was intellectually and morally superior to the leader of all peoples. It is difficult to believe that a party leader who insisted that every Soviet writer should become a Communist "after having taken serious inner decisions" and "should test himself daily with community work" could revive our national culture.[15] Vadim Kozhinov demonstrated that even Bukharin, the most sincere romanticist among the old Leninist guard, had neither the inner tact nor culture for that.

However, we can hardly be surprised that these Communists, whose personalities were formed at the turn of the century under the influence of the thesis of uncompromising antagonism between the old and the newly born worlds, had no insight into the nature of culture and the ways

---

* The clergy were physically annihilated, the theologians isolated from the people. In 1925, about 2,000 distinguished experts in theology, including the authorities in religious philosophy, were deported from the country. Not only the Russian Orthodox clergy were victimized: out of 166 Buddhist monasteries that had functioned prior to 1917, none existed by 1941; out of 20,000 mosques, only 1,000 survived.

† K. B. Radek (1885–?1939), V. I. Lenin's associate, was active in the Trotskyite opposition.

of its development. Even our contemporary Otto Latsis firmly believes in the need to "destroy old bourgeois culture." He is convinced that the true challenge is to fill as soon as possible the resulting spiritual vacuum with "developed proletarian consciousness," to erect as soon as possible the building of a new socialist culture on the ruins of the old bourgeois one.

This escapes my understanding. We live at the end of the twentieth century. Nevertheless, apparently serious people still believe that had we provided for "stable proletarian consciousness" and "had we reached a higher level of proletarian consciousness" there would have been no Stalinism and we should have secured the boosting of Soviet economy as well as rapid social and cultural progress.* These very sentiments are still being expressed today, when all humanity has already realized that no changes in property relationships, no purity of class consciousness proper, can make up for a lack of competent, resourceful people capable of reasoned and independent judgments. They cannot make up for the lack of workmanship, intellect, and expertise.

Is it not obvious that all the verbiage about pure proletarian consciousness and the conflict between stable proletarian and unstable petit-bourgeois consciousness is nothing but mysticism? Is it not clear that after the struggle with the so-called bourgeois or petit-bourgeois intelligentsia had destroyed the country's intellectual potential, after the "destruction of bourgeois culture" had ruined Russia's productive forces, neither the staunch revolutionaries nor pure proletarian consciousness could have provided for our more or less adequate progress? Vladymir Shubkin is perfectly correct: It is unrealistic to suppose that a few staunch revolutionaries could substitute for an abundance of scholars and scientists, philosophers, distinguished industrialists, production managers, people of culture and letters, composers and singers. This author notes that "the men of science and culture who decided in favor of emigration had been educated on the great traditions of Russian culture, especially that of the nineteenth century. They measurably built up the intellectual potential of Europe and America. Their emigration meant an enormous and often irreparable loss for our culture and our genetic pool."[16]

---

* Otto Latsis notes, "A more or less long period of unstable proletarian consciousness in the initial stages of socialist construction should be regarded neither as accidental nor as characteristic exclusively of the underdeveloped countries with a large rural population. One should view it not as chance but as a social regularity, a manifestation of some specific stage in the development of proletarian consciousness, some intermediate level. Revolutionary class interests have already been identified but there is insufficient experience to completely eliminate petit-bourgeois influence. Old bourgeois culture has already been thrown away but a new, socialist culture has not formed yet. The objective of the party is to provide the working class with methods which make it a higher level of proletarian consciousness, minimizing the inevitable drawbacks" (Latsis, "The Turning Point," 170).

There was, of course, a way out. There is always a way out. It was charted by Lenin in his last works. We could have been saved only by a policy of national reconciliation, the reconciliation with the country's intelligentsia in the name of saving a Russia that was exhausted and ruined. But the Ironsides, with very few exceptions, were opposed to such a concession. They, like Stalin, dreamt of a miracle. They dreamt that all men of letters, without a single exception, should roll up their sleeves and set about building communism.

Our tragedy is that there was actually very little even of the pure proletarian consciousness that is the source of historical optimism for Stalin's idea of a turning point in our history. Indeed, in my view, the very idea of some peculiar, sterile proletarian consciousness is another myth fostered by the intelligentsia, similar to the myth about the exceptional cultural and ethical standards of the Ironsides. It is well known that the most skilled and best educated, and therefore the most affluent part of the working class, cannot develop pure revolutionary consciousness because they are terribly afraid of a forcible revolution. Lenin himself often noted that it is not by chance that the most resourceful and the best educated and skilled workers gravitated toward menshevism. They preferred "bourgeois," "huckstering" cooperation to the revolution. As for the poor, unskilled part of the proletariat, they could never develop pure proletarian consciousness because they lacked both the culture and knowledge for that.

This country simply did not face the danger of the pure proletarian consciousness being dissolved in the impure peasant, petit-bourgeois consciousness, because the former never existed in Russia in measurable amounts.

Otto Latsis insists that in the early twenties the Communist workers of Petrograd* had specific immunity to all sorts of leftist theories, that they would never support Zinoviev's leftist platform on their own. The author of the article "The Turning Point" believes that it was the most proletarian part of the party that was least liable to petit-bourgeois influence.[17]

But it is not clear from where this pure proletariat of Leningrad could have originated if it had not existed in the Petrograd of 1917, that is, before the beginning of the Civil War.

The authors of the recently published essays and articles are generally journalists by background and should, therefore, think in specific terms and interpret abstract notions as the actions of actual people under

---

* In May 1924, Petrograd was renamed Leningrad. This is a reference to the workers of Leningrad.

specific circumstances. It is paradoxical that they prefer instead to play with socio-philosophical categories, hoping that in this way they will come closer to the mysteries of our socialist history.

When I read all the discourses about the struggle and the antagonism between the "pure" industrial proletariat and the "impure" petite bourgeoisie, with which we have all been sick and tired since the time of leftist oppositions, I just want to cry out, "Come on, where is your conscience?" Just recall where and how our revolution took place. Recall all those miserable slum dwellers in Vyborg,* whose very way of life gave rise, above all, to hatred, malice, and lust for revenge. Remember all the suffering and torment that made Russian workers roar with anguish on the verge of the October Revolution. These people, embittered with poverty and humiliation, half-starved and weary, could hardly have recognized the responsibility for their actions and behavior, to say nothing of having insight into the historical meaning of the revolution's dramatic results. Maxim Gorky recalled,

More than once, at night rallies in the Petrograd district, bolshevism was opposed to socialism. I heard attacks on the intelligentsia and a lot of other rubbish. One should keep in mind that all this was happening in the very center of the revolution, where the ideas were sharpened most keenly and wherefrom they would shoot across the underdeveloped, illiterate country.[18]

These are Gorky's very words. He sympathized with the proletariat, supported the workers, but could not remain a mere onlooker when "a certain part of the working mass, excited and manipulated by the leaders who had run amok, showed the spirit and the methods of a caste [and] resorted to violence and terror—the violence against which its best leaders had been fighting so bravely for so long."[19]

I would like to repeat that Stalin actually had no need to dissolve the hereditary proletariat in the impure peasant mass. This process had taken place in Petrograd and in Moscow back during World War I. Maxim Gorky wrote, "Trench warfare annihilated dozens of thousands of the best workers. They were replaced by people who came to work at defense enterprises to avoid military service." In Gorky's view, they were alien to proletarian psychology, politically underdeveloped, lacking the urge inherent in a proletarian to create a new culture.

They are driven exclusively by bourgeois ambition to arrange their personal well-being, as soon as possible and at any cost. These people are organically unable to accept and to carry through the ideas of pure socialism. There are some plants at which workers have started stealing and selling copper machine parts. There is considerable evidence to suggest the wildest anarchy among the working mass.[20]

---

* The Vyborgsky district is a working class district in Petrograd.

I think Gorky could not have afforded to slander the working class of Petrograd. Had it been slander, had the consciousness of Petrograd workers reached the heights of social stability described in Otto Latsis's articles, the new Soviet government would not have had to resort to the harsh methods of coercing them to work, which turned out to be necessary immediately after the October Revolution. One should keep in mind that Lenin, confronted with the large-scale resistance of workers to the new order immediately after the revolution, had to develop a whole system of measures toward coercing them to work. In his view, the experience of such coercion could be different for society as a whole.

In one place half a score of rich, a dozen rogues, half a dozen workers who shirk their work (in the manner of rowdies, the manner in which many compositors in Petrograd, particularly in the Party printing-shops, shirk their work) will be put in prison. In another place they will be put to cleaning latrines. In a third place they will be provided with "yellow tickets"* after they have served their time, so that everyone shall keep an eye on them, as *harmful* persons, until they reform. In a fourth place, one out of every ten idlers will be shot on the spot. In a fifth place, mixed methods may be adopted.[21]

Nikolay Bukharin did not foster any illusions about the Russian working class and the purity of its proletarian consciousness either. During the Civil War he, of course, set little store by the existing working class and set his Communist hopes, above all, on the future one. As for the workers who were fated to become the forerunners of communism, Bukharin believed that they had to reconcile themselves to coercion to work. "One should proceed from the fact," observed the author of *The Economy of the Transitory Period*,

that in the working population there are some groups completely corrupted by capitalism, self-interested to the utmost. But even relatively wide strata of the working class bear the stamp of the commodity-capitalist world . . . Hence, *coercive discipline* is absolutely inevitable. Its coercive nature will be the stronger the less the given stratum or the given population group is characterized by voluntary inner discipline, i.e., the less revolutionary it is. Even the proletarian vanguard, united in the revolutionary Communist party, establishes such *coercive* self-discipline in its own ranks . . . The elimination of the so-called "freedom of labor" is one of the basic coercive forms of the new type for the working class itself . . . As it cannot reconcile itself with the correctly organized planned economy and planned distribution of labor.[22]

I would like to repeat: We should not interfere with anyone's beliefs. One might even believe that the Bolsheviks of Petrograd of the October Revolution and the Civil War period were saints thanks to their pure

---

* A document testifying that its carrier was deprived his or her civil rights.

proletarian consciousness. One might believe that they did their best and even better than their best to resist leftism, revolutionary maximalism, and impatience, to resist the temptation to take revenge and to loot the looters. But, in my view, you cannot impose the myth bred in your soul on other souls. Indeed, there were brave and courageous people devoted to the revolution and ready to die for it at any time. But at the same time they behaved like other people did, and they actively, and sometimes enthusiastically, contributed to stoking the fire of the Civil War. They did not lose the chance to deal with the bourgeoisie of Petrograd, whom they hated, did they? No, they did not miss this opportunity. They acted in keeping with the threat used at that terrible time by the newspaper *Pravda:* "Each of our dead will be paid for by hundreds of bourgeois dead."

Today, unfortunately, there are no longer any white spots in our post-October history that could really soothe our spirits. Nikolay Bukharin was one of the leaders of the October Revolution who opposed the general secretary after Lenin's death and who made the largest contribution to opposing leftism. Despite this, in the twenties, as a Bolshevik he put it down to his party's credit that it had complied in every way with the desire of the revolutionary masses. In his 1925 article "The Road to Socialism and the Union of Workers and Peasants," Bukharin wrote,

The decisive contribution was made by the unanimous efforts of workers and sol-diers, the soldiers who were one bone and one flesh with our peasants. The sol-diers wanted peace—and so did the peasants, the peasants longed for land—so did the soldiers; *the peasants craved to deal with the landlords—so did the soldiers. All these demands were supported, popularized by the working class and its party. They became its top-priority slogans*[emphasis added by author].[23]

It's up to you. Those who want to may, of course, go along with Otto Latsis. They may believe that the 2 percent of the party membership—that is, the Bolsheviks who had joined the party before February 1917, the so-called Ironsides who took all the key positions in the party and the state—could really resist the leftist urge to destruction of the revolution-ary masses. They may believe that the Ironsides alone really could keep the revolution within the frame of reason and sufficient measures.*

---

* "They accounted for only two percent of the party membership but they were the Iron-sides and had enormous political experience, and they took all the key posts in the party and the state. They ought to have kept the revolutionary locomotive on the rails during the most difficult period of the revolution. Only after that could the role of a personality or several personalities on whom the success of the entire cause depended diminish to the normal standards. Was it feasible for several thousand people who were the party leader-ship? Yes, it was, provided they didn't interfere with one another" (Latsis, "The Turning Point," 127).

I personally prefer to side with Bukharin. who had enough courage to tell the truth. He admitted that the Ironsides (those who, quoting another revolutionary leader, "toughened the revolutionary energy of Petersburg workers and soldiers,") were ready for anything in the name of victory, up to "supporting" physical violence to their former exploiters, up to "supporting" the robbing of the thieves.

Nikolay Bukharin at least cannot be caught in a lie. He spoke aloud the truth that was also voiced by Korolenko* and Gorky, who refused to accept "Trotsky's furious dance on the ruins of Russia." He reminded us of the fact that (especially in the first post-October months) both the so-called Bolshevik intellectuals and nonintellectuals were contaminated with the anti-intelligentsia feeling characteristic of the masses. When the workers of Petrograd insisted on Red terror they got the support of the party leadership, did they not? We cannot prove that the Russian workers were less enthusiastic than the peasants about plundering the plunderers, can we? Maxim Gorky, who watched this expropriatory confusion in Petrograd, actually quoted Korolenko, who described expropriation procedures in Poltava province. The author of "The Stormy Petrel" wrote,

One of the loudest and most favorite slogans of our particular revolution was, of course, the slogan "Plunder the plunderers." And so they are looting—beautifully, artistically; no doubt, history will tell with great enthusiasm about the process of Russia's self-robbery. Churches and war memorials are being plundered and sold; canons and rifles are being sold; commissariat reserves are being ransacked. The palaces of former grand dukes are being robbed. Everything that can be robbed is being robbed; everything that can be sold is being sold.[24]

It is paradoxical that we are currently trying to debunk Stalin by relying on the interpretation of ethics and the spiritual development of the individual formulated by him and his epoch. See for yourselves. When was it established that a so-called iron will, devotion to one's principles, and so on, was evidence of high morals? The answer, of course, is in the thirties, when Stalin and his fellows-in-arms—Yezhov, Beria, and some others—were glorified. Before the revolution, Russia had regarded the Ironsides as people with hardened souls, incapable of compassion and mercy. Indeed, an iron will has always been esteemed in history by all nations. But all nations could also distinguish the will from the conscience, men of steel from men of feeling. In contrast, we somehow came to the conclusion that a strong-willed revolutionary capable of self-denial, able to sacrifice himself or herself for the sake of the revolution's victory, should necessarily be a person of conscience with high moral principles.

---

* V. G. Korolenko (1853–1921) was a Russian author and publicist.

The Ironsides are often described today as "the votaries and devotees of the idea," who were devoted to it under any conditions to the hour of their death. In contrast, it is stressed that from the very outset nothing was allegedly sacred to Stalin, that socialism was not dear to him. In this way we are brought to the conclusion that, morally and intellectually, Stalin was measurably inferior to other representatives of the old guard and, therefore, belonged to a less worthy category of people.

Let us now consider the factual aspect of this issue, though it would be easy for me to prove that Stalin believed in the feasibility of communism and world revolution not less but more than many others, such as Bukharin, did at a later time. Had it been otherwise, he would not have taken grain away from starving countries, like Czechoslovakia. The moment Stalin saw a chance to promote world revolution, an offensive on capital on the global scale, he immediately seized this opportunity. In my view, had Trotsky or Radek, Kamenev or Zinoviev been in Stalin's shoes in the post-war period they would have failed to do as much as he did to expand the bridgehead of the world revolution to which they had devoted their lives. We have no grounds to assert that Stalin, in contrast to the other leaders of the October Revolution, betrayed the idea of the world revolution.

A Deficit of Revisionism

But let us for the moment abstain from judging whether Stalin was or was not a votary and a devotee of the idea. Let us abstain from the discussion of whether he was sincere in his belief that violence and execution were the most adequate methods for implementing the ideal of a classless society, or whether he resorted to them simply as the result of innate villainy. It is more important for us now to decide to what extent zealous devotion to an idea—in this particular case to the idea of a world revolution, and readiness to do anything for its sake—can be regarded as a mark of high moral and ethical development.

First of all we must rehearse a few self-evident remarks on devotion. The devotion to an idea per se can, of course, result from absolutely different motives. It can be a manifestation of goodness, but it can also be a manifestation of evil. It may result from great suffering and hard labor of the brain and heart, but equally it may reveal an idle brain and soul and the inability to work. It may result from the underdevelopment of someone's personality and lack in independence and self-confidence. It may be the result of despair, the wish to lean on something, to escape loneliness and depression. But I would like to reiterate that it can be a manifestation of the highest intellectual and ethical development.

I believe this should especially be taken into consideration in Russia because futile daydreaming is, of course, our national characteristic. We can be extremely easily tempted by some global idea. The less it has to do with reality, the better. This is because our realities have always been very bad and no one wants to deal with them. We, in this country, should be afraid above all of belief in something. We were warned against it by such distinguished thinkers as Gogol, Herzen, and Chaadayev.* As Nikolay Berdyayev† is still little known in this country I would like to refer to some of his comments on the matter. He stressed that "conservatism and stagnation had converged in our path with the liking for innovation and the latest European schools which we had never really mastered."[25] As Berdyayev noted in "Vekhi," our *raznochintsy*‡ followed by our socialist intelligentsia, had a special weakness for accepting without any analysis ideas that promised to settle Russian problems, to eliminate poverty and autocracy. The Russian intelligentsia, as he put it, "was always willing to accept an ideology which centered on the problem of distribution and equality."[26]

Blind faith may eventually result from elementary laziness. It is unnecessary for such a devotee to think about the agonizing contradictions of human history and the human soul. Devotion protects us from disagreeable thoughts, from the unpleasant truths that destroy the comfort of romantic faith. It eventually makes it unnecessary to study the world, or people, or to investigate the hidden depth of the human soul. Maxim Gorky, who well knew the Russian soul, wrote that

we are all willing to come to believe in something as soon as possible. To believe in a good "lord" capable of "reasoning" and establishing a kind order inside and outside . . . The norodnichestvo made a honey-cake of a Russian peasant and we willingly believed them—our peasant is superb, a true Chinese, he is much superior to a European peasant.

In this country, Gorky insisted, people believe not because they know and love but simply for the sake of peace of mind. Meditative faith is futile and abortive; it is "dead."[27]

Staunch people who go to the end and remain true to their principles and oaths are worthy of respect. One may disagree with their beliefs, but they should never be put on a par with the cynics who change their con-

---

* P. Ya. Chaadayev (1794–1856) was a Russian religious philosopher.
† N. A. Berdyayev (1874–1948), one of the leading Russian religious philosophers, lived in emigration since 1922.
‡ *Raznochintsy*—people from different social classes that were officially recognized in Russia at the end of the eighteenth and nineteenth centuries (such as the clergy, petite bourgeoisie, clerks, merchants, etc.)—engaged in nonmenial work.

victions like a pair of gloves. Even if this is blind faith and fanaticism, it deserves to be taken seriously as a manifestation of human culture.

You have to be really strong-willed, a true person of steel, to openly conflict with government in Russia. Not everyone can endure the results of this choice, the belief in the feasibility of a different life.

But faiths differ. It is imperative at least to distinguish faith in moral ideas, in something that has been tested by the lives of many generations, from faith in various political ideas, faith in what is desirable and possible. The belief in a specific personality, in Christ or in Buddha, differs greatly from the faith in the feasibility of, for instance, collective grain factories in agriculture. It is up to you who will be your god and in what way you shall love him or her: whether you prefer blind faith or enlightenment by theology.

But it is a whole different ballgame to discuss the zealous belief in the need to destroy bourgeois culture and the old world, to eliminate the market relationship, and so on. Under these circumstances blind faith is equivalent to crime. My argument is that in this case your faith is outside-oriented; it touches upon the fates of many people. Its very existence provokes people to action. In such a situation intellectual maturity is manifest not in faith but in doubt, in the ability to maintain a critical distance that allows the individual once again to reflect upon arguments that look superficially quite convincing.

When you assume the responsibility for popularizing something that has never existed and cannot yet be tested by practice (especially if you call yourself a materialist), you simply ought to use to the utmost your capacity for intellectual doubt. You should do this even if you have seen for yourself that people are tired of the old way of life and are looking forward to a new one. You ought to make sure at least mentally that this new way of life is feasible. You ought to think at least for a moment about the habits and feelings of those whose happiness you desire, and to match these habits and feelings to the new patterns you are making for them. The fact that people are tired of their old life-style, that they hate it and are looking forward to a new one, cannot by itself guarantee that they can live differently, that this alternative way of life is feasible.

Indeed, it is not enough to seize power; it is necessary to keep it. But today we are aware that this is not enough either. Difficulties arose where we had not expected them. It is even more difficult to prove the feasibility of an alternative life-style, to prove that the dream may come true, to prove that people can live in a different way, that there can be neither rich nor poor, that all can be completely equal.

You should, of course, look for the answer to the question, "And can people live differently?" before you start destroying the old world and the established order. It is also self-evident that the devotees of an idea who are more concerned about its practical implementation than about gaining insight into their faith and their ideas are incapable both of such reasoning and such a responsible attitude toward revolution.

Isn't it true that there is nothing more dangerous than the arrogance and self-confidence of people who have challenged the established world order? It is true that history is in continuous progress, and it is impossible to preserve life and human civilization without periodically throwing away concepts that have become obsolete and are obstacles to progress. Reforms and revolutions are necessary for maintaining society's spiritual health. But how can one determine which doctrines have really grown outdated and should be replaced and which should be simply modernized? How can one determine, for instance, that the process of self-development has exhausted itself, that from this particular moment all development has stopped and the movement has really gone downward? The nature of social life, like human nature, is universal. Beneath the obvious there is the hidden, the eternal X, which confuses the plans of those arrogant theorists who have come to believe that they know and understand everything.

It is impossible to determine precisely the potential of some social system until it has completely decayed by itself.

The blunder may result from your likings and your original aims. If you believe from the very outset that the social institution under study is doomed to oblivion, that the collisions and conflicts you observe are death throes, then you will naturally press for the forcible destruction of the foredoomed institution and set all your hopes on some other social institution that has never yet existed. But if some part of your heart is in harmony with the society in which you live, if you appreciate at least something in your present life, then you will probably give it another chance and will try to release its latent potentialities with the help of reforms.

A serious revolutionary, a reformer who assumes the responsibility for the destiny of millions of people, not to say civilization itself, cannot but reflect. The revolutionary should not be limited to mere belief in the correctness and sanctity of a chosen ideology or concept. A revolutionary who is a true intellectual must ask himself or herself thousands of questions before plunging into a maelstrom that will shatter the world. Could it be that everyone before us was deluded and only we know the truth? Isn't it dangerous to throw away pills prescribed by other physicians without knowing for sure that your medicine will cure the patient? Am I correct in my calculations? Have I a clear insight into the nature of the human soul? Do people really seek equality?

I may be wrong, but I would think that the morals of those who simply and zealously adhered to a preselected idea and never doubted it should be evaluated in a revised terminology. Such expressions as "moral and intellectual standards," in the exact meaning of these words, are out of place here.

When I attended lectures on the history of Marxist-Leninist philosophy in the early sixties, students were taught to view as a merit the fact that Russian Social Democrats, especially the Bolsheviks, were, unlike their German colleagues, true disciples; that they firmly believed in, and followed in every respect, the commandments of the classics. At that time we did view it as a merit and in our seminars condemned Bernstein* for the doubts he expressed.

But today, twenty-five years later—when all the mysteries of our post-October history have been divulged, when we know that the victims of the cataclysms endured by the country in the twentieth century may be counted in dozens of millions, when it has become obvious that socialism as built by Stalin was not vital from the very outset—I regret ever more often that revisionism has not taken root in Russian soil.

Of course, these reflections come with hindsight. But we must at least today tell ourselves the truth, we must understand what has happened to us. Certainly, millions of victims in the Civil War, the atrocities of which have shocked the world, can be accounted for by their hatred of former masters, which accumulated over centuries of humiliation and resulted in an uncontrollable outbreak of anger. But they can also be accounted for by the zealous belief that it is feasible and necessary to exterminate the proprietorial instinct from the human spirit. They are accounted for by the firm belief that all acts may be justified to retain the bridgehead for the future joint attack with the awakened proletariat of the West on a capitalism that is doomed by history. They are accounted for by the firm belief that any actions that promote our advance toward communism, toward the aims charted by the founding fathers of Marxism, are perfectly excusable. There would have been fewer victims but for the conviction that the new had to be built on the ruins of the old; that so-called bourgeois, mercantile cooperation or family work on land or the instinct of ownership would be out of place in the emerging socialist society.

---

* E. Bernstein (1850–1932), one of the leaders of the 2d International, was the first German Social Democrat to begin a revision of the basic tenets of Karl Marx's philosophy.

There would have been fewer victims in the Civil War, and the war itself would have been different, if it were not for the dogmatic, orthodox hostility of the Ironsides to the individual farmer and the middle peasant.* There would have been fewer victims but for their naive belief that society could feed itself without those hard-working farmers, the true owners; the belief that rural proletarians working on large socialist farms would be able to secure a happy future for humankind. Had not the Bolsheviks initially aimed at "neutralizing" the middle peasant, had they from the very beginning decided in favor of the union with him or her there might have been, as Gavriil Popov, a prominent Soviet economist, remarked, "no serious civil war" in this country.[28]

The class struggle in the villages stoked the fire of the Civil War, which broke out in the summer of 1918. One should bear in mind that it was deliberately provoked by the towns. In promoting class struggle in the villages, the party leadership was guided not only by the excusable wish to save the proletariat and the Red Army from starvation, but also by the urge to extend the socialist orientation of the revolution and to make it permanent in character. The Committees of the Village Poor (Combeds) were set up not only to get grain but also "to split the village," "to make the October Revolution of the towns a true October Revolution."[29]

The old guard, the Ironsides, went out of their way to implement the teaching on class struggle as soon as possible, to involve all working people in the continuing process of destroying the old world and bourgeois culture. Everyone must make his choice, said Lev Trotsky on July 4, 1918, blessing the members of a food requisition detachment for a "crusade against the kulaks."

"The choice essentially boils down to the Civil War," Trotsky continued, "and our party is in favor of the Civil War. The Civil War has centered on grain. Soviets, take the field!"[30]

Grigori Zinoviev adhered to the same views in his numerous messages to the village poor. According to him, the revolution in the village started right then—with the transition of power to a "true working peasant" who owned nothing, to the "blackbone"—to the poor. The leader of the Petrograd party organization said that poor peasants were to play the major role not only in the Russian village but also in the future world revolution. But their position in rural areas was such that had we held elections to local Soviets they would not have been elected. Therefore, Zinoviev noted, it was necessary to "make short work of villains" and the Combeds should have been set up by "the agitators sent from the center."[31]

---

* A middle peasant in Russia was a peasant of average means.

The zealous belief of the Ironsides, especially in the initial stage of the revolution, overcame reason in everything: their assessment of the readiness of world imperialism for socialism; their evaluation of the Russian worker's wish to live and to work in a Communist way; and their assessment of the people's capacity for innovations. The Second Party Program was the most graphic evidence of the victory won by the old guard's faith and devotion over reason. This program reflected their hope to make a single leap from capitalist to Communist Russia. I agree with those who assert that had Lenin been healthy he would have without fail reconsidered the program of 1918, which aimed directly at building communism in Russia. But our concern is different. Is the orthodox nature of this program, the Ironsides' aspiration to adhere to Marx's aim of eliminating the market and the fiscal-commodity relationship, of building a classless society and nationalizing all means of production, a manifestation of their high moral and intellectual standards? In my view, it is not. Any reasonable person must agree with Gavriil Popov that, in retrospect, it is difficult to call this program a meaningful and logically composed document. This author notes,

To us, thinking over some pages of the Second Program seventy years later, it is obvious that the old world, which was allegedly ready for the new system, for some reason has not collapsed. It has yielded to the new formation only the regions that abound in antagonisms but clearly lack the economic basis for socialism or in the countries in which socialist armed forces have entered. But can we agree that the given characteristic of imperialism was, probably, correct for its epoch? It seems to me that even then, in 1919, it was wrong to assert that imperialism was ready for socialist transformations: the scope of the deadlock confronted by imperialism at the turn of the century and that of the contradictions and horrors resulting from it were mistaken for the level of the socialization of productive forces. But the deadlock of the system is just another argument in favor of reforms. It is not an argument in favor of a specific reform alternative. Imperialism came to a deadlock in the first quarter of the twentieth century. But does it mean that socialism was the only way out of the deadlock?[32]

Today, at the end of the twentieth century, we have developed an insight into many phenomena and processes. For instance, Edward Bernstein was a doubting Marxist who called upon German Social Democrats to reject Marx's theses on the need to destroy civil society and bourgeois civilization.* It would be easy to prove that he had much higher moral

---

* Marx was, of course, to the hour of his death devoted to the "Manifesto of the Communist Party," which taught the proletarians to destroy everything that had hitherto protected and secured private property. (See Karl Marx and Frederick Engels, *Selected Works* [Moscow, 1971], 1:108–36.) He proceeded from the belief that it was no longer possible to stop the process of the degradation of civil, burgher society launched by the formation of industrial

standards than Lev Bronstein (Trotsky).* Trotsky was an orthodox Marxist who zealously believed with all the Ironsides, to the hour of his death, in the need to restructure all the fundamentals of bourgeois civil society. And he urged his followers to clear social soil in such a manner that "everything would disintegrate" and nothing old could survive.†

It would be easy for me to demonstrate that the doubting Marxist Edward Bernstein, who tried to convince us that large enterprises are not always superior to small ones, especially in agriculture, and who tried to substantiate, contrary to what Marx said, the vitality of individual farming, had much higher spiritual and moral standards than Lev Bronstein and his fellow Ironsides.‡ They died with the conviction that Marx was always correct, that the individual farmer was doomed, and that nothing but grain factories, centralized labor organization in agriculture on the national scale, and the complete transformation of the peasant's very nature could save the country from poverty.§

---

capital. He believed that bourgeois civilization with its cult of private property and the family home, with family education of the children, freedom of conscience, and civic rights was actually doomed. In his early article "On the Jewish Question," Karl Marx declared the basic principles of his teaching, saying, for instance, that he rejects "the so-called" rights of man, "as they" are nothing but the rights of a member of civil society, that is, the rights of egoistic man, of man separated from other men and from the community. See Marx and Engels, *Collected Works*, 3:146–75.

* "But what does this struggle and the elimination of civic society mean?" Edward Bernstein asked and answered his question himself: "No one thinks that civic society as a civically civilized form of community should disappear. On the contrary, Social Democrats do not intend to destroy this society and turn all its members into proletarians: rather they press for the improvement of the social status of the worker, raising it up to that of a citizen and thus spreading civic rights. They press for a truly general civil society. Social Democrats do not wish to replace civil society by proletarian society. Their only wish is to replace the capitalist system by a socialist one" (Edward Bernstein, *Social Problems* [Die Voraussetzungen des Socialismus und die Aufgaben der Socialdemokratie] [in Russian] [Petrograd, 1906], 181–82).

† Lev Trotsky insisted that society should "continuously shed its skin." Any stage of transformations logically follows the previous one and directly results from it. Revolutions in economy, technology, knowledge, family, everyday life, and morals develop in close harmony with one another and prevent society from reaching an equilibrium." See Lev Trotsky, *Permanent Revolution* (in Russian) (Berlin, 1930).

‡ Edward Bernstein wrote, "If the continuous advance of technology and the increased centralization of enterprises in an ever larger number of industries is a fact which even an inveterate conservative can hardly ignore today, it is equally obvious that in some sectors small and middle enterprises have proved their vitality alongside large ones. . . . And, finally, as far as agriculture is concerned, the tendency in the size of farms throughout Europe and partly America, apparently contradicts everything that has been so far suggested by socialist theory. Whereas industry and trade revealed only a slower movement towards larger production than the theory had envisaged, the trend in agriculture was either toward stability or a direct decrease in the size of farms" (Bernstein, *Social Problems*, 82–87).

§ "To emancipate the peasant from the pressure of elemental forces on his consciousness, we should change his peasant nature completely. This is the objective of socialism" (Lev Trotsky, *A Squeaking Machinery: Popular Explanation on the Right—and the Left Wings*).

In my view, the doubting Bernstein had higher moral standards than the Russian Ironsides, with their zealous devotion to Marx's commandments. Not only because he took into account the interests of those of the minority, whose noble proletarian origin was not written on their faces. Not only because he respected the wish of a peasant to remain a peasant and that of a petty trader to remain the petty trader. Not only because he treated them on a par with all other members of society. But because he was also able to see things as they were.

He realized, for instance, that the legal basis of the so-called civil society (that is, the right of the minority to disagree and the rights and freedoms of the individual, a legal basis ignored by many Marxists owing to its "bourgeois level") was in fact the foundation of modern civilization, and its destruction would entail terrible cataclysms. He realized that the replacement of one type of class domination by a different one changed little and could not by itself lead to democracy.* He realized that, contrary to Karl Marx's forecast, the civil bourgeois society, which had evolved over centuries, managed to withstand the pressures of entropy and destruction exerted by a redundant industrial population and their working environment. He saw that bourgeois society found some potentialities for subordinating these pressures to its values, norms, and principles, and integrating them into the traditional bourgeois way of life. Contrary to the superficial arguments of such Ironsides as Lev Trotsky in favor of permanent revolutions in morality and family, these institutions have even been consolidated as we reach the twenty-first century. Hence, it has been shown that traditional virtues should not be viewed as "a provincial convention" and that those who had transgressed the "Do not kill!" principle most often became the victims of their own moral relativism.

However, we may demonstrate that a doubting Marxist always has higher moral standards than a devotee of Marxist dogma, using as an illustration the history of the Bolshevik party itself. Just ask yourself,

---

* "What is democracy?" Edward Bernstein asked himself in his favorite manner. "The answer to this question seems quite obvious: on the face of it, it can be simply translated as 'popular government.' But having thought a little, you come to understand that this definition is formal and superfluous. Nearly everyone using the word democracy means something more than simply a form of government. We shall approach the subject a bit closer if we reverse the definition and spell democracy as 'absence of class domination.' In this way we shall describe a state of society in which no class enjoys any special privileges as compared with society as a whole. . . . Today we regard as 'undemocratic' the suppression of majority by minority though originally it was believed to be perfectly compatible with popular government. . . . The behavior of the tyrannical majority in the epochs of a true civil war differs drastically from the domination of the majority in modern democracy" (Bernstein, *Social Problems*, 172–75).

Which Lenin had more compassion and morality: the one who sacrificed the well-being and the daily bread (and, therefore, the lives) of hundreds and thousands of people to his belief in the principle of "labor in common on a common farm," or the one who sacrificed his former faith in the idea of a single national syndicate to save the lives of workers and peasants?*

Which Lenin had more feeling and higher moral standards: the one who, intoxicated by victory, declared (in keeping with Marx's behests) a holy war on all those who had fallen into the habit of working autonomously—that is, peasants, merchants, and artisans†—or the one who realized that we should be more afraid of starvation than we should of the petite bourgeoisie?‡

In my view, it is Lenin the apostate who is more humane; the Lenin who came to understand that human life had greater value than theoretical dogma[33]; the Lenin who came to doubt, even on his deathbed, the correctness of Marx's theses on direct harmonization of the interests of society and the individual.[34] I can trace greater humanism and morality in this Lenin, who dared to transgress the authority of dogma in the name of life, the one who dared to appear "unprincipled."

What of Bukharin, a left-wing Communist who during the Civil War encroached on the sanctum of the homeland, who glorified the craziness of national self-annihilation and destruction?§ Even Bukharin can be pardoned for his grave sins. Not only because he was very young when he committed them, but also because he saw his equals in the children and grandchildren of the kulaks in the twenties and realized that they were

---

* "We must recognize the fact," Lenin said at the 10th Party Congress, "that the masses are utterly worn out and exhausted. What can you expect after seven years of war in this country, if the more advanced countries still feel the effects of four years of war? In this backward country, the workers, who have made unprecedented sacrifices, and the masses of the peasants are in a state of utter exhaustion after seven years of war. You must have a worker and a peasant who can work; yet in most cases they are in no condition for it, they are exhausted, worn out" (Lenin, *Collected Works*, 32:224).

† "To fight to instill into the people's minds the idea of Soviet state control and accounting, and to carry out this idea in practice; to fight to break with the rotten past, which taught the people to regard the procurement of bread and clothes as a 'private affair,' and buying and selling as a transaction 'which concerns only myself' is a great fight of world-historic significance, a fight between socialist consciousness and bourgeois-anarchist spontaneity" (Lenin, *Collected Works*, 27:254).

‡ "We must not be afraid of the growth of the petite bourgeoisie and small capital. What we must fear is protracted starvation" (Lenin, *Collected Works*, 32:237).

§ "Old society in its state and production forms breaks down, disintegrates completely, falls apart in every respect. History has never seen such an enormous breaking. But the proletarian revolution could not do without it. This revolution will reunify the disintegrated elements in a new way, in new combinations, in keeping with new principles and will turn them into the foundation of a future society" (Bukharin, *The Economy in the Transitory Period*, 5–6).

equally entitled to live on the land their forefathers had inhabited for centuries.*

There is no question that it is possible to explain why, compared with their German counterparts, Russian Social Democrats developed the ability to have faith in and to serve the cause of Marxism rather than doubt its basic tenets. It is now clear why they bitterly opposed any attempt to reinterpret certain provisions of Marxism. Unlike Marxists who defend their convictions and interests in the framework of parliamentary democracy under the protection of the law, Marxists who are engaged in an underground revolutionary struggle against monarchy and are subjected to persecution do not have this kind of freedom and cannot look at the texts of their teachers from the outside, as it were. For Russia's Social Democrats, particularly the Bolsheviks, Marxism represented not only a source of knowledge about the laws of historical development and the contradictions of capitalism but also a source of faith in the ultimate triumph of their cause and hope for an early liberation from the depravities of Russian capitalism and retribution for all their sufferings and trials. They could not doubt Marx in his conviction that the epoch when "capitalist private property would be no more" and "expropriators would be expropriated" had come.† For them, Marxism was a justification of the violent surgical treatment of Russia's ills. It was their alternative prompted by the atmosphere of violence in the country. Yes, it is true that violence bred violence and that there was no end to it. But the atmosphere of violence and the violent means of achieving the objective were certainly not conducive to a broad intellectual outlook on life. Militant Russian Marxists were incapable of a sober self-appraisal and a critical reevaluation of the ideas they had armed themselves with. A person lifted to the heaven of hope by the tornado of revolution and enraptured by the festival of the downtrodden and the exploited simply has no time for and is incapable of taking a look around. As the revolutionary situation in Russia matured, left-wing Russian Marxists were increasingly unwilling to undertake and indeed had little time for a sober-minded interpretation of Marx's writings. Their hearts were longing for the service of Marxism, which they regarded as a symbol of faith rather than anything else.

---

* Nikolay Bukharin finished the description of his theory, which involved the integration of the well-to-do peasant into socialism, with the following sentimental phrase: "The kulak's grandson may, eventually, be grateful to us that we have treated him in this way" (Bukharin, *Selected Works*, 133).

† This is a reference to the final section of chapter 22, vol. 1, of *The Capital*, where Marx says, "The knell of capitalist private property sounds. The expropriators are expropriated" (Marx, *Capital: A Critical Analysis of Capitalist Production* [Moscow: Progress Publishers, 1978], 1:715).

In that situation the intellectual choice was very limited – either to become a revolutionary and, guided by the Marxist teaching of the proletarian revolution as a locomotive of history, to promote its cause or to become an academic looking at the revolution from the outside. The 1905 revolution forever severed the thin philosophical threads that connected the official wing and the militant wing of Russia's Marxists. Stunned by what they believed to be unimaginable atrocities of the revolution, the former abandoned Marxism for good* while the latter turned into committed and active champions of Marxist ideas.

Full credit must be given to those official Marxists who "handed in their resignation" and preferred to preserve their freedom of thought rather than become the makers of history. They realized that their choice was an exception to the rule rather than otherwise. They knew that the attitude toward Marxism as a symbol of faith, which emerged in the wake of the 1905 revolution, and the belief in the approaching kingdom of truth on earth, with Marxism as its foundation, was inevitable. Berdyayev wrote, "Who is to blame for the intellectual decadence of the Russian Social Democratic movement? The culprit is here for all to see – the monarchy and its atrocities which have determined the character of the Russian revolution. The government's violent reaction systematically cultivated the idea of a social revolution and fostered the psychology which transformed political passions into religious fervor and politicians into fanatics."†

In that situation a self-sacrificing faith in Marxism was almost inevitable. It was something a dedicated and honest revolutionary, longing for a festival of history, could not resist. One other fateful circumstance was mentioned above: None of the militant, "ironsided" Marxists in Russia had the basic philosophical education or the level of knowledge in the history of human culture necessary to make an objective assessment of Marx's role in the history of social philosophy and to correlate his notions of the future with the ideas of the great utopians.

They should not be blamed for that. We know that Trotsky, Sverdlov, and Zinoviev spared no effort to educate themselves. But a miracle could not happen. The most they could achieve was to learn the basics of

---

* Nikolai Alexandrovich Berdyayev (1874–1948) was a Russian bourgeois mystical philosopher, existentialist, founder of the so-called new Christianity, and ideologist of Vekhism. In the opinion of Nikolai Berdyayev, it is generally impossible to develop Marxism and to remain a Marxist at the same time because "every effort of a free mind leads to a decisive crisis and decomposition of the doctrine" (Berdyayev, "On the History and Psychology of Russian Marxism," in *Philosophical, Social and Literary Essays (1900–1906)* [Petersburg, 1906], 384).

† Ibid., 384–85.

Marxism and admire its integrity and organic beauty.* But they had neither the intellectual power nor the desire to gain a profound insight into the inner drama of Karl Marx's teaching or understand the many contradictions that had already become obvious even in their time and the logical inconsistencies between certain aspects of his socioeconomic theory. The Ironsides did not respond to the scientific criticism of Marx's teaching. They ran from the "bourgeois pestilence" of all those arguments, proofs, and facts, which even early in the twentieth century were sufficient to undertake a reevaluation of certain provisions of Marxism and cleanse it from everything obsolete.

The Ironsides ignored not only what we now refer to as "Western" and primarily German literature exposing the contradictions of Marxism but Russian literature, too. A serious scholarly dialogue between the liberal and the militant factions of Russian Marxists on the internal contradictions of the theory of Marx and Engels did not happen.

Finally, if we really want to get at the truth, we must tell ourselves the most important of all truths. We cannot really call people morally and intellectually developed if, being in their right mind, they could agree with Marx that there are no laws, no crimes, and no moral standards but only the laws of history and the interests of the liberation of the proletariat. In this case their young age is no excuse. Young Lenin was sincere, when, following Sombart,† he insisted that "in Marxism there is not a grain of ethics from beginning to end"; theoretically, it subordinates the "ethical standpoint" to the "principle of causality"; in practice, it reduces it to the class struggle."[35]

But if the leaders of Bolshevism voluntarily put themselves beyond good and evil, what is the point in distorting the history of our party and the country and of regarding their actions in the framework of a system of coordinates, which they did not accept and could not care less about?

---

* In this respect, a comparison between the style of Marx and the style of Lenin in Trotsky's article "Lenin as a National Type" is particularly revealing: "Marx's style itself—rich and beautiful, a combination of power and flexibility, wrath and irony, austerity and refinement—carries in itself the literary and aesthetical accumulations of all previous socio-political literature, beginning from the Reformation and earlier times. The literary and oratorical style of Lenin is terribly simple, utilitarian and ascetic, just his entire lifestyle. . . . The whole of Marx is in *The Communist Manifesto*, in the preface to his *Critique* and in *The Capital*. Even if he were not the founder of the First International, he would ever remain what he is today. His scientific work is only preparation for action. Even if he had not published a single book in the past, he would have entered history for ever as he is entering it now—the leader of the proletarian revolution and the founder of the Third International" (Trotsky, "Lenin as a National Type"[in Russian] [Leningrad, Gosudarstvennoye Izdatelstvo, 1924], 3–8).
† Werner Sombart (1863–1941) was a German philosopher.

In itself, Marxism, with its struggle against moral dogmas and the eternal and immutable moral law,* is certainly not the fruit of an individual's evil will. It was born of the crisis that gripped European civilization. Not only Marx but Nietzsche, too, revolted against the prejudices of morality. Russian Bolsheviks equally share the responsibility for the insanity of the First World War, which created the moral and psychological conditions for the harsh punishment meted out to the old and hated world.

It is common knowledge that nothing in this world takes place without a cause. The revolutionary immorality of Marx and, later, the Bolsheviks had objective historical foundations. But this does not mean that the Bolsheviks did not really have a choice. It is not true that in their situation an intellectually developed person could not act otherwise. Their choice is not exempted from moral judgment.

A person's intellectual development carries no presupposition that he or she should always be guided by the revolutionary sentiments of the restless masses and recklessly plunge into the whirlpool of the struggle. There are situations where a person's intellectual and moral development presupposes a totally different type of behavior, particularly when there are grounds to believe that an escalation of revolutionary restlessness would lead to chaos, the destruction of the foundations of human life, or a general catastrophe. The great Russian author V. G. Korolenko tried, as far as he could, to stop the imminent pogrom in Russian and prevent the plunder of the plunder, because he understood that hate and violence could not stimulate progress. I have no doubt in my own mind that, both morally and intellectually, he stood head and shoulders above the Russian lawyers, publicists, socialists, and the leaders of the October Revolution who fanned the fire of hate and enmity in the soul of the Russian paupers and their desire to rob the rich of their wealth.† With respect to

---

* "You cannot make the old laws the foundation of the new social development, any more than these old laws created the old social conditions," wrote Karl Marx (Marx and Engels, *Collected Works* [Moscow: Progress Publishers, 1977], 8:327).

† In his third message to A. V. Lunacharsky, V. G. Korolenko wrote, "Just as the lies of the dictatorship of the nobility, which replaced the significance of the peasantry as a class by the image of a good-for-nothing and a drunkard, your formula replaced the role of the organizer of production, albeit a bad organizer, by the image of an unmitigated robber. . . . In our country the robbery instincts were first fanned by the war and later by the disorder which is inevitable in the course of any revolution. Any revolutionary government must struggle against them. This was also prompted by the feeling of the justice. . . . You did not do that. Due to tactical considerations you sacrificed the duty in the face of the truth. Tactically, it was to everybody's advantage to fan the popular hate to capitalism and direct the popular masses against capitalism, just as a military unit is directed against a fortress. And you have not stopped short of distorting the truth. You passed what was only part of the truth for the whole truth. And drunkenness did take place too. And now this has born fruit. You have seized the fortress and given it away to be plundered" (*Novyi Mir,* 1989, 10:205–6).

Korolenko's unassailable moral stand, Trotsky, Kamenev, Zinoviev, Sverdlov, Radek, Lunacharsky, and Stalin all look like so many twin brothers.

In 1918 the leaders of the October Revolution thought they had the right to take away the fruits of labor and in many cases even the lives of well-to-do farmers despite all the notions of justice, morality, and legality. But if so, then why in 1929 did Stalin not have the right to take away the fruits of labor and in many cases even the lives of the same well-to-do farmers despite the same notions of justice, morality, and legality? In both cases the notions of morality and justice were sacrificed to the interests of revolutionary progress and a speedy transformation of Russia's class structure.

No one will ever be able to prove any substantive difference between the actions of the future Red Army marshal Tukhachevsky, who in 1918 and 1919 used army artillery against the farmers who were insisting that the fruits of their work belonged to them, and the actions of Stalinist henchmen who wiped out whole villages that revolted against forced collectivization.

On January 6, 1919, the Orgburo* of the Russian Communist Party (Bolshevik) called for "mass terror against rich Cossacks and their total extermination" and "mass terror against all Cossacks who participated, either directly or indirectly, in the struggle against Soviet power." No one will ever be able to prove that the Orgburo was more moral or humane than the Stalin's Politburo, which in 1929 set the objective of eliminating the kulaks as a class. In both cases the leaders of the party were convinced that history gave them the right to decide the destiny of other people and determine who could live on this earth and who was doomed to die. From the moral point of view, both the leaders of 1919 and the leaders of 1929 were criminals who launched a campaign of genocide against their own people.

The moral relativism of Marx and Engels and their teaching on class morality† should be condemned for putting in question the eternal values of morality and justifying violence against people and the values and traditions of a civic society. Marx questioned the fundamental principles

---

* Organizational Bureau.

† F. Engels wrote, "We therefore reject every attempt to impose on us any moral dogma whatsoever as an eternal, ultimate and for ever immutable ethical law on the pretext that the moral world, too, has its permanent principles which stand above history and the differences between nations. We maintain on the contrary that all moral theories have been hitherto the product, in the last analysis, of the economic conditions of society obtaining at the time. And as society has hitherto moved in class antagonisms, morality has always been class morality . . . (Engels, *Anti-Duhring*, 2d edition [Moscow: Foreign Languages Publishing House, 1959], 131).

of democracy and the Christian idea of the original spiritual equality of people. He believed that those who embarked on the road of salvation* were in some way socially deficient, and this must certainly be condemned, too.

Stalinism will live on until we free our minds of the conviction that there are people or whole classes of people who do not understand their interests as well as we do, who cannot decide their own destinies or are incapable of organizing their own life. It will continue to survive until we abandon the notion of genuine and nongenuine classes. Today, the revival of the traditional values of a civic society in our country is inextricably linked with the revival of the Christian tradition to regard any other person as equal to you and as a sovereign personality enjoying equal rights. We are increasingly aware that nothing is more valuable than the life and joy of those who have been blessed to come into this world.

---

* The reference here is to the nihilistic attitude of young Karl Marx to the basic principle of Western democracy: the idea of spiritual sovereignty and equality of every person irrespective of the level of his or her intellectual development. He wrote that "man in his uncivilized, unsocial form, man in his fortuitous existence, man just as he is, man as he has been corrupted by the whole organisation of our society, who has lost himself" cannot be equal to man who is "a real species-being" (Marx and Engels, *Collected Works* [Moscow: Progress Publishers, 1976], 3:159).

NOTES

1. G. Pomerants, "Mother's Question," *20th Century and the World*, 1989, no. 3:24.
2. I. Klyamkin, "Why It Is Difficult to Say the Truth" (in Russian), *Novyi Mir*, 1989, no. 2:205.
3. Ibid., 211.
4. M. Gorky, *Untimely Thoughts: Notes on the Revolution and Culture* (in Russian) (Petrograd: Cultura i Svoboda Publishers, 1918), 109.
5. Quoted in N. Sukhanov, *Notes on the Revolution* (in Russian), book 7 (Berlin-Petrograd-Moscow, 1923), 203.
6. Ibid., no page number available.
7. Sukhanov, *Notes on the Revolution*, 23.
8. Gorky, *Untimely Thoughts* (in Russian) (Moscow-Petrograd, 1921), 58.
9. Ibid., 73.
10. V. V. Kozhinov, "The Major Threat," *Nash Sovremennik*, 1989, no. 1; V. Shubkin, "Difficult Farewell," *Novyi Mir*, 1989, no. 4.
11. See Lenin, *Collected Works*, 29:192.
12. See Otto Latsis, "The Turning Point" (in Russian), *Znamya*, 1988, no. 6:70.
13. Ibid., 127.
14. Karl Radek, *Portraits and Pamphlets*, (in Russian), Book 1 (Moscow, 1933), 317.
15. Ibid., 320
16. Shubkin, "Difficult Farewell," 171.
17. See Latsis, "The Turning Point," 155.
18. Gorky, *Untimely Thoughts* (in Russian) (Moscow-Petrograd, 1921), 48.

19. Ibid., 67.

20. Ibid., 92.

21. See Lenin, *Collected Works*, 26:414.

22. Nikolay Bukharin, *The Economy of the Transitory Period* (in Russian) (Moscow, 1920), 143–45.

23. Bukharin, *Selected Works*, 150.

24. Gorky, *Untimely Thoughts* (in Russian) (Moscow-Petrograd, 1921), 82.

25. N. Berdyayev, *Philosophical Truth and the Truth of Intelligentsia* (in Russian) (Moscow: Vekhi, 1909), 1-2.

26. Ibid., 3.

27. Gorky, *Untimely Thoughts*, 51–52.

28. See Gavriil Popov, "On the Aims of the Second Program," *Sotsialisticheskaya Industriya*, February 4, 1989.

29. See V. I. Lenin, *Collected Works* (in Russian), 37:179, 354.

30. L. D. Trotsky, *Works* (in Russian) (Moscow-Leningrad, 1926), 17:404.

31. G. Zinoviev, *What Shall We Do in the Villages?* (in Russian), (Leningrad, 1919), 14.

32. Popov, "On the Aims of the Second Program."

33. Lenin, *Collected Works*, 33:439–40.

34. Lenin, *Collected Works*, 33:467.

35. Lenin, *Collected Works*, 1:420–21.

Conclusion:
The Philosophy of Limits
Instead of the Philosophy
of Dreams

I am deeply convinced that no matter what happens in this country in the future we shall never return to the primitive understanding of the individual that stoked the fires of Stalin's regime, a state of totalitarian uniformity deprived of alternatives. The philosophy of perestroika, in my view, essentially consists of a new, more realistic and more tolerant attitude toward the individual. We have come to understand that people are not made of steel and cannot be melted in the crucible of revolutionary storms. And it is an even greater waste of time to try to remake them by coercion, to force humans to be altruistic and class-conscious by order and decree. As a matter of fact the reverse is true: Human nature vigorously resists external pressure and fosters, above all, precisely the properties it is urged to reject. We can see for ourselves that human nature is fantastically resourceful when protecting persecuted traits. World, and especially socialist, history viewed in these terms reveals dozens of the most unexpected and inconceivable methods of mimicry and the camouflage of both natural selfishness and the concern for self-interests.

The lessons of the Stalin era are most striking in this respect. The altruism and self-denial of millions of people ultimately served the appalling selfishness of one evil man, his aspiration for absolute power, his wish to be the focus of attention, to impress the whole world, and to mask his mediocrity. This universal lesson of the Stalin era is, unfortunately, insufficiently studied so far: We are still afraid of philosophical generalizations. We should say that the departmental selfishness of the stagnation years was equally appalling and demonic. The joy of one egoistic person awarded the title of Hero of Labor could be sometimes bought at a shocking price: the tipping of the environmental balance with the ensuing suffering of thousands of people as the result of climatic changes and air pollution.

Fortunately, we are no longer naive; we have learned to distinguish true from sham collectivism and to concentrate on the moral motives of people's actions.

We are currently coming to understand that Andrey Platonov, the author of the long-suppressed novels *The Foundation Pit* and *Chevengur*, was perfectly right: Participation in the renewal of the world does not necessarily ennoble all those who are involved. Some of them, having lived through the revolutionary upheavals, become embittered, malicious, intolerant, and disrespectful of the personal dignity and honor of others, rather than nobler and kinder. In fact, many people became spiritually degraded while "building the new house."

We are gradually giving up the idealization of the human being. We have realized that our knowledge of the human soul and its passions, inherited from the Enlightenment, is far from being complete. We acknowledge today that the process of remaking human nature is much more complicated than many thinkers believed in the past. And we are no longer afraid of incurring reproaches for revising the established doctrines and undermining hitherto indisputable authority. It is evident that we used to overestimate the positive impact of the socialization of the means of production on human morals. Hence, we have to accept the low and unpleasant truth that bursts the bubble of our most heartfelt dreams: "To make a person work—pay him." But in my view, our idea of morality itself was inaccurate and insufficiently meaningful.

We are today much wiser, kinder, and, above all, more tolerant to the individual than we were in the past. Vladimir Mayakovsky, a distinguised Soviet revolutionary poet, used to compare an individual to a zero. And what is more, the individual was always to blame for everything: He could neither know the truth nor live on his own. The old man from Andrey Platonov's *The Foundation Pit* is afraid to go into the street in his bark sandals. "Aha, they would say, you are wearing bark sandals, so you are poor! But if you are poor then why do you live alone rather than congregating with the other poor?"

Today we have managed to spotlight all the adverse effects of such a nihilistic approach to the principle of individual autonomy (i.e., the wish to retain independence and personal freedom). By no coincidence, Soviet intellectuals and the vast majority of our youth have been so unanimous in their protests against the attempt of Nina Andreyeva, supported by the editorial staff of *Sovetskaya Rossiya*, to discredit this idea. For instance, the distinguished Soviet writer Chinguiz Aitmatov notes that "we have given preference to everything associated with the collective and team spirit. As the result we have lost a lot of the individuality, personality, and identity of the human being. We should proceed from the belief that the surrounding world exists if the individual person exists." We have realized there can be no genuine culture without an independent, autonomous personality—though it is true that the right to spiritual autonomy is fraught with certain flaws, including spiritual ones.

We have come to understand that the idolization of the collectivist spirit morally and spiritually damaged not only the individual who could not express himself or herself and had no autonomy and independence, but also society at large. You cannot appreciate the work done if you do not appreciate the one who did it. The underestimation of the individual and his or her personality inevitably entailed the underestimation of talent and skill. This is a major reason for the progressive loss of professional excellence and the increasingly degraded quality of work. A society incapable of an objective assessment of the individual and his or her abilities cannot develop an efficient production organization. Hence, such a society cannot preserve the basis of its social being. The thesis that the majority, the collective, is always right was used to justify numerous cases of injustice. It favored the spread of clannishness and helped to make short work of honest and, above all, gifted people. As the poet Evgenyi Evtushenko put it, "Oh, the majority, the majority, you have been wrong so many times, you have corrupted and ruined so many people that you are no longer the God."

One of the unexpected discoveries of perestroika—discoveries that for the first time in decades have allowed us to base our economic and cultural policies on real, rather than imaginary, human feelings and motives—was the realization that "power lies in the word of the minority" (i.e., that a society that does not guarantee rights to the minority is doomed to failure). We have come to understand that peace, culture, and progress rely on the interests of the individual. It is impossible to create something worthy without individual initiative, the developed need for self-expression, and, therefore, without self-identification and some distancing of the self from other people. Note that ten or even two years ago very few people could have foreseen the brave and resolute acceptance of the importance and intrinsic value of individuality by Soviet society. It was a true revolution in our established concepts of the world and the human being.

It has turned out that only a free person, an independent personality, can be a real collectivist, can indeed uphold the interests of society. A collectivist with an underdeveloped personality, just one of the many who is afraid to be unique, is an obedient slave of the majority rather than a true collectivist. Such obedient slaves of the majority paved the way for Stalin's dictatorship.

We have realized that the individual's inherent need to distinguish himself or herself, to draw attention to his or her personality, and to compete with other individuals does not at all threaten the foundations of our social being. On the contrary, it is the force that guarantees social progress and motivates it. We are no longer shocked by the appeals to encourage competitiveness among individuals and enterprises. Neither do we spurn attempts to provide the economic, political, and social conditions for the competition of intellects, talents, and abilities. Clearly now, people do not seek leveling-off as the antithesis of competition. Recognizing that everyone is entitled to equal basic rights, people, nevertheless, do not strive for equal (i.e., identical) results in proving their value. On the contrary, bold competition in this field, in their view, is necessary and only fair. Life is partly the competition of personalities. An individual must be given an opportunity to show his or her worth. It is their normal, legitimate right, if we understand by this their right to self-realization rather than the exploitation of others' work. Every individual experiences ineradicable yearning for such competition.

We have realized it is impossible to reestablish a wise and humane attitude toward the individual without a certain reappraisal of values. Now we are facing the acute problem of ideological guarantees, the protection of the individual's identity, his or her uniqueness and autonomy. We should convince ourselves that there is nothing criminal in the individual's aspiration for personal happiness, prosperity, and a full life. We should accept the priority of each individual's current problems as against those that might be faced in the future.

It is extremely important to reconsider our attitude to our contemporaries; to stop looking down on them from the standpoint of the human being of the future; to stop looking down on everyday life with its chores. It is probably time to examine more carefully "the human being of the past," to acknowledge that human beings were not more stupid than we are today and to profit from their experience. To sum up, it is time to have confidence in the individual, in human nature. At the present juncture it is unnatural to wish to sacrifice our natural resources—human interest, efficiency, skill, talent, and initiative—to the speedy perfection of human nature, as we did in the past. Individuals who are unable to take care of themselves can hardly be expected conscientiously to promote social well-being.

True, not every individual capable of upholding his or her personal interests is at the same time able and willing to serve the common cause. However, we should also keep in mind (and today we can say this for sure) that, with very few exceptions, the romantics who neglect their own welfare are, in principle, unable to contribute expertly and wisely to social well-being.

Few people today are ready to believe the myth of the peasant or petit-bourgeois origin of Stalinism with its extremes of destruction. Common sense persuades many of us, even those who are not experts in the field, that Stalin rushed headlong into Soviet history as a result of a different, not at all patriarchal, line of development. He came into our life on the bandwagon of the romantic concepts of the individual and socialism. Stalin relied on modernism: a passion for uniformity, total patronage, and an obsession with gigantism. In other words, Stalinism marks the culmination of the antitraditionalist line.

At a certain moment in our post-October history these two lines— patriarchal and modernist—merged. This was during World War II when the socialist homeland turned to the Russian past for help. But this was, as we can see, a temporary alliance. Stalin's coercive, accelerated modernism failed to take root in Russian soil. Only thus can we explain our present return to the Leninist doctrine of socialism as a system of civilized cooperators, the attempts to find a plausible form of returning land and initiative to the peasant and to make the worker a joint owner of the means of production.

But if, as I assert, everyone knows where to look for the roots of Stalinism, why then do many people still try to avoid a serious discussion of this issue? In my view, the explanation is as follows: The modernist line that carried the ominous figure of Stalin into Soviet history is closely related to our most sacred ideals. Hence, we fear that criticism of the substance of Stalinism might shake them. For example, the writer Vykulov acknowledges that "for above half a century we have been ruthlessly robbing the *muzhik* (a common Russian peasant) and killing his peasant soul." He agrees that Stalinism was no less than the genocide of Stalin and his cronies against their own people. But despite all this he still doubts whether it is expedient to talk about it. "Can the soul withstand such revelations? I am afraid that it will collapse under the burden. Will it not avert the people, in the first place, from our ideals, from our dearest beliefs?" the writer asks.[1]

I have no grounds to doubt that Vykulov is perfectly sincere in his comments on the evil of Stalinism. But it escapes me why he, a Russian writer, does not fully believe that his people can live without lies and myths. What is the value of his dear ideals if we must continue to resort to half-truths to save them? Is it not dangerous to found our national destiny and the beliefs of the young on deliberate lies?

It might seem that we are again building for ourselves the trap that already ensnared Nikita Khrushchev. We first develop a distorted image of our contemporary as one who is allegedly unable to understand the historical truth and to gain insight into the dramatic substance of the revolution, who cannot distinguish genuine values from sham ones or tell an error from a crime. Then we transfer our mistrust for Soviet people onto Soviet history, filling it with myths to be ultimately exploded by the time bomb we ourselves have planted. We are really an amazing nation completely lacking the ability to learn from our mistakes.

We have been punished so many times for the lies and half-truths that it would seem much easier to gulp our history's truth to the dregs. Wouldn't it be easy to tell about everything that has prevented us from averting misfortune and, having dispensed with all lies, to get down to work? But we do nothing of the kind. Even when we can do this, when we have all the necessary conditions for such a purifying shock, many people prefer to mark time. Or they create new myths and impose on the Soviet people new idols—the martyrs Radek or Kamenev—to replace that of Stalin.

It is generally difficult to understand why we are so very afraid to "erode" the socialism born of a dream, the impulse of the soul, while permitting many people to mistreat the socialism of truth and to slight it. Why has a half-truth got the right to be called an ideal whereas the truth has never gained this high honor? I am deeply convinced that we have from the very outset failed to think everything out. For instance, why should we regard noncommodity production, or the peasants who have been coerced to give up their peasant way of life, as the features of the ideal while truth, pragmatism, excellence, efficiency, and initiative should be classified as the values of the so-called middle level? Can a society that has not learned to appreciate truth, talent, and initiative succeed in a big way? Can a society in which such values as mercy, tolerance, and compassion have long fallen into disuse be viewed as spiritually healthy?

All our misfortunes, including the atrocities of Stalinism, may be rooted precisely in our long-established lies. They may draw on our failure to honor truth and, above all, the truth of our own socialist history and its lessons. What are we afraid of? I shall never forget how the custodians of our ideological purity baited the philosopher Henry Batishev in 1970 for his article on the indisputable priority of truth among all social values! Why can all the civilized nations afford to accept the whole truth about their history? Why can they afford a free discussion of their history and its main political figures? And why do we always seek to preserve without fail the icons, the idols of impeccable leaders set up by Stalin to serve his political self-interests? We have already realized that such thinking will take us nowhere in the twenty-first century. Then what is wrong? Who said that people have a greater respect for a canonized idol than for a normal human being with all his flaws and errors? Most probably the opposite is true. People suffer today from a general unwillingness to discuss the reasons for the atrocities of the Stalin era. They confront the revelations about Stalin's devastation but fail to ask, "Why did this happen?" Only thought can eliminate fear and purify our souls. But, as I have tried to show in this book, we are making little progress in this matter.

The one general conclusion we can possibly formulate from the lessons of Stalinism is that we need to stop deceiving ourselves. We should put an end to cheating and fostering myths. A clash of interests cannot, of course, be avoided. But it can be more easily resolved if spotlighted by truth. We should have more trust in truth. The nations that have taken the risk are still there and have been living a worthy life. We need truth about everything: the individual, his or her soul, our history, beliefs, and potential. But, above all, we need truth about our actual aims.

In my view, the philosophy of the future to which we and the rest of humanity are advancing today will lean most heavily on humility in the face of the truth. We cannot hope for salvation otherwise. The human soul will be unable to stand any new myths that tempt people by promises of easy solutions to their problems.

People are already tired of the futile process of continual "building." They are tired of perpetual contemplation of unreal, immaterial advantages. They are tired of the nonstop expectations of a miracle. People yearn for a rational and just life. They yearn for efficient work, high living standards, pragmatic and cheap management. To everything there is a season. The carnival of history in which fantasists run amok while millions of people waste their lives standing in line for their daily bread cannot last forever. It is time to put an end to this abuse and to have respect for the people. It is high time for Russia to give birth to enterprising individuals who can both think and work hard and improve the efficiency of Soviet agriculture and industry.

Politics has already witnessed a change toward rationality and pragmatism. Now the imperative is to make it irreversible by changing our philosophy, our social and historical thinking.

Today, when we are doing so much to restore justice and to exonerate the innocent, it is time to rehabilitate "the present" for the population of Russia. We cannot scorn reality forever and sacrifice it to our ambition to realize a fairy tale. We should not measure ourselves, our neighbors, or world history by an artificial yardstick—the dream of irresponsible visionaries.

I am not suggesting at all that we should reconcile ourselves to the evils of life, the horrible individualism, the inheritance of Stalinism and the stagnation years. I am simply saying that we should turn to the individuals who exist now, take a closer look at them, and try to understand what has made them what they are. We must learn to love them, to acknowledge their rights to preserve their identity and to seek personal happiness. At the same time we must help them to believe in their powers and to identify their talents. We must accept their right to think the way they do.

True, real humanism nowadays lies, above all, in the tolerance of a pluralistic concept of human happiness. Forms of self-realization and asserting oneself can be different. We must have confidence in the individual and his or her initiative as well as trust the individual's ability to distinguish the rational from the absurd, good from evil, and beauty from ugliness.

We have got to know that alongside the problem of equality that has dominated the consciousness of the people of the New Age there are other vital problems: It is imperative to conserve nature, family, life in general. We must find proper stimuli to work; we must encourage effective work and the faculty for innovations. We face the problem of controlling humanity's savage instincts, etc.

It is, of course, a difficult task to assert and popularize the philosophy of life and peace we are developing now by eliminating Stalinism and deepening our insight into perestroika. In contrast to the philosophy of pure socialism and the pure human being that ideologically and spiritually paved the way for Stalin's adventurism, our new social thinking does not promise to work wonders. On the contrary, it has assumed the thankless task of teaching people common sense and showing them the limits of their resources and, most important, the limits inherent in nature and social activity. Our new philosophy can be called the philosophy of the limits of human ambitions.

We should also acknowledge that the ideological and spiritual atmosphere at the beginning of this century was more favorable than the current one to the development and popularization of the concept of pure socialism and the pure human being. Then people did not know much about themselves: Numerous methods of personal development and techniques for treating deep-seated human diseases had not yet been tested. Hence, they were generally very hopeful about the future, and they were quick to believe various speculations into the as yet vague unknown.

The spiritual situation at the end of the century is dramatically different. This century, much more than all the preceding millenia, has taught humankind about the limits of its resources and the contradictions of social existence.

It turns out that the fruit of knowledge is really fraught with danger. Chernobyl, undoubtedly, has gone beyond the scope of human disasters. It has given us a new insight into the wisdom of the past and the meaning of ancient culture.

It turns out that the price of technical progress and the amenities of modern civilization can be extremely high. The treasury of natural resources has been fast depleting. Contemporary people can actually visualize the prospect of self-annihilation as the result of a nuclear war, a prospect simply unthinkable to the naive inhabitants of the earth at the turn of the century. We have made great progress in gaining equality. The Russian revolution has generally accelerated the democratization processes all over the world. But we have simultaneously faced dozens of even more complicated problems: the threat of an environmental holocaust, the food problem, the upsurge in national fanaticism.

And what is most important, we have made no headway in socializing the younger generations, in developing a well-rounded personality with a deep-seated mechanism to control, for example, the urge to abuse alcohol or drugs or to commit a crime.

Today, at the end of the twentieth century, we are even less able to cure the most dangerous social diseases than we were one hundred years ago.

We used to think, as Marx put it, that humanity sets itself only such tasks as it can resolve. Now we are aware that the logic of history's development does not always coincide with that of thought. People sometimes set themselves impracticle tasks. An individual can contemplate the unfeasible, but nature deals only with the practical.

The new philosophy teaches that destruction of any culture will not create anything, let alone anything "Great." The large numbers of the dead do not bear witness to the thoroughness of a revolution. According to the new philosophical school, the objective of history is not to sacrifice as many lives as possible to "progress" in order to prove by blood and death its devotion to the "Great Cause." On the contrary, it seeks to avoid unnecessary sacrifices and to meet the greatest economic and political challenges at the minimum price.

We should not deceive ourselves. We should not take pride in our readiness to suffer for the right cause. A nation that cares nothing for the price of progress but seeks progress "at whatever price" cannot hope for recognition and respect in the contemporary world. Not by mere chance does Christianity, the most profound world religion, condemn suicide. The same reason may account for the lack of international respect for the nations who can, as Chaadayev put it, "all of a sudden, without the slightest cause" indulge in self-annihilation.

The new philosophical school does not discover anything new. It simply reminds us of what was already known in the distant past:

- we can meet great challenges only by hard and meaningful work;
- priority should be given to intelligence, excellence, and talent;
- we should not listen to the prophets who promise to turn stones into bread and who try to condemn those who work hard.

Intelligence, creativity, talent, and hard work are the only shamans that can really work wonders.

The new philosophical school teaches us to be circumspect, to try to understand the motives of people who lived before us, to be careful with their traditions and experience. We must attempt to overcome the difficulties we identify and treat the diseases of human society. We must be tolerant of the ideological search of our predecessors and their incomplete knowledge of what is true and good.

The new philosophical school does not negate the future. It teaches instead that the stability of the future depends on the stability of the present. And therefore we should always be concerned with the health of what we call human civilization, created by the hard work of previous generations.

The new philosophical school does not negate either the existence of the law or its place and role in society. On the contrary, it calls for an extremely serious and respectful attitude toward the law. But the law should not be understood as a supernatural force that pulls nations from the pit of historical nonbeing and places them on the heaven of world civilization. The law should not be misunderstood as fate, as something unavoidable. The law does not guarantee the miracle required by political adventurers.

The law should rather be viewed as the defender of life, as an insurmountable barrier to the ambitions of various "shakers-up" of life. It marks the limit of human possibilities, something that a person must take into account and cannot overstep.

NOTE

1. Vykulov, *Literaturnaya Rossiya*, December 4, 1988.

Index